LIVING THE WORD WAY

LIVING THE WORD WAY

A Journey of Hope and Encouragement

ARLINA YATES

Scotland Media Group,
3583 Scotland Road, Building 70,
Scotland PA 17254

Paperback ISBN 978-1-941746-30-1

eBook ISBN   978-1-941746-31-8

For Worldwide Distribution, Printed in the United States.

1 2 3 4 5 6 / 19 18 17 16

Dedication

To those who prayed and to those who encouraged.
Together we dedicate this book to our Lord Jesus Christ.

What People Are Saying…

Endorsements

Arlina's thoughtful shepherding through God's Word has guided many into a richer appreciation of scripture. Reading from multiple books simultaneously has enriched understanding. Her weekly devotional insights are truly inspiring. This is a wonderful passageway for both scriptural novices and veterans alike.

Rev. David L. Ritterpusch

Living the Word Way came into my life at a time I needed a lifeline and transformed my relationship with God and fed me daily. I have been through the program several times, always gleaning new gems and finding God's word to be refreshment to my soul. I am now a pastor and share this treasure with all in my circle of influence so they too can experience God in a satisfying and intentional way.

Donna Hildebrand

Arlina Yates is your Spirit-led guide in Living the Word Way, an exciting new daily journey through the Bible. As you explore, each Word Way devotional reveals fresh insights, draws you closer to the LORD, and deeply refreshes your soul. Whether this is your first or umpteenth time savoring God's Word, expect a changed life.

Michele McKnight Baker,

Author of Sandpaper Sisters, and Soldier's Heart

…About the Bible Reading Program:

This is just what I needed! I wanted to let you know that I love doing the study this way. One chapter a day is not so overwhelming, and I can handle it and enjoy it.

Joyce, Pennsylvania

If you've landed on this website thinking, Bible-reading group? Been there, read that, and have no extra time for it—it may be worth a rethink. From personal experience, it's well worth making time for, and I've discovered that God has a way of making old passages (and even "boring" ones) suddenly have new meanings within our current situations and to burst back to mind in future times of need.

Carrie, Michigan

I want to thank you for giving me the opportunity to read the Scriptures. I find myself doing more meditating through this study and learning more about what God wants me to do and more about how to live my life according to His teachings.

Margie, Pennsylvania

...*About the Devotionals:*

These writings have encouraged my heart so many times, and I have found I can print them or forward them to hurting souls, and they devour them like they are starving. It causes them to pick up a Bible. How awesome is that?

Donna, Pennsylvania

Another wonderful, sensitive, honest, inspiring commentary!

Reverend John, Arizona

Does speaking to me for God just come naturally to you? What will I do when this is over?

Bob, Alaska

Thank you so much for this week's thoughts. I'm going to print them out and read through it often.

Kathy, South Africa

Thank you, thank you, thank you for taking the time to pray about this, and then writing me this awesome explanation. It took me a few days reading over your email and then back over the story and really letting it all sink in. It's amazing to me how much I have learned about myself from this one story, and this is just the beginning of the journey! WOW!

Angel, California

Once again you have sent such comforting words at a time most needed. You have such a gift for getting to the heart of scripture and applying it to everyday life and circumstances.

Diane, Washington

Try to Resist the Urge to Skip this Introduction

In our complex and ever-changing world, there is a longing for the type of encouragement, guidance, and hope found in the Bible. That longing often goes unfulfilled because some people read and know only bits and pieces of the Bible while others have no knowledge of it.

But it doesn't have to be that way. The devotionals contained in this book will walk you through the entire Bible and share the help and reassurance found there.

Life-changing is a term used often and loosely, but those who read the entire Bible and apply what they read to their lives know it really is one of the most exciting, influential, and yes, life-changing actions anyone will take. It was for me!

If you would like to read the Bible chapters associated with each devotional, turn to the next page for tips on getting started on your Bible-reading journey. If not, the first devotional awaits you.

Getting Started On Your Journey through the Bible

The Reading Program

This program is designed for individuals or groups who want to read the entire Bible and make what they read relevant to their life situations. The reading schedule is based on reading one chapter each day and moves between the Old Testament and New Testament each week to show the relationship between these two sections of the Bible.

Choosing a Bible

If you do not already have a favorite Bible translation, you may want to read the New Living Translation (NLT) Life Application Bible because it is easy to understand without sacrificing accuracy from the original Hebrew and Greek texts.

Life Application Notes

Life Application Notes are included in many different Bible translations. The Life Application Notes help you understand what you are reading and enables you to connect the Bible to your everyday life. Life Application Notes are one of the key reasons that people are able to read the entire Bible when they were unable to do so in the past. So no matter what translation you choose, a Bible containing Life Application Notes will be useful.

Your Commitment

Even more valuable than the Life Application Notes to your reading success is your commitment to read the entire Bible. People find reading and reflecting on one chapter a day an achievable goal. If you are determined to read the entire Bible, you will, and it will change your life for the better.

xiv   *Arlina Yates*

Bible Reading Schedule (see Appendix A)

The Bible Reading Schedule gives you the chapter selected for each day and allows you to track your reading progress.

Devotionals

The devotionals contained in this book are based on each week's seven Bible chapters. They were written to encourage you in your relationship with God, to answer questions that may not be addressed in the Life Application Notes, and to supplement your knowledge of the Bible. They may be used along with your Bible reading or as stand-alone devotionals.

Tips for Reaching Your Goal of Reading the Entire Bible

- Pray about reading. Ask God to help you find the time to read, give you understanding of what you read, and help you put God's Words into action.
- Set secondary reading goals for yourself. If you cannot read every day, can you set a time to catch up each week? Each month?
- Keep your Bible in a highly visible place so that you are more likely to make it part of your daily routine.
- Find someone who will encourage you to keep reading or even read with you.

What does God want to say to you today? Read the Bible to find out.

THE JOURNEY BEGINS

Our Greatest Need

Genesis 1–5; Matthew 1–2

Adam and Eve had never experienced trouble, but that was exactly what was brewing. As they bit into the fruit from the special tree, a new feeling came over them—one they did not like and could not explain. They could ask God about it when He came to be with them later in the day, but there was no time to think about that visit now. Gathering fig leaves was their current priority. . . .

When people think of Adam and Eve's story, it is the fruit eating and the dreadful consequences that get most of the attention. But eating the forbidden fruit was just the early part of Adam and Eve's story, not the essence of it. Woven between their disobedience and God's punishment are two unchanging factors: God's constant love for Adam and Eve and His desire to continue their relationship. We see proof of this immediately following their punishment when "the Lord God made clothing from animal skins for Adam and his wife" (Gen. 3:21).

Clothing that Makes a Difference

Clothing may seem like a trivial matter to us compared to the introduction of sin into the world. But clothing demonstrated God's continued love for Adam and Eve and His concern for all aspects of their lives.

God made clothing for Adam and Eve because He cared about their *emotional* needs. Because of their sin, Adam and Eve became aware of their nakedness and were troubled by it. So God made clothing to ease their minds.

Clothing reflected God's care for Adam and Eve's *physical* needs. Before they sinned, there had been no thorns and thistles to hurt their skin; now there were. So God made clothing to protect them from harm.

And clothing showed God's attention to Adam and Eve's *practical* needs. Fig leaves weren't durable enough to be clothing, and Adam and Eve would have spent much of their time replacing their coverings. So God taught them how to make clothing, giving them a new and needed skill.

A Greater Need

Before God took care of Adam and Eve's emotional, physical, and practical needs, He wanted to attend to their greatest need—a restored relationship with Him. Adam and Eve's sense of failure could have kept them from any relationship with God, for we see that one of their first actions toward God after disobeying was to hide from Him. But God did not allow them to remain helpless and confused. He called to them, "Where are you?" (Gen. 3:9).

God, of course, knew where they were. The real question was whether Adam and Eve would run *away* from God because of their sin or whether they would run *to* Him in recognition of their desperate need for Him. Adam and Eve chose wisely and came out from among the trees to be in God's presence.

Yes, punishment awaited them, but love greater than the sting of that punishment also awaited. Adam and Eve had failed to obey, but God's love, forgiveness, and care for them were far greater than their failure.

Genesis 4:25 tells of the continuing relationship between Adam and Eve and God, for it says that when Eve gave birth to Seth "she said, 'God has granted me another son in place of Abel, the one Cain killed.'" Eve gave God loving credit for what brought her much joy, the birth of another child. These few words point to the enduring relationship between God and Eve.

As we read through the Bible, we will learn many things about having a personal and loving relationship with God; for just as God wanted to be with Adam and Eve, He wants to be with us. And that is what this book is all about.

Week 2

Five Words

Genesis 6–9; Psalms 1–2; Matthew 3

The simple message stood out as I entered the sanctuary for a friend's funeral, for it was both humbling and captivating. Hanging prominently at the front and made up of only a few words, it said:

KNOW WHOM YOU STAND BEFORE

The "WHOM" in that message was, of course, God. It is God before whom we stand each day of our lives. And it will be God before whom we stand when our days on this earth cease to be. What a difference it would make if we would be diligent in remembering these few words as we make our way through this life.

All Scripture points us to whom we stand before so that we can know our Lord better and grow closer to His likeness. The more we truly know God, the more we long to know Him because we were created to be fulfilled by our relationship with Him. And what a beautiful relationship it can be.

There is much to know about our Lord. Keep studying the Bible and see how God reveals Himself to you.

Week 3

Expectations

Genesis 10–14; Matthew 4–5

Expectations. We all have them. Expectations of God. Expectations of friends, family, co-workers, casual acquaintances, even strangers. We expect something to work in a certain way. We expect a particular level of service in a business transaction. We expect specific responses to our actions. Yes, it is safe to say we have expectations. And, probably, it is also safe to say that we often have negative reactions when our expectations are not met.

Based on their long history together, Abram may have had an expectation of what acreage his nephew Lot would choose when they agreed to divide the grazing land they shared. His expectation would have been based on many factors. Abram had watched over Lot after Lot's father died. He had protected and guided him, shared his riches with him, and shown him love and friendship. Abram was also the leader of the family in a culture that honored its elders. It would have been logical for Abram to expect Lot to choose the second-best land and leave the best for Abram.

But Lot chose the best for himself.

Abram had a choice, too. He could choose how he would react to what was probably an unexpected outcome. He could have felt cheated by Lot's choice and become angry. He could have attempted to influence Lot to make a different choice. He could have demanded his right to have the best land.

Although we are not told about Abram's thoughts, we are told about his reaction. And Abram's reaction is a good model for us when our expectations are not met. After Lot chose the best land, Abram seemed to harbor no ill-will toward Lot. He displayed no resentment. He spent no energy trying to assert his rights. He acted on the belief that he did not have to look out for his own best interests...he could trust God to do that.

God was the silent witness to Lot and Abram's conversation and to Lot's choice of land. And God honored Abram's selfless reaction to Lot's choice and to having his own expectations go unmet. Abram may not have had the "fertile plains of the Jordan Valley" (Gen. 13:10), but God had land for him. "After Lot was gone, the Lord said to Abram, 'Look as far as you can see in every direction. I am going to give all this land to you and your offspring as a permanent possession'" (Gen. 13:14-15).

In this story, we see two of God's most important messages, ones that are found again and again in the Bible. The first message is that we can trust God to meet our needs—as He did for Abram in providing good grazing land. The second message is that we should treat others as we want to be treated—even when their actions or decisions do not conform to our expectations.

Our sense of annoyance when our expectations are not being met can serve as a trigger to focus on God and what *His* expectations are for us in these situations. Who knows how God will use these times of frustration in our lives? The one thing we can know is that as we put our trust in God, we can expect His help in dealing with our unmet expectations.

WEEK 4

What...Me Worry?

Genesis 15–18; Psalms 3–4; Matthew 6

Jesus said, "That is why I tell you not to worry..." (Matt. 6:25).

Now I don't know about you, but my family bloodlines include thorough and accomplished worriers. They could have won Olympic Gold in worrying. With a background like that, these verses have deep meaning to me because I, too, used to excel in worrying and have seen firsthand the serious damage caused by worry.

God tells us not to worry. In other words, don't be anxious, concerned, uneasy, apprehensive, nervous, fretful, troubled, losing sleep, bothered, or fearful about the circumstances of your life. Do you ever struggle with any of these emotions over a situation? God says don't bring the turmoil of worry into your life.

You may think, *Easy to say, not easy to do. My family problems, health problems, relationship problems, money problems, future, past, mistakes* (you can add your own "worries") *are serious.* God still says, don't worry.

Why not worry? Because, as Genesis 18:14 asks, "Is anything too hard for the Lord?" Anything? Can we trust God with our problems? Is there any possible reason to say to God about any troubling situation,

"Thanks, God, I'll take it from here…it'll be better off in my hands than Yours"? The basic question becomes, do we believe in God enough to trust that He is who He says He is and that He will do what He says He will do for us?

Sarah thought she had a good reason not to trust what God told her. Most people would have agreed with her. Based on her beliefs, abilities, and knowledge, there was no solution to her problem of not being able to conceive a child. Because she thought her situation was impossible, she did not believe that God could do what He said He would do for her and Abraham. Turns out she was wrong.

Probably most of us are like Sarah at times. After all, one of Satan's most effective tools is to get us to doubt Christ so that we are robbed of our joy and our witness. How do we fight back? How do we learn to trust more and worry less? Here's what I've learned through years of hard times, years of failing to trust, and years of learning to trust.

When I first sense that something is troubling me, it becomes the signal to start asking myself a few questions. I need to determine if my worry is associated with something that I have done but should not have done. Or have I failed to do what I should have done. If so, I need to get busy and stop something or start something. If my worry involves a sinful action, I need to ask God's forgiveness and possibly make something right between myself and others.

If all is clear on that front, then I need to pray, asking God to help me to deal with my fear and to trust Him, regardless of the circumstance. Many times, we have trouble trusting, but God is more than willing to help us trust in Him and rest in Him. Don't be afraid to ask, God is not stingy with us, nor does He ignore those who depend on Him. We may need to ask God to remind us of the many times that He has cared for us through hard times in the past. We may need to ask Him for patience to see us through, if the situation is long-term. We may need to ask that He help us understand what our real need is. For example, do we need healing? Maybe. Do we need increased faith and trust? Undoubtedly. Finally, we need to force ourselves to take our worry and redirect it to recalling the blessings that we are enjoying from God. Having trouble thinking of any blessing? Ask God's help.

Here's the bottom line. Has God ever once proven His love and ability to care for you in the past? If so, you know that He can be trusted to do so in the present and in the future. And practice does make perfect. While my ancestors practiced worrying, I'm working on practicing trust.

Here's to a week, and a lifetime, of more trusting and less worrying.

Week 5

Healing

Genesis 19–23; Matthew 7–8

"Suddenly, a man with leprosy approached Jesus. He knelt before Him, worshiping. 'Lord,' the man said, 'if you want to, you can make me well again.' Jesus touched him. 'I want to,' he said. 'Be healed!' And instantly the leprosy disappeared" (Matt. 8:2-3).

Bible verses talking about healing always grab my attention. So Jesus' statement that He wanted to heal the leper made these verses stand out.

Jesus was true to His word. He healed the leper and many like him. Yet not every sick or injured person on earth was healed during Jesus' time here, as healing does not always come to us. This is an issue that often shakes people's faith. How does Jesus saying no to our request for healing connect to the Matthew verses where Jesus says, "I want to [heal you]"?

One possibility is a difference in timing. When we ask for healing, we want relief as quickly as possible. While Jesus does want to heal us, He may ask us to wait for healing to occur. He may even ask us to wait until our days in Heaven, where He has promised to heal us of all our suffering and pain. Waiting can be hard, but physical and emotional suffering can lead us to a place of value, a place where we can draw nearer to God.

And that is what makes the beginning words of Matthew 8:2-3 so important. They tell us the leper "knelt before Him, worshiping." This leper needed healing, that is obvious, but before all else he worshiped Jesus. Jesus was more important to him than his physical well-being. The Bible doesn't tell us, but I believe that even if the leper had not been healed, he would have continued to worship Jesus because he had found something more valuable than freedom from illness.

How can I be so sure of this? Because my words are based on years of having Jesus say *no* to complete physical healing for me but yes to allowing me to know Him better. Without the physical issues, I doubt I would have sought God as much, and that would have been my great loss. You too may have firsthand knowledge about suffering or bear the anguish of seeing someone you love suffer. Do we desire healing for ourselves and for others? Of course we do! And yet, let us not undervalue that which can give us peace in the midst of our physical and emotional burdens—the comfort and spiritual healing of knowing Jesus more intimately and worshiping Him.

Week 6

Do I Have a Story for You!

Genesis 24–27; Psalms 5–6; Matthew 9

Eliezer, a respected and trusted servant of Abraham, was on an important mission for his master. He had been sent to find a wife for Abraham's son Isaac. Eliezer prayed for God's help to accomplish this task, and God answered Eliezer's prayer even before he had finished praying. What was Eliezer's reaction? He fell on his knees in worship and thanks for God's answer to his prayer. But he didn't stop there. He immediately told others what God had done for him (Gen. 24:12-48).

Eliezer's story reflects two key building blocks of our Christian life: prayer and telling others what God has done for us. Both of these acts seemed to bring Eliezer joy, and they also seemed to be completely natural for him.

This seemed so simple for Eliezer, but even something simple, something that can give us joy, can be difficult the first time we do it. We do not know if Eliezer was uneasy before he spoke to others about

God for the first time, but this is often the case for Christians who want to share their faith but who fear not having the right words or looking foolish.

But there is no doubt that if we are willing to confront any fear we have about sharing with others our personal experience with Jesus, God will help us as we take our first, halting, scary steps in that direction. Matthew 9:10 tells us that this is exactly what Matthew did when Jesus called him from his life of sin. He was called in the daytime and by that evening had gathered his friends to hear about Jesus, and he never turned back from telling what Jesus had done for him. Telling others about his relationship with Jesus was not an unpleasant task for Matthew, but a joyous one.

In Matthew 9:27-31, we are told another story about Jesus healing two blind men. What did they do after being healed and being told by Jesus not to tell anyone? They immediately told everyone what Jesus had done for them. They couldn't help themselves. They had been given something too valuable to keep quiet about it.

Eliezer, Matthew, and the two blind men did not have deep discussions of great theological truths with others. They simply told what Jesus had done for them to those who were willing to hear. For those whose hearts were not yet open to hear, the lives of these witnesses had to model the story until it was time to tell it in words.

Eliezer started with prayer, and Matthew 9 comes back full circle to that important practice. The end of the chapter tells of Jesus urging His disciples to pray that God would send people to tell others about Him. That counsel, spoken thousands of years ago, is for us today, as it has been for those before us and will be for those who come after us. We have a job to do. The world is in chaos, and fears abound. We who believe have the answer to this turmoil. We have something of great value in our relationship with Jesus Christ.

Has it changed our lives? If so, like Eliezer, we can pray for help to do the job we have been given—telling others about Jesus. That is a prayer totally in God's will, and we can be assured that He will answer it swiftly as He did Eliezer's prayer.

A Significant Number

Genesis 28–30; Psalms 7–8; Matthew 10–11

Have you felt it too? Maybe it was while standing before an ocean or looking over an endless landscape or gazing at the stars. Whatever the trigger, there are times when we simply feel insignificant—our frailty, our smallness in the universe, our limitations compared to our Creator driven home.

And yet we are not insignificant to God. In Matthew 10:30, Jesus tells us that "the very hairs on your head are all numbered." Think about that. The hair on our head is not a fixed number. It changes as we lose hair and grow hair. Except when we are losing a lot of hair, we humans don't give the number of hairs on our head a lot of thought. In the scheme of life, it doesn't seem that important to us. But it is important to God. Why? Because we are important to God, even down to details we would consider insignificant. Who do you love the most in this life? Do you know how many hairs are on that person's head right now, yesterday, last month? Do you know anything even close to that type of intimate knowledge about your loved one? God does.

Matthew 11 ends with words about Jesus' compassionate love for us. It says, "Then Jesus said, 'Come to me, all of you who are weary and carry heavy burdens, and I will give you rest. Take my yoke upon you. Let me teach you, because I am humble and gentle, and you will find rest for your souls.'" In other words, Jesus is saying, come, let Me love you and guide you. Come, let Me love you and lead you when your life is pleasant and show you the way when it is not. Come, let Me love you and go before you when you are dealing with issues much greater than the number of hairs on your head.

It may be that it is impossible for us to understand fully the love God has for us because it is beyond our capacity as humans to love the way God does. Even when we feel fervent love for someone, it can only be a pale imitation of the pure, unselfish love that God has for His children. Often we feel we must be deserving of love to be loved, and how do we earn the love of a Being as powerful and astounding as God? We can't, but we can do what Jesus says. And He simply says, come, be loved, be guided.

WEEK 8

Raeann

Genesis 31–35; Matthew 12–13

Several years ago I had the profound joy of visiting someone who was dying of multiple brain tumors. Yes, Raeann was dying, and, yes, our visit was joyous. Raeann had become a follower of Jesus Christ. She spoke about what a difference her belief in Jesus had made, both in her life and in her fear of dying. She knew that her day of judgment was going to be a joyous occasion because of Jesus. This had not always been Raeann's story.

For her first forty years, Raeann had been neutral about Jesus. Even when dealing with a rare and deadly form of breast cancer two years earlier, she remained neutral. But something happened. God continued to seek her while friends and family continued to tell her about Jesus. One day she said "yes" to Jesus and became a new person.

With that "yes" Raeann entered into a relationship with Jesus that offered incalculable value for this life and the life to come. The joy of her new relationship with Jesus replaced the hopelessness, fear, and regret that hovered near her during the years she lived on the edge of death. Raeann's death would not bring the "weeping and gnashing of teeth" that Jesus warned about for those who die without accepting His forgiveness of sin (Matt. 13:42,49). Raeann had been rescued!

But Raeann's story didn't end with her rescue. She still had this life to complete, and she needed more seasoned Christians to help her grow in her knowledge of God and to ensure that her growth in Christ was not choked out by the hardships of this world (Matt. 13:21). How do we become the kind of believers that Raeann needed in her new journey with Christ?

Ways to fulfill our responsibility as believers:

You are already taking one important step if you are reading through the Bible, God's living word to us (Heb. 4:12). It's easy to glance over the word "living" when applied to Scripture. But it is exactly that, and by reading and studying all of it, our lives are enhanced and changed in a different way than when reading only selected portions. Reading all of God's Word is one way to gain the knowledge of Jesus that He says we need in Matthew 13:12.

Pray. Pray that God will cause us to care deeply about unbelievers and their fate. Pray that God will prepare their hearts to accept the good news of Jesus Christ and that we will have the courage to tell them the story of our relationship with Him. Pray that all believers' understanding of Jesus grows.

Take action. We need to be conscious of whose hearts have been prepared by the Holy Spirit to hear about a relationship with Jesus. Not everyone is receptive, so we need God's help in knowing when we should be planters, harvesters, teachers, or one who prays behind the scenes on behalf of others.

Jesus revealed His thoughts on this subject in Matthew 12:30, a verse that caused me to stop and think hard. He said, "Anyone who isn't helping me opposes me, and anyone who isn't working with me is actually working against me." Those are strong and even harsh words. But, in reality, we do make a difference for all eternity to the people whose lives we touch either by our action or inaction.

We've been called to action by Jesus. What is our answer?

WEEK 9

It's All Right

Genesis 36–40; Psalm 9; Matthew 14

Jesus' disciples were in a boat far from land. They were alone, for Jesus was on shore. The disciples were in that boat because Jesus had instructed them to go ahead of Him to the other side of the lake, and they had obeyed. But now they were fighting for their lives because strong winds and waves threatened to drown them. In their despair and distress they felt abandoned. They were exhausted and close to giving up.

And then they saw something walking toward them on the water. More trouble—a ghost! The waves and wind were already enough to sap their spirit and their strength, and now they were sure that a specter from the dead was headed their way. Whatever it meant, it could not be good, and they were terrified.

But then they heard a familiar voice over the crash of the waves and the howling of the wind. It wasn't a ghost headed toward them, it was Jesus. "Jesus spoke to them at once. *'It's all right,'* he said. *'I am here! Don't be afraid'"* (Matt. 14:27). The wind did not calm down immediately. The waves did not stop hitting the boat. Jesus still was not beside them. But it was all right. And it is all right because Jesus is who He says He is, and He keeps His promises.

Have you been tossed about by the winds of adversity? Have you felt the sting of despair? Have you sensed hope slipping away? Have you been confused when hard circumstances came your way even though you knew you were an obedient child of God? Have you experienced the pain of God's silence when you wanted to feel His presence?

In the midst of overwhelming life situations, remember Jesus' three short sentences. Believe them, for they are true. Let the words flow over you and sink deep into your mind and heart. Hear Jesus say them to you:

"It's all right."

"I am here!"

"Don't be afraid."

Trust through the Trials

Genesis 41–45; Psalm 10; Matthew 15

I wish I were more like Joseph.

A beloved son of a wealthy father, he was sold by his brothers into slavery—a slavery that was so grueling that it often led to death. How's that for sibling affection and a change in life status?

Joseph went on to live the humble life of a slave with integrity, but was then imprisoned when he refused to yield to the adulterous advances of his master's wife. How's that for justice?

While in prison, he befriended a fellow inmate who promptly forgot him upon his own release. How's that for appreciation?

These devastating experiences didn't play out over a few days or months, but over many years. How's that for quick relief?

Any one of these experiences would cause many people to question God's goodness, if not cause outright disbelief in that goodness. What was Joseph's reaction to those painful early years in Egypt, the place he called "this land of my suffering" (Gen. 41:52)? Did he blame God and turn away from Him? Did he want revenge against his brothers who had started his cycle of pain and suffering? Was he consumed with anger toward the wife of Potiphar or bitterness toward his fellow prisoner who had forgotten him?

Genesis 45 tells us the answer. Joseph, whose position had been stunningly reversed from an imprisoned slave to an influential Egyptian ruler, meets with his brothers. He orders everyone else out of the meeting room. Joseph knows who his brothers are, but they do not recognize him. As quiet settles over the room, Joseph begins to weep loudly. Could it be that he was remembering the day he was sold as a slave by these brothers or the many painful years that followed? Through the deep sobs, he tells them, "I am Joseph, your brother whom you sold into Egypt" (Gen. 45:4).

Even through his tears, Joseph would have seen the mix of emotions on his brothers' faces. Their shock, confusion, disbelief, and finally fear could not be hidden, for they know that it is now Joseph who holds their lives in his powerful hands. Joseph rushes to explain, saying, "Don't be angry with yourselves that you did this to me, for God did it" (Gen. 45:5). Joseph, understanding the role God played in his life, has forgiven his brothers.

And with these words, we realize that Joseph was not only at peace with his brothers but with all the people who played a part in his years of pain. He had come to the conclusion that it was God who "did it," God who had allowed each painful circumstance to take place in his life.

Regardless of his present affluence and influence, the agony of those years surely would have caused him to distrust and hold a grudge against God...wouldn't they? But Joseph saw a bigger picture. He understood that God "has sent me here ahead of you to preserve your lives. God has sent me here to keep you and your families alive so that you will become a great nation" (Gen. 45:5,7). No grudge, just trust.

And that is why I want to be like Joseph. I want to forgive those who wrong me. I want to be obedient to God's commands, even when life is rough. I want to see and believe in the higher purposes God has for me, even when I encounter hard times. I want to be unshaken in my belief that, yes, God is good, even when my circumstances are not.

How does this kind of faith develop? It doesn't simply appear but is built up in our lives through each adversity and painful situation we face. What do you face today?

Despite our circumstances, let us pray that God will help us to believe His promise that all things will work together for good for those who love Him. And when Satan causes us to doubt that this could ever be so (and he will), let us pray yet again for strength to continue believing. Then let us walk forward, understanding that, like Joseph at the beginning of his severe and multiple trials, we do not know how the story will end or the good that can eventually come from it.

I'm not a Joseph yet, but I want to be. How about you?

WEEK 11

Don't Be Afraid

Genesis 46–50; Matthew 16–17

Verses 1 through 9 of Matthew 17 are the familiar words about Jesus' transfiguration, but as I tried to picture the scene with fresh eyes, many thoughts and questions came to my mind.

Does it surprise you that the disciples did not seem to be afraid of Jesus as His face changed so much that it "shone like the sun, and his clothing became dazzling white" (Matt. 17:2)? What was it about Jesus that prevented them from being alarmed in spite of this startling change? Could it be that something about His loving nature was still visible through the intense light? And what was it about this light? It was sun-like and dazzling, but the disciples were still able to look at Jesus. Humans, who cannot look directly at the sun without being blinded by it, could look directly at Jesus as the light poured from Him. Is this how Jesus will look when we see Him in Heaven?

What did Moses and Elijah look like when they appeared before the disciples? We aren't told that they shone like the sun as Jesus did. And how did the disciples know who they were? Again, was there something about their appearance that made it obvious to Peter, James, and John that they had been joined by these two important Jewish leaders? And, again, why weren't they afraid? They knew Moses and Elijah had died many centuries earlier, and yet, suddenly they "appeared and began talking with Jesus" (Matt. 17:3). Is instinctively knowing others who were previously strangers and talking with them another small glimpse of what Heaven will be like?

Now in spite of being thrust into this unusual situation, the disciples were not afraid. In fact "Peter blurted out, 'Lord, this is wonderful!'" (Matt. 17:4). This is wonderful! What will be our first thoughts and impressions in Heaven? What will it be like to see Jesus and others we have known? Could it be that "This is wonderful" will be our first thought, a thought that will convey meaning that is only dimly understood here on earth?

But then the atmosphere changed. "Even as he [Peter] said it, a bright cloud came over them, and a voice from the cloud said, 'This is my beloved Son, and I am fully pleased with him. Listen to him.' The disciples were terrified and fell face down on the ground" (Matt. 17:5-6).

They were terrified! These were words spoken in approval, not disapproval, and yet they were terrified. They were terrified of the words of God—words that were, and are, living and powerful. Words like those that spoke the universe and our lives into being, words that portray the awesomeness and holiness of God, words before which no mere human can stand. The disciples had a glimpse of God's greatness and glory—a mere glimpse, and they could not bear it. God, the Creator and Sustainer, is too holy and too awesome and too perfect in comparison to humans for us to remain standing in His presence. There was no equality on that mountaintop.

But there was Jesus. "Jesus came over and touched them. 'Get up,' he said, 'don't be afraid.' And when they looked, they saw only Jesus with them" (Matt. 17:7-8). Jesus. *Only* Jesus—the name that speaks compassion, love, forgiveness, and reconciliation with a holy and mighty God when we seek it.

Each of us will stand before this holy God one day. In our smallness, we will be terrified. Except that Jesus will be there, too. He will be with us because we have believed that He is the way to God. And I believe He will assure us that, because of Him and what He has done for us, we "don't [need to] be afraid."

What a moment of profound recognition and great rejoicing that will be!

The One Who Always Is

Exodus 1–4; Psalms 11–12; Matthew 18

Do you ever feel battered, overwhelmed, and even hopeless because of the life-changing issues and problems facing you, your loved ones, your friends, or people you have not actually met? At times I do.

Barely a week goes by without multiple stories of people in pain, whose suffering is unmistakable. There is news of broken health, broken relationships, and death. My heart grieves deeply with each new message, and I am reminded once again how limited my ability is to make a difference. But I am also reminded how important it is for each of us to center our thoughts and trust on God during times that bring us to the end of our own resources, for only God can bring renewed hope to shattered and grieving hearts. Circumstances come to all of us that cause us to cry out to God for relief, understanding, solutions, and comfort for ourselves or others.

The Israelite slaves of so long ago would have understood these feelings. Exodus tells the story of their harsh mistreatment by the Egyptians and their intense suffering. God was not unaware of their pain and spoke to Moses about their plight: "Then the Lord told him, 'You can be sure I have seen the misery of my people in Egypt'" (Exod. 3:7). Here, and throughout the Bible, we are assured by God that He sees our pain.

The verse continues, "I have heard their cries for deliverance from their harsh slave drivers. Yes, I am aware of their suffering." What are *your* slave drivers? What is causing you misery or suffering? God is aware of your situation and pain. Like the Israelites, you may not see any possible way through your suffering or have any hope for a better day to come. Based on your abilities, you may see no possible escape, but we must be careful not to think of God as being restricted by the things that limit us.

God was not controlled by the Egyptians' power, and the last verses of Exodus 3 contain His promise that not only will the Egyptians let the Israelites go free but they will send them off with great riches. How absolutely impossible this must have sounded to the Israelite slaves when they heard it. This was a promise to turn their world upside down, to deliver them from slavery and poverty to freedom and wealth.

What was it that caused them to believe such a reversal in fortunes was possible? Was their belief based solely on the signs of the Lord's power that Moses could perform? Or was it that they chose to believe that God is who He says He is and would do what He said He would do? Is it possible that they understood the underlying power of God's name and knew that their trust could rest there? God says in Exodus 3:14 that His name is "I AM THE ONE WHO ALWAYS IS." Eternal, holy, just, powerful, never-changing, promise-keeping, loving, ever-compassionate, always hearing His children as they cry out to Him.

What we *do* know is that they chose to trust in spite of their circumstances, circumstances that gave no earthly reason for such trust. And it was because of that trust, that the leaders all bowed their heads and worshiped. Their circumstances had not changed but their focus had. In that moment of worship, the leaders did not know what lay ahead. They did not know that their lives were going to take a sharp turn for the worse before God's promise of their liberation would be accomplished. Worsening events would cause their faith and trust to falter, but those events never altered God's promise to them nor its eventual success.

Throughout the Bible we are told again and again that God hears our cries for help, that He watches everything closely, and that He is aware of our suffering. The Israelites' story is one of great suffering, coupled with great trust in God's deliverance and goodness. It was the type of trust that wouldn't make much sense if viewed through eyes that looked only at the circumstances in which these people found themselves. But it was a trust that was well-placed, even though the pain increased greatly before deliverance came.

We are not alone in having experiences that lead to feelings of brokenness and despair. Such experiences ripple through history. But thank God, we are never alone through these difficult times; God is with us. He knows, He hears, He cares, and He is able to turn our mourning into joy, if we can accept as truth His promise of ultimate goodness for His children.

"The Lord is in his holy Temple; the Lord still rules from heaven. He watches everything closely..." (Ps. 11:4).

WEEK 13

In God We Trust…Maybe

Exodus 5–8; Psalm 13; Matthew 19–20

What an amazing difference Jesus' touch makes in a person's life. Matthew 20:29-34 tells the story of two blind men who asked Jesus to heal them. It says that "Jesus felt sorry for them and touched their eyes. Instantly they could see!" (Matt. 20:34).

They could see! And then what happened? "Then they followed him" (Matt. 20:34). It didn't matter to them that they had been blind and now their eyes were struck by colors, shapes, depth, light, and shadows. It didn't matter to them that after years of darkness there was an entire world to learn about. It didn't matter to them that they were now in a position to begin accumulating material treasures their blindness had denied them in the past. Their eyes were fixed on Jesus. They had felt the Lord's touch, and they knew in an instant His love for them. They wanted more of the Master—not more of what was around them, not more of what their new way of life could provide—just more of Jesus' presence.

This was the essence of the rich young man's problem in Matthew 19:16-22. He had sight, but he was blind to the riches of knowing Jesus intimately. Life had provided a great deal of material wealth to him. His wealth allowed him to be self-sufficient. And yet there was something he sensed in Jesus that drew him, but there was also a barrier. He wanted to keep the status quo more than he wanted Jesus and what He offered. He didn't understand what he would be gaining; he only knew the price was too high for him to pay. His wealth was his god; it is what he trusted in.

Is there anything that we are trusting more than God? It is so easy to be like the rich young man and believe that what we own can make us safer or more secure. It is so easy to have more trust in something tangible than in the God we cannot see or touch. It is so easy to fall into the trap that what we control, what we know, how we look, where we've been, or where we are going is what gives us value. Our secular culture drives the point home to us constantly.

But in the midst of all of this is Jesus. As with the blind men, He wants to heal our eyes so we can see the incalculable value of Him. As with the rich young man, He wants to give to us what can provide the greatest joy in this life. Jesus says love Me more, trust Me more, believe in Me more than what you own or what you value. Jesus says let Me fulfill your true need—the need to know the One for whom you were created.

Like the blind men, let us have eyes and hearts attuned to Jesus.

WEEK 14

A Few Questions

Exodus 9–12; Psalm 14; Matthew 21–22

The religious leaders during Jesus' time on earth surely did their best to discredit and belittle Him. They were at it once again in Matthew 22.

These were the most educated people of their day. They were intelligent, clever, and busy people. How much valuable time did they waste thinking about, discussing among themselves, and attempting to carry out a plan to demean Jesus?

This time they had a few questions for Jesus. But with only a few words, Jesus took their well-planned attacks and reduced them to tools that He could use to teach about Himself and God. His answers left the religious leaders defenseless and speechless. And His answers left the crowds impressed.

His answers were startlingly simple. Taxes? "Give to Caesar what belongs to him. But everything that belongs to God must be given to God" (Matt. 22:21). Greatest commandment? "'You must love the Lord your God with all your heart, all your soul, and all your mind.' This is the first and greatest commandment. A second is equally important: 'Love your neighbor as yourself'" (Matt. 22:37-39). Resurrection of the dead? "Jesus replied, 'Your problem is that you don't know the Scriptures, and you don't know the power of God'" (Matt. 22:29).

"You don't know the Scriptures, and you don't know the power of God." The words reverberate through the many years and land squarely in my lap. How well do I know the Scriptures? How well do I understand the power of God? My honest answer: better than I used to but not nearly as well as I want to and need to.

Do I know the Scriptures well enough that they are a natural part of my thought process? Do I know them well enough that they guide my thoughts and actions? Am I able to recognize God's powerful presence in all the circumstances of my life, in both the blessings and the hardships? Do I understand the power of God enough to trust in His wisdom, justice, love, and forgiveness?

Jesus' answers to the religious leaders are still teaching us today, and we pursue knowledge about the Scriptures and the power of God as we read through the Bible.

Week 15

Memory Test

Exodus 13–16; Psalms 15–16; Matthew 23

The sea stretches before you. Can you feel the fear surging through your body as your muscles clench and your heart pounds? You're trapped. Completely and utterly trapped. You feel the thud of the horses' hoofs behind you. You hear the sound of the chariot wheels, the voices of your enemy, the uproar of the chase—ever closer, ever nearer. You search frantically for a way of escape. But it's useless; you are doomed. You can't go forward because deep and unyielding water blocks the way. You can't go backward because behind you the sounds of your terrible fate quickly approach. You know there is no escape, no hope. But you call out from the depth of your being for the Lord to help.

And in the midst of this unbearable chaos and inevitable devastation you hear Moses say, "Don't be afraid. Just stand where you are and watch the Lord rescue you. The Egyptians that you see today will never be seen again" (Exod. 14:13). Stand still? Just watch? Your terrified mind can't comprehend what he is saying as your frantic body calls for action.

God agrees. "Then the Lord said to Moses, 'Why are you crying out to me? Tell the people to *get moving!*'" (Exod. 14:15). Move where? Move how? There is no place *to* escape and no means *of* escape, but God has heard the prayers, and it is time for action.

You probably know the rest of this beautiful story. God blocks the path of the Egyptians, opens the Red Sea, dries the sea bed with a mighty wind, and leads His people to safety.

Why did God do this? We are given at least two reasons. Exodus 14:18 says, "When I am finished with Pharaoh and his army, all Egypt will know that I am the Lord!" The Egyptians would know, as would anyone else reading or hearing this story, that the Lord was not merely one of many gods acknowledged by the Egyptians but the one true God. The only God. The God of incredible power.

That same display of power was also to draw the Israelites, and other believers, into a trusting relationship with God. God wanted His people to understand His awesomeness, to put their faith in Him, and to believe without hesitation that He would care for them.

As we read through Scripture, it is evident that God, as our Creator, knew how often we would face times that frighten us, worry us, upset us, and turn our world upside down. He understood our frailty. He knew that each new problem could cause us concern and threaten to shake our trust in Him. How do we know this? Because almost every week we read the words, "Don't be afraid" and "Trust in God." Throughout the Old and New Testaments, the words are repeated over and over; the reminder is given.

Likewise, story after story backs up why we can, and should, trust in God's plan for our lives whether or not we are facing our own Red Sea with no way of escape. God knew these historical accounts are important to building our faith, and He directed the Israelites to set aside special days each year to remember, discuss with their children, and celebrate what He had done.

Why does God tell us to remember, to explain, and even to celebrate what He has done? Because remembering what God has done in the past for us can remove the worry and concern from today's issues. It brings assurance, builds thankfulness, and honors God. Remembering increases our faith and trust and helps us to say with the Israelites, "Who else among the gods is like you, O Lord? Who is glorious in holiness like you—so awesome in splendor, performing such wonders?" (Exod. 15:11).

Who else, indeed! It is good to remember.

Week 16

Paying the Price

Exodus 17–21; Matthew 24–25

To be in relationship with God and to serve God has value without measure for this life and our eternal life. But it is not without cost, as Matthew 24 so clearly states, and that cost will intensify as the time of Jesus' return draws closer.

Yes, it sometimes costs tremendously to follow Jesus. Jesus said, "The nations and kingdoms will proclaim war against each other, and there will be famines and earthquakes in many parts of the world. But all this will be only the beginning of the horrors to come. Then you will be arrested, persecuted, and killed. You will be hated all over the world because of your allegiance to me" (Matt. 24:7-9). We fear these things, and our minds shy away from the possibility.

But it is a reality, as persecuted Christians around the world know. And yet they steadfastly continue in their faith and loyalty to Jesus Christ. They count their relationship with Jesus as more precious to them than physical well-being or even life itself. The words of Matthew 24 are not abstract to them; they are a hard reality. How do they do it? The answer, I believe, is that none of us could do it without help—the help of the Holy Spirit. It is beyond an ordinary human's capacity to stand true and strong through these types of trials. But along with the trial (not before) comes the Holy Spirit's guidance, comfort, and strength.

Matthew 24 continues, as does the picture being painted: people led astray by false teaching, sin rampant everywhere, and love for God grown cold. Are there days when you feel like you're walking amidst this landscape? As followers of Jesus Christ we dwell among these conditions, but we must be different. We need active, vibrant, and clear-eyed faith to stay close to God. How do we develop this kind of faith? Through knowledge and diligence.

Knowledge comes from knowing God's word—words of the greatest value. Jesus says, "Heaven and earth will disappear, but my words will remain forever" (Matt. 24:35). It's no surprise that this verse is right in the midst of this chapter of horrifying prospects. God's word is a mighty gift and is able to provide us with reassurance and courage and bring us into the presence of Jesus. Jesus says that everything else we now know will disappear, be replaced, and be made new; but God's word stands as it is with no need for renewal. Revere it, and make it part of your life, as nothing is its equal.

Diligence begins through prayer and the Holy Spirit's help. It grows as we practice loving God and others. It grows through obedience to God. It grows as we trust God to lead us through both the good and bad times we face.

The chapter concludes with Jesus telling us to be ready at any time for His final return to earth. Thank God we are ready at all times when we trust Jesus as our Savior and acknowledge that He makes us acceptable to a holy God. Matthew 24:44 concludes with, "For the Son of Man will come when least expected." Although it may be unexpected, Jesus will not return until everyone at least has the opportunity to hear His plan of reconciliation and love, because God longs for each person to join His family. As we begin to more fully understand Jesus' sacrifice for us and the immense love behind that sacrifice, these verses compel us to share with others God's desire to be in relationship with them.

This chapter used to frighten me, as it may frighten others. Why? Because it is natural to fear pain and persecution. Because we wonder if we have what it takes to stand true. Because there are people we love who may not be ready for death or for Christ's return.

This chapter challenges us to wholehearted commitment while providing the hope of Heaven and our new life to come. And with that commitment and with that hope come reassurance and peace.

WEEK 17

Forgiven Failures

Exodus 22–26; Psalm 17; Matthew 26

"We will do everything the Lord has commanded. We will obey," vowed the Israelites after Moses read the Book of the Covenant to them (Exod. 24:7). They were sincere and believed what they were saying. Yet God knew they would not obey.

Even though God knew the Israelites would not keep their vows, God kept true to His. God still wanted to bless the Israelites. He did not abandon them but wrote His commands on special stone tablets to give to Moses so Moses could teach the people.

Many years later as Jesus and the disciples ate the Last Supper, He said, "'The truth is, one of you will betray me.' 'No!' Peter insisted. 'Not even if I have to die with you! I will never deny you!' And all the other disciples vowed the same" (Matt. 26:21,35). They were sincere and believed what they were saying. Yet Jesus knew they would abandon Him.

That same night "Peter declared, 'Even if everyone else deserts you, I never will'" (Matt. 26:33). Peter was sincere and believed what he was saying. Yet Jesus knew Peter would deny even knowing Him.

Even though Jesus knew the disciples would not keep their vows, Jesus kept true to His. Jesus still shared the Last Supper with His friends. He still asked them to go to the garden with Him as He wrestled with, and prayed through, the issue of His rapidly approaching crucifixion—the horrific sacrifice that would provide forgiveness for sin and salvation for all who repented and put their trust in Him.

Yes, our Lord is faithful to us even though He knows we will not always be faithful to Him. Our Lord loves us even though He knows we will not always love Him as we should. Our Lord will never fail us even though He knows we will fail Him. It is not a question of "if" we will fail, but "how" we respond after we have failed.

How did the Israelites respond to God's commands in the Book of the Covenant? They did not obey nor did they turn away from their disobedience. As punishment, they wandered in the desert for forty years and never received God's promise of living in the earthly home He had chosen for them. They traded obedience for aimless wandering in a scorched and hostile land, where they would not experience the blessing God wanted for them.

Unlike the Israelites, the disciples turned from their fearfulness and became wholehearted followers of Jesus Christ. They put their failures behind them and moved forward with God. Did they totally forget their disloyalty to Jesus? It is not likely. Think of how much it must have grieved Matthew to write regarding Jesus' arrest, "At that point, all the disciples deserted him and fled" (Matt. 26:56). Matthew was one of those disciples.

Peter's public acknowledgment of his failure came more quickly. As he waited in the courtyard to see the outcome of Jesus' trial, "Peter said, 'I swear by God, I don't know the man.' And immediately the rooster crowed. Suddenly Jesus' words flashed through Peter's mind: 'Before the rooster crows, you will deny me three times.' And he went away, crying bitterly" (Matt. 26:74-75).

But the disciples did not let these failures become their focal point. Their failures were a springboard to lives spent telling Jesus' story and His power to forgive and restore. And their deepening relationship with their Savior, through the Holy Spirit, gave them the courage to die a martyr's death rather than stop telling Jesus' story. Through their lives, and through their deaths, these men helped change the world forever.

Is there something that you carry close to your heart that you are ashamed of and grieved by? Don't let it become your focal point. As with the disciples, Jesus already knew about our specific sin when He prayed in the garden and when He died for that sin. He has not been caught off guard by our sins and will make us clean before God when we turn away from those sins and sincerely seek His forgiveness. Those confessed sins may haunt us at times, but they do not trouble God, for He has chosen to not remember them. With God, we can move past our failures.

No Barriers

Exodus 27–30; Psalm 18; Matthew 27–28

What must it be like to be so tenderly loved by someone that they take delight in thinking of you, desire only what is good for you, and are beside you offering help and comfort during each time of trouble?

Somewhere deep inside us we yearn for an all-encompassing love like this and even vaguely recognize its existence. And yet we aren't quite sure of what we long for, since love like this goes beyond our understanding. Love like this is greater than we can imagine because it is greater than the love we are capable of extending. But there *is* a love like this, and we *are* the object of this love when we are part of the family of God.

God loved the Israelites in this way. He desired to be always near them and gave instructions for building a tabernacle where His Spirit would dwell. Although the people could not interact directly with God, a high priest would be their representative with God.

Exodus 28 tells of the special clothing that the high priest was to wear. This clothing was symbolic, representing important aspects of the relationship between Israel and God. One of the most visible pieces was an ephod, or apron, which was worn on the shoulders of the high priest. And on this highly visible ephod were memorial stones, engraved with the names of the tribes of Israel. As Aaron the high priest came before God each day, he would "carry these names on his shoulders as a constant reminder" (v. 12).

Did God need the stones to remember the people He loved so fervently? Of course not. But the people, whose memories were short and whose hearts were fickle, needed to be reminded that they were continually in God's thoughts. Not sometimes, but at all times.

And so it is with us today. We sometimes forget how important we are to God. And sometimes our emotions mislead us into believing that we are not loved as much as God tells us we are. One of the greatest pieces of evidence of this love is that, unlike the Israelites whose access to God was through the high priest, each of us has been given the precious gift of access to God at any time.

This access was vividly illustrated at the time of Jesus' death. "Then Jesus shouted out again, and he gave up his spirit. At that moment the curtain in the Temple was torn in two, from top to bottom" (Matt. 27:50-51). The Temple's curtain, through which the high priest passed to come into the presence of God, was now opened wide to everyone. There were no longer any barriers between the people and God. Right of entry was available to all who accepted the invitation to come to God. That right of entry is still available to all who accept God's invitation.

Access to a god who was dead would mean nothing. But Jesus lives! (See Matthew 28.) And His last words in Matthew to His disciples and to us as His present-day followers, show once more His great love toward us. "And be sure of this: I am with you always, even to the end of the age" (Matt. 28:20).

With us always. Not sometimes. Always!

Changed Lives

Exodus 31–35; Acts 1–2

How was it possible for eleven scared and defeated disciples to become confident apostles—apostles who were steadfast in their beliefs and persuasive with unbelievers? The first two chapters of Acts tell us how.

First, they spent time with the resurrected Jesus. Yes, they had spent years in Jesus' presence, but after His crucifixion and resurrection there was a difference, and they knew it. They knew He had died. But now they knew He was alive and all He had taught them was true and life-changing.

Second, they had learned the importance of obedience. "In one of these meetings as he was eating a meal with them, he told them, 'Do not leave Jerusalem until the Father sends you what he promised. Remember, I have told you about this before'" (Acts 1:4). Was Jesus reminding them about the gift of the Holy Spirit or was He telling them once again not to leave Jerusalem until the gift came? Was staying in Jerusalem after Jesus returned to Heaven a test of their obedience and trust of Jesus? If so, they had come to the valuable place of complete obedience because after watching Jesus ascend into Heaven, "they walked the half mile back to Jerusalem" (Acts 1:12).

What was the next step in their transformation? They prayed and sought God's will for their lives. These weren't the falling-asleep prayers of their time in the garden of Gethsemane with Jesus before His crucifixion. These were the prayers of people who couldn't think of functioning without knowing God's direction. These were the prayers of people who found that communing with God was more important than anything else—anything!

A pattern of prayer, obedience, seeking God's will, and encouraging each other was developing. "On the day of Pentecost, seven weeks after Jesus' resurrection, the believers were meeting together in one place" (Acts 2:1). And God met them in that room with the gift of His Holy Spirit.

As then, there are many reasons why the Holy Spirit is given to each of us, but surely one reason is so we will have the Spirit's guidance in sharing with others about our relationship with Jesus Christ. Peter immediately seized that opportunity the next time he was with unbelievers. Without hesitation, he said, "'So let it be clearly known by everyone in Israel that God has made this Jesus whom you crucified to be both Lord and Messiah!' Peter's words convicted them deeply, and they said to him and to the other apostles, 'Brothers, what should we do?' Peter replied, 'Each of you must turn from your sins and turn to God, and be baptized in the name of Jesus Christ for forgiveness of your sins. Then you will receive the gift of the Holy Spirit'" (Acts 2:36-38). There's nothing ambiguous in those words.

And what was the result? Almost three thousand people believed and were baptized. There's nothing ambiguous about those results!

But new believers are exactly that. How are new believers transformed into believers with deep and unshakeable faith? They must be taught through words and actions. "And all the believers met together constantly and shared everything they had…all the while praising God. And each day the Lord added to their group those who were being saved" (Acts 2:44,47).

The apostles could have kept on with their daily lives, going about their jobs, content with their own relationship with Jesus, and safe in their knowledge that they had been made righteous before God through Jesus' death and resurrection. They could have taken time for other pursuits rather than spending so much time in prayer, learning about God through the Scriptures, encouraging other believers in their growth, and sharing with others the wonderful news of Jesus' plan of salvation. But what a lackluster life that would have been!

We are not unlike the apostles. Do we want a life that is alive with vibrancy, meaning, and excitement? Do we want a life where our faith is put into action and where those actions lead to stunning results? We have access to the same tools as the apostles. It is up to us to determine to what extent we will use those tools.

WEEK 20

An Awesome Glory

Exodus 36–40; Psalm 19; Acts 3

Can you hear the hum of the voices? Voices giving instruction, asking questions, and offering encouragement. Voices alive with eagerness, excitement, and anticipation. Voices discussing this great thing they are undertaking.

Can you feel the energy? There are many people gathered together—*purposefully* gathered together. They are a busy people with important work to do. These are the people creating God's holy Tabernacle and all that will be in it.

And yet weren't these the same people who had only recently created and worshiped a god made from gold? The same people who, although they had seen God's glory time and time again, wanted a god small enough for them to understand and even control. The same people God had said were "an unruly, stubborn people" whom He would destroy if He was among them for even a moment (Exod. 33:5). Yes, these were those same people, and, yes, thousands of their number had died as a result their disobedience.

The remaining Israelites were the same people, and yet they were a changed people. They had been through the purification of God's judgment; they had mourned for their sins and sought forgiveness. The days of the golden idol were behind them.

This was no small task they were taking on, and this was no small God for whom they were working. This was the one true God, and His dwelling place must reflect His glory and magnificence. While it is easy for us to gloss over the measurements and instructions for this Tabernacle, God was specific in every detail of the construction. This Tabernacle was precisely, deliberately, carefully, and symbolically planned. This Tabernacle was to be a message not only to the Israelites but to the inhabitants of the lands through which they passed. Its splendor, when contrasted with the nomadic, only recently freed-from-slavery people who worshiped there, would send a message to all who came within sight of it.

In total obedience to all God had instructed, the Israelites completed their work. "And so at last the Tabernacle was finished. The Israelites had done everything just as the Lord had commanded Moses. The Lord now said to Moses, 'Set up the Tabernacle on the first day of the new year'" (Exod. 39:32; 40:1-2).

The Tabernacle was beautiful, and it was meaningful, but it was an empty tent until God's presence brought it to life. "Then the cloud covered the Tabernacle, and the glorious presence of the Lord filled it. Moses was no longer able to enter the Tabernacle because the cloud had settled down over it, and the Tabernacle was filled with the awesome glory of the Lord" (Exod. 40:34-35).

This is what they had labored for. In this Tabernacle, and near this Tabernacle, the "glorious presence" and "awesome glory" of the one true God could be sensed. This was the end result of their journey from a disobedient people practicing idol worship to a forgiven people committed to genuine worship of the Lord.

God's awesome presence continues to dwell among groups of believers as they gather together to worship the Lord. More amazingly, God's presence also now dwells within each individual believer through the Holy Spirit. May it be said of us that the "glorious presence" of God is evident in our lives as people draw near to us.

The Highest Price

Leviticus 1–5; Acts 4–5

You gaze out over your herd of cattle. Your eyes are scanning for the best bull, one that is perfect in every way. Your eyes settle on the one. It is a valuable animal to you—a wealthy person.

You gaze out over your flock of sheep and goats. Your eyes are scanning for the best animal, one that is perfect in every way. Your eyes settle on the one. It is a valuable animal to you—a person of the middle class.

You gaze down at the small coins in your hand. Your eyes are fixed on them, for you will use them to buy a turtle dove or a pigeon. These coins are valuable to you—a poor person.

You gaze at the container of flour. Your eyes look at what would have been part of your meal. This flour is valuable to you—the poorest of people.

Leviticus chapters 1 through 5 tell us of the sacrifices to be made by Israelites when seeking forgiveness of their sins. Bulls, sheep, goats, coins, grains—these were not items of little consequence in their society. These sacrifices cost them dearly, both in the value of the sacrifice and in the all-too-public confession of their need for forgiveness.

And yet it cost the animals even more. It cost them their lives. As those seeking reconciliation with God placed their hands on the animal, they could feel the life of that animal slip away as the priest killed it. They could smell the warm blood as it was put on the altar as a visible reminder of the cost of their own sin. This wasn't an abstract or theological concept; this was a harsh reality.

We shy away from these images. And yet I wonder, *Would we be more aware of and repulsed by our own sin if it cost us more dearly than it often does?* It is true that we occasionally pay an immediate penalty for the consequences of our sin, but does that happen often enough to keep us vigilant against sin? What would our attitude be toward our sin if we saw the cost *each* time?

Jesus paid the price for our sin—a price too costly for any human to understand. This sacrifice was all at Jesus' cost and none of our own. It was *His* blood that was placed on the final altar. Peter, speaking in Acts 4:12, says clearly about Jesus, "There is salvation in no one else! There is no other name in all of heaven for people to call on to save them." Jesus makes us acceptable to God, in whose holy presence sin cannot exist.

Our praise should always rise to God for this amazing gift, and yet it may be that we often take it for granted. Jesus' excruciating death happened so long ago, and unlike the ancient Israelites, we do not have the visual reminder of that death to sensitize us to the awful cost. As benefactors of that sacrifice, may we actively remember the cost, receive the great joy of sins forgiven, and live in never-ending thankfulness for this remarkable gift.

Week 22

Bubbling Up

Leviticus 6–9; Psalms 20–21; Acts 6

Have you ever felt a joy so deep that you were overwhelmed by its intensity? Have you ever experienced a joy for which there were no words to tell of it? Perhaps you have, but did this joy continue undiminished in its intensity? Is it as strong today as when it first occurred? There is a joy like this. It is the incomprehensible joy of being in God's presence.

The joy of being in God's presence is a recurring theme throughout Scripture. David spoke of his joy when writing about his own relationship with God in Psalm 21:6. But as with all of us, David's joy was not a consistent feeling—as other Psalms show. In this life we are blessed to get tiny glimpses of the joy that awaits us when we are finally in God's presence in Heaven. But these glimpses are simply that, and even the glimpses get crowded out again and again by the pressure of life's circumstances.

Long before David's time, the Israelites prepared for the joy of being in God's presence. But before that happened, there were conditions they had to meet, and meet specifically, as Leviticus 9 details. Being in God's presence was not only a joy, it was a most remarkable gift that was not to be taken lightly. The people had to prepare for God's presence as we would prepare ourselves and our homes for an honored guest.

But the conditions had been met, and they experienced the deep significance of God's presence coming to them. "Next Moses and Aaron went into the Tabernacle and when they came back out, they blessed the people again, and the *glorious presence of the Lord appeared* to the whole community. When the people saw all this, *they shouted with joy* and fell face down on the ground" (Lev. 9:23-24).

They could not contain their joy at being in God's presence, and they shouted because of sheer exhilaration. Theirs was the kind of joy of which Jesus spoke during His Palm Sunday procession, when the religious leaders rebuked Him for allowing the people to praise Him as God. What did Jesus say about the joy of being in His presence? "He replied, 'If they kept quiet, the stones along the road would burst into cheers!'" (Luke 19:40). Even inanimate objects want to express the joy of being in God's presence.

We were created *by* God and to be *with* God. Being in His presence is going to make us want to "burst into cheers!" It is so sad when people think that Heaven may be boring. They may agree that we'll be in God's presence, but they cannot imagine enjoying all that singing, listening to harp music, floating around on a cloud with nothing meaningful to do. That *does* sound terribly boring, but that is far from an accurate description of Heaven or being in God's presence.

There is something deep within us that senses our need to be in God's presence. Sin has temporarily separated us from the ongoing, face-to-face presence of God; but at the moment of our death, or our Lord's return, that separation will no longer exist. And for the person who has prepared for God's eternal presence, there will be great and astonishing joy. It will be a joy that causes us, like the Israelites, to shout from the sheer delight of it. It will be a joy that keeps bubbling up and up and up. We've not yet known a joy like this, at least not on a consistent basis, but we *will*. Now *that's* something to look forward to!

WEEK 23

Stephen and the Stones

Leviticus 10–14; Psalm 22; Acts 7

"The Jewish leaders were infuriated by Stephen's accusation, and they shook their fists in rage. …Then they put their hands over their ears, and drowning out his voice with their shouts, they rushed at him. They dragged him out of the city and began to stone him" (Acts 7:54,57-58).

How had Stephen come to this point? It could have been avoided. It would have been so simple. Perhaps a few less direct words concerning his beliefs about Jesus would have been prudent. Perhaps more sensitivity to the beliefs of the people to whom he spoke would have been in order. Perhaps a bit more discretion would have been wise. Couldn't he have been as effective by allowing his good deeds to speak for him and for Jesus, rather than his words?

In a word, no. Stephen had a message to share. His life had been changed, and he wanted *everyone* to know what he now knew as absolute truth. Acts 6 and 7 tell the story of Stephen standing firm in the face of bitter opposition. He stood firm because he loved others and wanted them to understand the life-changing and life-giving message of Jesus Christ's death, resurrection, and provision for our salvation. Stephen stood firm regardless of any personal consequences.

And so he was stoned to death. Reason tells us overwhelming fear should have been the predominant emotion during those minutes of extreme peril. But that was not the case. Instead, Stephen faced those stones and the people who threw them, with his face aglow "as bright as an angel's" (Acts 6:15).

How was Stephen able to not fear the hatred of the crowd and his certain death? It was because Stephen had his eyes fixed on Jesus, not his dire circumstances. We are told that "Stephen, full of the Holy Spirit, gazed steadily upward into heaven and saw the glory of God, and he saw Jesus standing in the place of honor at God's right hand" (Acts 7:55). He knew that his faith was not misplaced.

Perhaps Stephen, on his own, could not have gathered the courage to speak the words of truth that infuriated the crowd and began this confrontation. But *God* could give him the courage, and He did.

In his own strength, Stephen could not have risen above the laws of physics, which bind humans to this earth, to see into Heaven. He could not have ignored the physical pain and torture of rocks hitting him with such force that life departed from his battered body. But God could help him to look beyond and bear these circumstances.

By himself, Stephen could not have moved beyond the emotions that would naturally occur toward those determined to kill him. But God could give him the ability to do so and did. Astonishingly, Stephen's last earthly words cried out to God for mercy, rather than condemnation, for those who killed him.

Fear did not mark Stephen's death—peace and forgiveness did. The manner in which Stephen died was a compelling witness even to those who hated the followers of Jesus—including Saul who observed what happened.

Stephen's unwavering faith, and witness to that faith, made a tremendous difference. He was the first of many through the years who have paid greatly to follow Christ. Their stories humble us. But their stories should also challenge us and make us consider what our response would be in similar circumstances. Like Stephen, and like countless others since Stephen, may we be as reliant on our Lord and as steadfast in our faith.

WEEK 24

An Unusual Day

Leviticus 15–18; Acts 8–10

It defied the laws of science. How does a living, breathing human being disappear into thin air? But it happened. It happened the moment after Philip baptized the treasurer of Ethiopia, a eunuch: "When they came up out of the water, the Spirit of the Lord caught Philip away…" (Acts 8:39).

If it were you or me instead of the eunuch left behind, how long would we stand there not moving a muscle, trying to make sense of the impossible? Would the joy that we had known moments before ever return, or would we remain shaken to our core; unable to accept what had happened? Acts 8:39 tells us, "the eunuch never saw him [Philip] again but went on his way rejoicing."

Let's make sure we have the story straight. The eunuch saw a human being disappear into thin air. This had to be the most astonishing thing that he had ever witnessed, but it seems to have made little impact. How could this be? The only explanation is that the eunuch had experienced something more life-changing than the mere disappearance of a person. He had experienced a personal encounter with the Son of God, and his eyes had been opened to an awesome truth.

It began as the eunuch made his way back to Ethiopia from worshiping God in Jerusalem. Seeking to know God better through the Hebrew Scriptures, he was reading the writings of Isaiah. Suddenly Philip was running alongside his carriage, asking if he understood what he was reading. "The man replied, 'How can I, when there is no one to instruct me?' And he begged Philip to come up into the carriage and sit with him" (Acts 8:31). Good decision!

What words did Philip use to instruct him? They may have been similar to the words used by Peter when speaking to Cornelius in Acts 10. Words that never lose their power to change a life—words such as: "…*there is peace* with God *through Jesus Christ,* who is Lord of all. He is the one all the prophets testified about, saying that everyone who believes in him will have their sins forgiven through his name" (Acts 10:36,43). The eunuch, who had been reading Isaiah's detailed prophecy about Jesus in the Hebrew Scriptures, *did* believe that Jesus could forgive his sins. And his new commitment led immediately to his public declaration of this belief when he asked to be baptized. It was the assurance that his sins *were* forgiven that gave this prominent government official such joy and peace.

What about us? Are we rejoicing at what Christ has done for us? Do we remember what it was like when we first believed and knew that our sins were forgiven—when the burden of those sins was lifted from us and given to Jesus? When was the last time we felt sincere joy at the thought? Take time to remember and to be grateful.

And what of the second person in this story—Philip? Even more than the Ethiopian he must have been affected by what happened. Surely he, too, had to be in total shock. He was after all a man of flesh and bones and muscles, but in the blink of an eye he was miles from where he had been. What must it have felt like to be transported supernaturally and instantly to another place? He may still have been wet from the water in which he was standing as he baptized the eunuch! Was he overcome with terror at this strange thing that had happened to him?

No, it sounds like Philip brushed himself off from his unusual means of travel and got down to business immediately. Acts 8:40 says, "Meanwhile, Philip found himself farther north at the city of Azotus! He preached the Good News there and in every city along the way until he came to Caesarea."

It is hard to stop someone who is passionate about spreading the gospel. Philip was passionate, and he had a story to tell—a life-changing and life-giving story, the most important story that anyone can ever hear. Like Philip, we have the same story to tell. And as with the eunuch, there is someone we know who needs to hear it. Let's get down to God's business!

Could You Repeat That?

Leviticus 19–22; Psalms 23–24; Acts 11

If repetition makes something important, then there are three points in our reading this week that God wants us to fully grasp.

Two times we are told, "You must be holy" (Lev. 19:2; 20:26). That's fairly straight to the point. What does God want from us? He wants us to be holy—without sin. The word "must" cautions us that being holy is not a suggestion, it's a command. So God has made it perfectly clear what we are to be, but why? Why is it so important that we be holy? God answers that question in the second half of these verses: "because I, the Lord, am holy."

So how do we achieve being holy? Leviticus 20:8 tells us how to do this: "Keep all my laws and obey them, for I am the Lord, who makes you holy." The need to obey God's instructions is found throughout Leviticus 19–22. And yet the directive to be obedient in these chapters is balanced by God's acknowledgment that we must look to Him to obtain holiness.

God knows that even with the purest of intents and the deepest of desires, we are incapable of obeying to the extent that we would be considered sinless. And so we are told seven times it is actually the Lord who makes us holy (Lev. 20:8; 21:8, 15, 23; 22:9,16, 32). And that is the whole crux of the matter. We can't be holy without Jesus. It is impossible. Our desire to obey is a sign of our alignment and relationship with God, but it is only God who makes us truly holy. It is God, through Jesus Christ, who makes us sinless and worthy to be in the presence of our holy God. (See 1 Corinthians 1:2.)

God does not take His holiness lightly. He says, "Do not treat my holy name as common and ordinary. I must be treated as holy" (Lev. 22:32). God's name and God Himself are not common but awe-inspiring. We need to sense His magnificence and acknowledge the greatness of our God. Twenty-seven times God states, "I, the Lord, am your God" or "I am the Lord" (Lev. 19:3, 4, 10, 12, 14, 16, 18, 25, 28, 30-32, 34, 36, 37; 20:7,8,24; 21:12; 22:2, 3, 8, 9, 16, 30, 31, 33). Twenty-seven times of anything says *pay attention!* We need to get this thought firmly established in our minds—the Lord is our God! And with that simple acknowledgment we come to admit that He is worthy of our worship, worthy of our trust, and worthy of our obedience.

Where does each of us stand in our desire to be obedient to God? Without question, if we are seeking to obey God, there are going to be many times when we will be doing what God wants rather than what we want. It seems hard to subjugate our will to God's until we've practiced for a while and experienced the pleasure of obedience. For there can be joy in obedience, and that joy makes obedience seem not only natural but desirable.

Without question, the obedient person is going to stand out. It can't be any other way because God's standards are vastly different from this world's standards. And the differences that obedience makes may cause us to be rebuffed by people we associate with and even by people we love. But it will also draw other people to both us and to God—people who want to know why our actions and words are different.

With the desire to obey and be holy comes a constant awareness of God. And with that awareness comes more love for God's character, attributes, and nature. And with that love comes more thankfulness to Jesus, the One who makes us holy before God.

WEEK 26

Humility

Leviticus 23–27; Psalm 25; Acts 12

It was an important day, probably the most important day of the year. It was the Day of Atonement, the day when the Israelite nation and each of its people approached God to demonstrate repentance of their sins, to make amends with God for breaking fellowship with Him, and to have their relationship with God restored.

And on this crucial day there was a crucial step that each Israelite had to take. They were told by God, "On that day you must *humble yourselves*, gather for a sacred assembly, and present offerings to the Lord by fire" (Lev. 23:27).

Humbleness was the requirement to approach God, and this attitude was not taken lightly by God. God added, "Anyone who does not spend that day in humility will be cut off from the community" (Lev. 23:29).

Serious business, this humility thing. But why? Why was humility so vital to approaching God for the Israelites? And why, even after Jesus' sacrifice, is it still so essential for us today as we approach God?

There are many reasons. Most importantly, humility allows us to understand our position before a holy and mighty God. It provides us with the proper awe and respect for God. It gives us the proper perspective.

Humility allows us to be submissive to God's will for us. It allows us to hear God rather than hear ourselves. Humility allows us to be teachable. In humility, we accept instruction, or even rebuke, from God and others and recognize that we don't always know better.

Humility allows us to recognize our sin and our need for God's forgiveness. It keeps our focus on what *we* need to change, not on what changes *others* need to make. Humility allows us to seek both God's forgiveness and others' forgiveness when needed and to be thankful when we receive forgiveness.

Unlike the Israelites, because of Jesus we have the privilege of approaching God at any time and in any place. But what hasn't changed is the need for humility as we approach God. The problem is that humility doesn't tend to come naturally to most of us.

Where are we on the humility scale? Are we ready to defer to God, to listen, to be taught, and to seek forgiveness when needed? Humility must be purposely practiced. God has great things for His children, but it all starts with a humble attitude.

WEEK 27

Comfortable with Change

Numbers 1–5; Acts 13–14

It was time for the message of Jesus Christ to move far beyond Israel and Syria, and God had picked the two men for this special mission. As the prophets and teachers of the early Syrian church met together in worship, prayer, and fasting, "…the Holy Spirit said, 'Dedicate Barnabas and Saul [Paul] for the special work I have for them'" (Acts 13:2).

It surely was a special work. But it was also a work that would turn Paul and Barnabas' world upside down. What were their reactions to the news that they were going on a long journey—long in both time and distance? What were their reactions to leaving their obviously important work in Syria and embarking on the unknown? Did they wrestle with concerns about their future, their safety, leaving behind their friends, and entrusting their work in Syria to others? Did they bargain with God, trying to swap this great unknown work for something familiar?

It appears that Paul and Barnabas were so attuned to the Holy Spirit and so trusting of God's promises to them that they went with gladness, not looking back but feeling secure in God's mission. We are told that "after more fasting and prayer, the men laid their hands on them and sent them on their way" (Acts 13:3). Case closed for Paul and Barnabas.

What would *our* reaction be to God's directive to make a drastic change in our location and lifestyle in order to serve Him more fully? Think about that carefully. I want to be able to say that I would be like Paul and Barnabas, but I wonder if I actually am that trusting of God. And if I am not, what is holding me back? The answer to that question may identify the barrier that is possibly keeping me from being all that God wants me to be.

But Paul and Barnabas had no barriers that kept them from readily obeying God. They and another helper, John Mark, set off to do what God had directed. Surely God's blessings would be given to them after their willing obedience. And blessings there were! As Paul and Barnabas spoke to the crowds, many people accepted as their own truth the fact that "in this man Jesus there is forgiveness for your sins. Everyone who believes in him is freed from all guilt and declared right with God" (Acts 13:38-39).

Although there were many blessings, there were also numerous adversities. There were hardships that caused a younger and healthier John Mark to leave the journey, illness that was severe enough to be, in Paul's own words, "revolting" to others (Gal. 4:14), angry mobs that ran Paul and Barnabas out of their towns, an attempted stoning, and an actual stoning that caused Paul to be left for dead. Let's think about these harsh conditions and put ourselves in their place. Would we be confused? Would we be resentful? Would we question God?

Why, after they had given everything to God, would He allow these horrendous things to happen to them? Where was God's love and protection from harm? Those questions often echo all around us. When our trust and focus falter in the face of difficulties, our hearts whisper, "Why?" or declare, "It's not fair!" But that was not Paul and Barnabas' story.

It seems that they did not even consider such thoughts, for we are told that after Paul had been left for dead from his second stoning, "he got up and went back into the city" (Acts 14:20). He went right back to the place where his life had almost ended—back to, once again, tell the Good News and to encourage and strengthen the new believers. Talk about persistence in the face of adversity and keeping one's attention fixed on one's purpose. This was beyond human persistence; this was God-given persistence.

What is even more amazing is that this was only the first of three journeys! How hard would it be to sell journeys two and three to most of us after suffering through the hardships from journey one?

What a difference their lives made and still make. Have you ever thought about how many Christians' genealogies, even today, could be traced back to Paul and Barnabas' missionary journeys? Maybe even your own? Their story has shown us the way to a life with purpose and meaning. It takes many small steps in trusting and obeying God before we can even come close to the trust and obedience of these giants of the Christian faith. But this kind of life starts with one small step and grows with each step that follows it. It doesn't matter where you are in the journey; it only matters that you are moving forward.

There is much to admire about Paul and Barnabas. Are we willing to follow their lead?

WEEK 28

Let's Talk

Numbers 6–9; Psalms 26–27; Acts 15

Occasionally in our Bible reading, a verse, or fragment of a verse, will be riveting to us. It's as if the words were written to answer a deep longing within, a longing of which we may not even be aware. Three verses from the psalmist David were like that this week for me. They are verses that offer comfort and hope.

The first verse is from Psalm 27:8. David says to the Lord, "My heart has heard you say, 'Come and talk with me.'" Can you hear what David hears? Can you hear the tenderness in God's invitation to come and talk? There is no demanding tone in God's words, and there are no barriers erected. David needs no special formula or specific language to gain God's attention. There is only the love of the Creator saying, "Come and talk *with* me." Be genuine and honest with Me. Tell Me what troubles you, what brings you joy, and about your day. Come and rest a bit in My presence.

And the response from David is trusting and confident: "And my heart responds, 'Lord, I am coming.'" "I am coming"—not reluctantly, but quickly and happily. David is coming to the place where he knows there will be welcome relief, greater joy, fuller understanding, and a deepening relationship with God. Does your heart long, as David's did, for this comfortable relationship with God? It is ours to have. Just come and talk with our God.

One of the benefits of coming often to talk with God is that we will begin to have an inkling of His unique love for us, as David did, when he declared, "For I am constantly aware of your unfailing love" (Ps. 26:3). A true understanding of God's constant, dependable, and enduring love would be life-changing. Because no human can love like this, we can only scratch the surface of understanding a love like God's for us, His creation. But even a surface knowledge begins to show us the depth of God's love. And as we become more aware of this love, we learn to trust where it will lead us each day.

David knew this, for he said, "I have trusted in the Lord without wavering" (Ps. 26:1). If you are like me, there are moments when you trust and there are moments when you waver. That tiny worry that nags at the back of our minds, that mounting anxiety over a particular situation, and those feelings of discouragement are examples that we are wavering in our trust and forgetting how deeply we are loved.

But we *are* deeply loved by God, and these three Scriptures show us that love. As we remember them, our lives will have a serenity and joy that can only come from following the guidelines of these verses.

Talk often with God. *"My heart has heard you say, 'Come and talk with me.' And my heart responds, 'Lord, I am coming"* (Ps. 27:8).

Know that you are loved. *"For I am constantly aware of your unfailing love"* (Ps. 26:3).

Allow the knowledge of that love to translate to trust. *"I have trusted in the Lord without wavering"* (Ps. 26:1).

As these verses take root in our thoughts, our thankfulness will increase as we begin to more fully understand the value of our relationship with God.

Straight Talk

Numbers 10–14; Acts 16–17

Last week we read about David's thoughts on talking with God and his keen awareness of God's love and trustworthiness. This week we again encountered these central themes, but we hear them from different sources and viewpoints—Moses' and God's.

In Numbers 11, Moses and God had a discussion about the ungrateful Israelites who were once again complaining, this time about the lack of variety in their diets. Moses' time with God wasn't one of praise and worship but a down-in-the-mouth, heartfelt lament. "And Moses said to the Lord, 'Why are you treating me, your servant, so miserably? What did I do to deserve the burden of a people like this? Where am I supposed to get meat for all these people? They keep complaining and saying, "Give us meat!" I can't carry all these people by myself! The load is far too heavy! I'd rather you killed me than treat me like this. Please spare me this misery!'" (Num. 11:11,13-15).

Do you almost feel yourself bracing for God's reaction? Moses had accused God of fairly serious neglect. In an instant Moses could have developed leprosy, the ground could have opened and swallowed him, or he could have been struck dead as others had been before him. But that was not God's reaction. Instead God told Moses how He would help him bear the burden of leading the people. God provided a solution for Moses' weariness, with no reprisal for Moses' complaints.

God's reaction to Moses is in direct contrast to His reaction to the Israelites' complaint of not having meat. God tells Moses that He will provide meat for the Israelites' diet, but He also tells him of the price the Israelites will pay for their complaining: "You will eat it for a whole month until you gag and are sick of it. For you have rejected the Lord, who is here among you, and you have complained to him" (Num. 11:20).

What was the difference between Moses and the Israelites' complaints to God? Why didn't God punish Moses for his frustration with leading the people when He punished the Israelites for a similar frustration with the monotony of their diets?

One glaring difference is that the Israelites did not talk with God, as Moses did, about the things that troubled them. They complained among themselves. Yes, Moses had questions of "why" and "where." Yes, there was even a large dose of self-pity when he told God to go ahead and kill him, but there was also a plea to God for help with "this misery." Moses was completely candid with God, but it was God to whom he talked.

The most amazing part of this story is that, after God did not condemn Moses but told him instead that He would provide help for him and meat for the nation, Moses *argued* with God that it would be impossible to obtain enough meat to feed the vast number of Israelites because that much meat did not exist. Moses was on quite a roll that day!

And what was God's reaction? Once again, God did not chastise Moses for asking the honest question of "how" but asked him in return, "Is there any limit to my power?" (Num. 11:23).

God asks the same question to us today. And we answer, "No." But when we do the gut check, is our actual answer, "Maybe"? Do we believe, deep down inside, that there *is* a limit to God's power or at least a limit when it comes to *our own* situations? Isn't it easier to trust in God's unlimited power when it is in the abstract than when it is in the personal places of our own lives?

I don't know about you, but at least for me, I fear that this is too often the case. The true limitation, though, is in our ability to trust in God's power and love for us, not in God's actual power or His actual love. Are we putting a limit on God's power in our lives by not being open with Him like David and Moses? Like David and Moses, we don't have to clean up our feelings, our hurts, our confusion, and our lack of trust when we talk with God. God, who cares tenderly for us, will hear and answer our cries of "I don't understand," "Help me," "I'm afraid," "I'm confused," "I'm lonely," and even "Help me to trust You."

We only need to be honest.

WEEK 30

Different Pages

Numbers 15–18; Psalms 28–29; Acts 18

They couldn't have been on a more different page. God clearly saw it one way and the Israelites another.

Numbers 16 tells the story of the Israelites once again rebelling against God and Moses and Aaron. This time Korah, an important

Israelite leader, along with two other leaders (Dathan and Abiram), had decided to challenge Moses and Aaron's spiritual authority and their right to lead the Israelite nation. Korah, Dathan, and Abiram obviously had the ability to persuade others because they were able to incite a rebellion throughout the camp against Moses and Aaron. They seemed oblivious to the fact that they were ultimately challenging God's leadership, since it was He who had appointed Moses and Aaron to these positions of authority. God brought swift death to these three men, their families, and 250 of their ardent followers.

That should have been a vivid object lesson for the Israelites, one that caused them to walk carefully for a time. But in less than twenty-four hours they were blaming Moses and Aaron for these peoples' deaths instead of acknowledging God's judgment on them for their rebellion against Him. Their amazingly short memory of God's judgment for unrepentant sin was instantly reawakened as a plague swept through the camp, causing another 14,700 deaths before Moses and Aaron could come between God's anger and the people.

By Numbers chapter 17, God wanted to put an end to any more rebellion, and He wanted it to be obvious whom He had chosen as the spiritual leader of the people. God made His intention clear by taking a wooden staff from each of the twelve ancestral tribes and stating that His designated leader's staff would sprout buds. Overnight, the piece of dead wood that was Aaron's staff not only buds, but the buds bloom, and the blooms produced almonds.

God was trying to make His message completely clear to these hardheaded people. And why was this message so important to God? God Himself said why: "This should put an end to their complaints against me and prevent any further deaths" (Num. 17:10). It seems that God's heart was grieved not only by the peoples' continual rebellion but by the resulting deaths. God's mercy was greater than His anger. In spite of their rebellion and their lack of trust, God still loved these people and wanted to protect them from death and suffering.

But the people misinterpreted the message. God told them what He wanted, so there would be no mistake, no rebellion, and no additional deaths. And what was their reaction? "Then the people of Israel said to Moses, 'We are as good as dead! We are ruined! We are all doomed!'" (Num. 17:12-13).

God said He wanted to "prevent any further deaths." The people said, "We are as good as dead!" God said, "Life." The Israelites said, "We are all doomed."

Aren't we like the Israelites? Sometimes we do not see God's plan for our lives, and we do not understand the path we are asked to walk, so we interpret things through our own life's experiences and our own eyes' bleary lenses. We're focused on what *we* see and know, not on how *God* sees or leads. We say, "Pain, suffering, confusion, and fear." God says, "Trust, growth, hope, and life."

We need God's help to correctly read our own life story as it unfolds each day.

WEEK 31

Who Are You?

Numbers 19–23; Acts 19–20

"I know Jesus, and I know Paul. But who are you?" (Acts 19:15).

"But who are you?" Normally this wouldn't be a particularly frightening question, but these words were spoken by an evil spirit, a demon. Can you hear the voice of this demon—mocking, cold, powerfully questioning the seven sons of Sceva?

These seven Jewish exorcists traveled from town to town claiming to drive out evil spirits through incantations. This was their business, their claim to fame, their path to power and social position.

They had heard of Paul and the powerful miracles of healing and casting out of evil spirits that he performed through the name of Jesus Christ. The seven sons recognized an opportunity when they saw one, so they decided that they, too, would invoke the name of Jesus Christ when trying to cast out evil spirits. The name of Jesus Christ was only another incantation for them, another gimmick among many to bring into play. There was no relationship to Jesus for Sceva's seven sons, but there was the possibility of true financial gain, if this name worked the way it did for Paul.

And so they came upon a man possessed by an evil spirit. This time using the name of Jesus, the seven sons told the evil spirit to come out. Because of the sheer power of the name of the Lord, the demon did come out, but "he leaped on them and attacked them with such violence that they fled from the house, naked and badly injured" (Acts 19:16).

The seven sons did not realize they had stepped into the midst of a spiritual battle by invoking the name of Jesus against the evil spirit. The evil spirit had to obey the mighty name of the Lord, but the seven sons learned in a few short moments how dangerous spiritual warfare can be if you are not personally committed to Jesus Christ.

Why did the evil spirit know Paul and not the seven sons? It was because Paul was its sworn enemy. Paul wasn't safely observing on the sidelines. Paul had chosen sides, and he was in battle. Paul clearly states his battle plan in Acts 20:20-21: "Yet I never shrank from telling you the truth, either publicly or in your homes. I have had one message for Jews and Gentiles alike—the necessity of turning from sin and turning to God, and of faith in our Lord Jesus."

Paul knew his loyalty to the message of his commander, Jesus Christ, would lead to numerous times of jail and mistreatment. In many of these instances, Paul would be in worse shape than the seven sons after the demonic attack, but that never stopped him from telling others about Jesus Christ.

Do Satan and his followers know us like they knew Paul? Before reading this account, I knew the importance of being known by God, but I had never considered the significance of being known by Satan and evil spirits. Now it seems like a worthy goal.

Have we, like Paul, firmly chosen sides? Are we in such harmony with Jesus that we are known to the demons as Christ's followers and their steadfast enemies? Like Paul, are we such faithful, consistent followers of Jesus Christ that we are on our enemies' radar screens? Are we making a difference for Christ each day upon this earth through our prayers and our actions?

Don't let it be asked of us, "But who are you?" Let our alignment to Christ be evident, strong, and true through the choices we make each day. Do you want to be known as an enemy of Satan? Tell and live one message—the Good News of Jesus Christ.

Moving Beyond the Intellectual

Numbers 24–27; Psalm 30; Acts 21–22

"The will of the Lord be done" (Acts 21:14).

These words of trust are easy enough to say during the times when life is going along pretty much as we'd like. But what about the times when it is not? What about the times when we are faced with crisis, confusion, rejection, pain, or loss and find it hard to believe that this is the will of the Lord for us? What about the times that knock us off our feet and prompt us to ask, "Why, Lord, if You love me"?

Paul could have asked that question frequently. He knew what it was like to be ill, lonely, in pain, hungry, tired, and hated as he traveled to tell others about Jesus Christ. He knew what it was like to be innocent, yet punished. He knew the sting of friendships lost through death. He had experienced all of these.

And he was prepared to experience it once more. As Paul made his way back to Jerusalem from his missionary journey, he knew he was headed straight into unfair treatment, physical suffering, and undeserved imprisonment. Fellow believers knew it, too. Two different groups of people begged Paul not to continue on to Jerusalem but to save himself from these horrendous times.

Paul understood their deep concern for him. He knew how much they longed to protect him, but Paul had an important message for them. "Why all this weeping? You are breaking my heart! For I am ready not only to be jailed at Jerusalem but also to die for the sake of the Lord Jesus" (Acts 21:13).

Paul's heart was not broken by his friends' predictions of hardships but by their lack of trust in God's plan for him. Paul knew it was God who gave his life meaning and purpose, and he was not willing to trade any aspect of that relationship for the possibility of safety or ease. As he and his friends parted, they reinforced Paul's trust in God's plan with the words, "The will of the Lord be done."

Like Paul, each of us will face tough situations common to all people. It is during these times that the words "the will of the Lord be done" brings peace to us or the awareness that we never truly believed them.

Are we subconsciously clinging to the belief that somehow we can control our world or our circumstances? When things begin to go against us, do we believe that God has let us down *or* do we believe that He is worthy of our trust? Are we able to rest in our belief that God does, in fact, keep His promise that all things work together for good for those who love Him, even when harsh realities seem to say otherwise?

It is during the times when we are genuinely suffering that it is most difficult to say, and believe, these words. But it is also during these times of testing, and retesting, that our faith can move beyond the intellectual and the theological into the core of our being.

This isn't only true for biblical times or for extraordinary people. This is true for *all* who keep reaching to God during the painful experiences and crises of our lives. We may never be wrongly imprisoned, and we may never be beaten for our faith, but we are going to be tested by the hardships of life. We are going to lose people and things that we hold dear, we are going to become ill, we are going to be confused over circumstances, and we are going to run into situations that frighten us. Sometime, maybe many times, our world is going to be shaken and turned upside down.

It is during these times that we can begin to learn authentic trust in God's plan for our lives, as He molds us to become more like Him and helps us to show others what faith can mean. We hate having to learn it through pain and difficulties, but we seldom learn it while our world is serene and unruffled. But with that learning comes genuine peace, genuine comfort, and the ability to say with conviction, "The will of the Lord be done."

WEEK 33

Unintended Influence

Numbers 28–32; Psalm 31; Acts 23

Paul was in Jerusalem, and Paul was in prison. Paul was not in prison because he was a threat to the people of Jerusalem but because they were a threat to him.

It began a few days after Paul's arrival in Jerusalem, when a great riot occurred due to the misinterpretation of Paul's teaching. The riot grew in intensity, and the mob tried to kill Paul. The Roman regiment commander, whose duty it was to keep the peace in Jerusalem, ran into the midst of the riot with his troops. His action saved Paul's life, as the crowd temporarily quieted in the face of absolute authority.

When the commander intervened, he did not know who Paul was or why he aroused such fevered reactions among the crowd, but he reasoned that such intense emotion had to be triggered by a serious crime. The commander arrested Paul until he could determine what that crime was.

The commander's attention was on Paul, but Paul's attention was elsewhere. Paul continued to focus on preaching the message of salvation through Jesus Christ to the crowd. Ignoring the fact that he had just been arrested, he requested permission to address those who had tried to kill him. Hoping to learn more about the cause of the riot, the commander agreed.

As Paul spoke, the riot restarted. Unfortunately for the commander, he knew no more about why the mob wanted Paul dead at this point than he had at the beginning. He ordered that Paul be jailed, and the next day he had Paul taken before the Jewish high council of religious leaders, hoping to determine his actual crime. Once again, Paul's words were divisive, and the council members began to fight bitterly among themselves. Before long, their attention, and fury, turned back to Paul, and he was almost ripped apart as opposing sides of the council pulled on him. Paul was once again taken back to jail for his safety.

So all sides were left in a quagmire. Paul was back in prison. The commander still did not know why Paul roused such violent feelings among the Jewish people. And to the religious leaders' consternation, Paul was still alive. Something had to happen to break this stalemate.

And so a plan was formulated. More than forty people went to the leading priests and other leaders and told them that they had "bound themselves with an oath to neither eat nor drink until they had killed Paul" (Acts 23:12). All that was needed to put their plan in action was to get Paul away from the safety of the prison. The leaders could help by asking the commander to bring Paul to the council to be questioned. The plotters would murder Paul before he made it there.

But they were unaware that "Paul's nephew heard of their plan and went to the fortress and told Paul" (Acts 23:16). Paul directed his nephew to tell this news to the commander, and upon hearing it, the commander ordered more than 400 soldiers to move Paul that night to the safety of the town of Caesarea.

The plotters never knew that they had been overheard. And they never realized that all they hoped to accomplish was destroyed by one young man of little consequence to them.

The plotters' goal was for evil. As God's children, our goals and actions should be intended for good. Even though we have different goals, we are like the plotters in that we never know who is listening to what we say or observing what we do. We do not operate in a vacuum, and it is sometimes easy to forget how much influence our words and actions can have on intended, or unintended, audiences. We never know how inconsistencies in our lives can harm unknown observers. Because of this we need to strive for transparency in our thoughts and actions, so that we have no qualms about anyone hearing what we say or seeing what we do.

If the thought of anyone observing how we act, knowing what we do, or hearing what we say causes us to pause, then it may be the perfect reminder that we need to change how we are thinking, talking, or acting.

As Paul's watchful, but unobserved, nephew changed the course of the conspirators' plans, our plans and the way in which we conduct ourselves can change the lives of those we do not notice but who are observing us. Bringing each of our thoughts and actions into alignment with God's principles is a continuing challenge for all of us but worthy of our effort.

WEEK 34

Pulling Up Stakes

Numbers 33–36; Deuteronomy 1; Acts 24–25

"The Lord our God said to us, 'You have stayed at this mountain long enough. It is time to break camp and move on'" (Deut. 1:6-7).

Moses was reviewing with the Israelites their journey toward the Promised Land since leaving Egypt. It should have been a happy story, for from the moment their journey began God had wanted the people to have the special gift of this bountiful land as their own. And to that end, God had shown Himself again and again to be the God of power, provision, and love—worthy of the people's trust.

But it *wasn't* a happy story because, in return, the people had built up a mountain of ungratefulness, disobedience, demands, fearfulness, and doubt regarding God's intentions. During their journey they had struggled not only with physical mountains but a mountain of their own making. Their mountain of doubt and disillusionment had blocked their view and dulled their senses to *who* God was and *what* He was.

However, they had "stayed at this mountain long enough," and they needed to "break camp and move on." Their fears and doubts and disobedience had left them stagnant at the mountain and far from the Promised Land for a long time. But there had been a way forward all along, and Moses stood before the people to remind them of this.

Moses said, "Don't be afraid! The Lord your God is going before you. He will fight for you, just as you saw him do in Egypt. And you saw how the Lord your God cared for you again and again here in the wilderness, just as a father cares for his child. Now he has brought you to this place. But even after all he did, you refused to trust the Lord your God, who goes before you looking for the best places to camp, guiding you by a pillar of fire at night and pillar of cloud by day" (Deut. 1:29-33).

There is nothing like a little action to destroy stagnation, and even though the people had been stagnant, God had not been. God was, and is, the God of action, and the people needed to be reminded of this. Look at all the action verbs describing God in the verses in Deuteronomy 1.

God is "going before you," He "will fight for you," "the Lord your God cared for you again and again," God "brought you to this place," He "goes before you looking for the best places," and is "guiding you." God was doing the heavy work here; He was taking all the actions needed for success and deliverance. And the action required of the Israelites was to "*trust* the Lord your God."

What about us? Like the Israelites, are we wandering in our own wilderness? Are there times when God seems too far away? Are we stalled and staring up at our own mountain built of fears, circumstances not of our doing, consequences of disobedience, or forgetfulness of God's goodness? If we aren't now, we most likely will be at some point. So be reminded that our God is the God of action—going before us, guiding us, fighting for us, caring for us, and helping us break past our mountains. We may not be aware of this activity, but we can be assured that it *is* occurring on behalf of those who love the Lord. And like the Israelites, the action that we need to take is "to trust the Lord our God."

"The Lord our God said to us, 'You have stayed at this mountain long enough. It is time to break camp and move on'" (Deut. 1:6-7).

Take the road of trust!

WEEK 35

Turn Around

Deuteronomy 2–5; Psalm 32; Acts 26–27

"Then we turned around and set out across the wilderness…" (Deut. 2:1).

The wilderness in this verse is a place that is lonely, inhospitable, confusing, and even life-threatening to those trapped in it. It represents a place of separation from the goodness of God. The words of this verse are profoundly sad, for they indicate a conscious decision to stop moving forward toward something good, an intentional turning away from the original direction, and movement toward something not good.

Why would anyone going in a direction leading toward a refuge deliberately turn around and head out to a wilderness that was isolating and harmful? Why would anyone in relationship with God turn away from that relationship?

The stories of both the Israelites and David give several explanations for their turning from the Lord, including disobedience to and mistrust of God. The Israelites turned around and set out across the wilderness when they wouldn't obey God and didn't trust Him to fulfill His promises. David turned around when he decided to deliberately disobey God by committing adultery and then arranging a murder to try to conceal the adultery.

Disobedience to and mistrust of God were two reasons why these people headed toward the wilderness, but there is probably at least one more; they did not know the reality of life in the wilderness. They were accustomed to the joys that came from God. They had no comprehension of what their daily existence would be like with the things they wanted, yet without the peace and comfort of God's presence. They were probably astounded at how bleak their lives became after rejecting God's good guidance, how devastating the wilderness was, and how harmful their actions were to themselves and others.

We still purposefully turn around and head in the wrong direction and for the same reasons as the Israelites and David. This verse has profound personal meaning to me. I've been there. Why did I turn away from God? It was because I decided I wanted something God said was wrong for me to have more than I wanted to keep living a life of obedience to Him. I can clearly remember the moment when I said to myself, "I want this more than I want to obey You, God."

At that moment, I turned away from God and set out across my own personal wilderness. Of course at the time, I didn't believe I was headed for the wilderness; I believed I was headed toward happiness. Looking back on it now, I wonder what ever made me believe that I was wiser than God about what would bring me happiness. Like others before me, I soon found out the misery of turning from God.

So, like the Israelites I wandered in the wilderness for many years— seven to be exact; not quite believing that God could forgive my willful disobedience. And, like David, I was weighed down by my guilt, overcome by the consequences of my wrong decisions, and ashamed for the damage my behavior had brought to the reputation of Jesus Christ (Ps. 32:3-4,10).

But like David, "finally I confessed all my sins" to God "and stopped trying to hide them" (Ps. 32:5). And with David, I can say that I know the joy of forgiveness of my sins. I know the delight of returning to the Lord and setting out again on the path that God desires for me. With David, I say, "Oh, what joy for those whose rebellion is forgiven, whose sin is put out of sight! Yes, what joy for those whose record the Lord has cleared of sin, whose lives are lived in complete honesty!" (Ps. 32:1-2).

The answer *how* to turn back was and is always available to those who have wandered in the wilderness, broken by sin's burdens. The answer is the same for us as it was when Moses told the people, "And if you search for him [God] with all your heart and soul, you will find him" (Deut. 4:29). Our search for God begins as soon as we turn back toward Him and away from the wilderness. God *wants* to be found, and He *wants* to restore any who have turned away.

These verses are deeply meaningful to those who have experienced the sorrow of separation from God caused by our disobedience and the joy of forgiveness that comes through heartfelt repentance. There is true elation in being able once again to live in complete honesty, no longer weighed down by guilt, facing each day with nothing to hide and nothing of which to be ashamed.

Thank God for His mercy, forgiveness, and restoration.

WEEK 36

God's Watchfulness

Deuteronomy 6–10; Psalm 33; Acts 28

"The Lord looks down from heaven and sees the whole human race. From his throne he observes all who live on the earth" (Ps. 33:13-14).

The Israelites should have been squirming at the thought of God watching them, for they were conducting their lives in direct opposition to how God wanted them to live. Even as God made plans for their well-being, He watched the people doing exactly what would cause them harm.

God watched the people as He prepared the Ten Commandments, His guidelines for their successful living. As God handed the Commandments to Moses, He didn't spend time reviewing what they had spoken about over the past forty days. God had more urgent concerns, and He told Moses, "Go down immediately because the people you led out of Egypt have become corrupt. They have already turned from the way I commanded them to live…I have been watching this people, and they are extremely stubborn. Leave me alone so I may destroy them and erase their name from under heaven" (Deut. 9:12-14). God had been watching. He wasn't being unfair to think about destroying the Israelites, for as He watched, He saw the people continually ignoring Him. Wiser people would have thought about God and stopped their foolish actions.

God's holiness demanded that the people be judged, and even their fellow Israelite, Moses, agreed when he declared to the people, "Yes, you have been rebelling against the Lord as long as I have known you" (Deut. 9:24). Only God's love and mercy prevented the complete destruction of these early Israelites.

As we honestly assess our lives, there will be times when we know that our actions and thoughts are not pleasing to God. At these times our awareness of being watched by God may bring discomfort or even fear. If so, we can learn from the Israelites' and our own mistakes and move toward the type of relationship with God that the unidentified psalmist wrote about in Psalm 33.

This psalmist wrote about fearing God, an emotion not often thought of as a positive in a relationship. But fear, as used in this Psalm, means to respect God's holiness, depend on His guidance, and trust in His immeasurable knowledge and wisdom.

The psalmist recognized another essential that turns being watched by God into a pleasurable experience. That essential is God's unfailing love: "But the Lord watches over those who fear Him, those who rely on His unfailing love" (Ps. 33:18). It is this coupling of "unfailing love," with the fear (or trust and respect) of the Lord that makes being watched by God a source of peace and security for us. As we begin to understand God's intense love for us, there is comfort in knowing that He cares enough to keep watch over us just as a doting parent keeps watch over his or her beloved child.

But this is almighty God who has promised to keep watch over us, not a human parent. We determine, by our beliefs and behavior, if this promise brings uneasiness or comfort to us.

Week 37

Walk and Cling

Deuteronomy 11–15; Romans 1–2

"Be careful to obey all the commands I give you; show love to the Lord your God by walking in his ways and clinging to him" (Deut. 11:22).

How do we show our love for God? The verse above specifically says that we do so by "walking in his ways." There are many ways of walking, but all walking begins with an action taken and continues by determinedly putting one foot in front of the other. But there is one type of walking that goes far beyond the norm; it is the confident walk of someone with head up, back straight, stomach in, stride firm. Doesn't walking this way portray a sense of purpose, action, and sureness? In the same way, walking in God's ways evokes images of standing tall and firm in our faith, moving forward with intent, and remaining upright even when knocked back.

But walking in God's ways implies something more. To walk in God's ways suggests not only walking but following in the same manner in which He would walk. This type of walk reminds me of a scene from a classic movie filmed in the 1930s. In this scene, a butler, who has an unusual walk, answers the door. "Walk this way," he says to the arriving guest, meaning, "Follow me." The guest does "walk this way," following the butler *and* imitating his exact walk. Like the guest, to walk in God's ways is to both follow Him and emulate Him. How's our walk?

Deuteronomy 11:22 mentions one other equally important action to show our love for the Lord our God. Along with walking, we are told to cling to God.

Clinging may carry with it an aura of weakness, but in reality, there will come a time when even the strongest and most self-sufficient person will cling to something. What are we doing as we cling, and what drives us to do it?

For starters, we aren't letting go when we cling to someone or something that we feel has great value to us. We will try our best to keep a solid grip regardless of the circumstance, and, as circumstances worsen, our grasp only tightens on whatever we cling to for security. When we feel something is worth clinging to, there is nothing as important to us as keeping our connection unbroken. Pride goes out the window as we turn all of our efforts and thoughts toward retaining that relationship.

Clinging is always a highly emotional response to something we feel we need. Clinging speaks of our reliance, our belief that this person or object will support us in our weakness and sustain us with its greater value. Are we wise enough to have a clinging relationship with God?

Walk with God and cling to God. At first glance, it may seem odd that these two commands would be linked together as a way for us to show our love for God, for they seem to be in direct emotional opposition to each other. Unlike walking, where we are in command of our movement and initiate the first step, clinging speaks of being carried by that which we embrace. As we cling, we are not in the lead; we are holding on.

But isn't that like God, who understands us so completely? Hand-in-hand walking and clinging complete the cycle of our experiences. There will be times when we *are* feeling confident and strong in our faith, and it will be with joy and anticipation that we walk in His ways. But there will also be times when we are *not* confident and do *not* feel strong. It is especially during those times when we must cling to God and draw from His strength and support. We have something of tremendous value to cling to. We have a relationship that truly completes us. It is a relationship with God through Jesus Christ and the Holy Spirit.

During the time of Deuteronomy, Jesus hadn't yet come to earth to live out God's commandments. Jesus showed His love for the Father by walking in obedience to Him and by clinging to Him for strength and direction. We have been given a flawless example of how to walk in God's ways through Jesus' life.

Walking and clinging. It makes perfect sense when you are following the perfect Guide.

Week 38

Time to Celebrate!

Deuteronomy 16–20; Psalm 34; Romans 3

"Then you must *celebrate* the Festival of Harvest to *honor* the Lord your God. …It is a time to *celebrate* before the Lord your God. *Celebrate with your whole family*" (Deut. 16:10-11).

"Another *celebration*, the Festival of Shelters, must be observed for seven days. …This festival will be a *happy time of rejoicing* with your family. For seven days *celebrate* this festival to *honor* the Lord your God. …This festival will be a *time of great joy* for all" (Deut. 16:13-15).

These verses tell us that God wants His people to come together to honor Him through the act of celebration—times of delight and excitement. The idea that our God wants us to celebrate may not always be how people think of our Lord since one of Satan's many deceptions is to lead people to believe that worshiping and serving God is boring, all-rules-and-no-fun misery. If that misconception is part of any Christian's belief system, then that person has yet to discover what it is truly like to follow the Lord.

Part of the confusion with associating God with celebrating is that celebrating can have contradictory meanings and outcomes. Let's think for a moment of the good aspects.

Celebrations usually mark things of importance in our lives. When we truly participate in a celebration, our thoughts are directed to the reason for the celebration, and this allows us a respite from other parts of our lives that sap our energy or cause distress. We look forward to celebrations because they are different from our day-to-day routines and enliven our senses. As we gather together with those we care about, we often create lasting and fond memories.

On the other hand, there are celebrations where the memories created are not good, where relationships are shattered rather than strengthened, or where someone's behavior causes embarrassment or even shame. But when our focus is to honor God, we retain the joy of celebrations and none of the aspects that cause pain or humiliation. In our celebration of God and His goodness to us, we not only uplift God but we are uplifted as well.

God's desire for the Israelites was that they would celebrate who He was, rejoice in what He did, and rest from their normal work schedule. These happy times weren't to be celebrated alone but were to include the entire community and especially each person's family—the children, the elderly, and those in-between.

Sharing our thoughts of God's goodness while celebrating together can bring joy. The psalmist understood this. In Psalm 34, David says, "Come, let us *tell* of the Lord's greatness; let us *exalt his name together*" (v. 3). In other words, let's take time to honor and celebrate the Lord while talking with others about Him.

Do we look forward to talking with our friends and family about what our relationship with God means to us? Is there anticipation and excitement at the thought of sharing what God has done in our lives or is doing right now? Do we rejoice together in answers to prayers? Do we celebrate the ways that we have been given to serve God? Do we discuss what we are learning about God, His attributes, and His words to us in Scripture?

Our stories about God can become the foundation of our lives and our families' lives. They can help younger generations learn the celebratory joy that comes with serving and honoring God.

Let's help them to learn that if they want excitement, if they want to make a difference with their lives, if they want to look at life through eyes not clouded by cynicism, if they want to grow wiser, if they want to truly have something to celebrate and rejoice over, then a life honoring God is the answer.

Celebrate God! Rejoice in Jesus! Find great joy in the Holy Spirit! And then talk about it. It will make a difference.

WEEK 39

What Makes a Promise a Promise?

Deuteronomy 21–24; Psalm 35; Romans 4–5

"Abraham never wavered in believing God's promise. In fact, his faith grew stronger, and in this he brought glory to God. He was absolutely convinced that God was able to do anything he promised" (Rom. 4:20-21).

There's so much to get our attention in these two verses. There is the strength of the words describing Abraham: "never wavered, faith grew stronger, brought glory to God, absolutely convinced." Powerful words! And then there is the focal point of these words—the promises of God.

Promises, whether made by God or people, are important to us. Promises have value to us because they relate to our desires. They set up an expectation that the person making the promise has the ability to make something happen. We cherish promises for the hope they bring. But that hope can only be as strong as the reliability of whoever is making the promise.

Abraham never wavered in believing in God and the reliability of His promises. Abraham was absolutely convinced—not convinced "most of the time," not "sometimes" convinced if the circumstances made sense, but unquestionably convinced. It didn't matter to him that circumstances made the promise appear unachievable. It didn't matter to him whether or not he saw progress being made on the promise. It only mattered that it was *God* who had made the promise.

Because of being absolutely convinced and unwavering in his belief in God's promise, Abraham's faith grew stronger, and he brought glory to God. That was the totality of it. In these verses we aren't told of anything else that Abraham did to glorify God or of anything else that helped his faith grow strong. Strength of conviction in God's promise covered it all. And that alone has caused Abraham's name to be recalled in honor throughout thousands of years. Can you grasp how astounding that is? There are few people who are remembered for eons. To be remembered not for something you created, discovered, or caused, but to be remembered for what you believed and for the strength of your belief is incredible. Even more importantly, it was that strength of belief that has caused God's name to be glorified ever since.

One important factor was necessary for Abraham to be unwavering in his belief of God's promise. Abraham had to know what the promise was. That may seem like an obvious point, but the manner in which Abraham "knew" this promise implies a depth to his knowledge, plus the willingness to act in accordance with any conditions that needed to be met for the promise to be fulfilled. Since he knew the promise, Abraham was then able to recall the benefits of the promise when doubts arose. His understanding of the promise, his recall of its benefits, and his fulfillment of its conditions helped keep his belief in the promise strong.

Abraham had one major promise from God—the promise to make his family into a powerful nation. We have the blessing of many promises made to us by God. But, like Abraham, we truly have to know *what* we are promised to be able to believe in those promises. The Bible is built upon the foundation of God's promises, and they are there for us to discover.

Abraham's belief that God would fulfill His promise caused his faith to grow stronger. This should be the case for us as well, but many times our faith becomes weaker, or is destroyed entirely, as our doubts begin to accumulate about God keeping a promise. However, it is not God's faithfulness that is lacking but our knowledge and belief. To increase our knowledge of God's promises, we need to determine their "who," "what," "when," "where," and "how."

First, we need to determine to whom a promise has been made. A promise may be for all people, for specific groups of people, or for an individual. While it is possible that we may benefit from the fulfillment of God's promise to other persons, not all promises apply specifically to us.

Second, what is the promise? Did you know that there are more than 1,000 promises in the Bible? Of how many are we aware? And how will it change our lives as we learn more about each of God's promises? In our study, it may be tempting to grab hold of promises that carry positive consequences and ignore those that don't, but promises can also serve as a warning to us. Both types of promises are important to our spiritual growth.

There is another "what" to promises, and that is what is required for the promise to be attained. Promises often carry an action that must be fulfilled by the recipient. We often want to claim the positive aspect of something promised while ignoring the requirement attached to it. We need to determine if a promise's fulfillment is conditional upon an action that we first need to take, and if so, take it.

Next, promises may be specific as to time or place. Some promises may be fulfilled in this life, while others will not be fulfilled until we join Jesus in Heaven. Some promises are for a specific time in our lives or a specific time in history.

Finally, promises have various ways to be fulfilled. Some promises may be specific and easily understood with the knowledge we possess. But others require complete trust in God's power because fulfillment is possible only because He has promised it. Are we able to trust God to be God and to work in ways we cannot understand?

We can grow in our knowledge of God's promises as Abraham did. We can determine to do what is required of us for their fulfillment. And we can recall them when our faith is shaken. Unwavering belief in God's promises assures us of growing faith, genuine joy, true peace in the midst of life's chaos, tender comfort in our sorrows, and boundless hope for our future.

WEEK 40

Weary, Exhausted, and Lagging Behind

Deuteronomy 25–29; Romans 6–7

"Never forget what the Amalekites did to you as you came from Egypt. They attacked you when you were exhausted and weary, and they struck down those who were lagging behind" (Deut. 25:17-18).

To the Amalekites, murder was a way of life, as they enriched themselves with the treasure of those they killed. More disturbingly, they were noted for the pleasure they took in killing. Except for God's intervention, the Amalekites most likely would have destroyed the Israelites at the beginning of their journey out of Egypt (Exod. 17:8-16).

The Israelites were vulnerable to the Amalekites' attack for two reasons. They were exhausted, and some lagged behind the main group following Moses.

It makes sense that the Israelites were exhausted. They had recently left a life of slavery where they had been brutally overworked. They were crossing a desert and had to stay on alert to attack by hostile groups such as the Amalekites. They had to learn new skills, find food and water in the desert, understand the new form of authority under which they would operate, and forge new bonds of trust. This new life offered the exhilaration of freedom, but exhaustion and stress were old foes. And with exhaustion came a falling back, a lagging behind.

God understood the physical, emotional, and spiritual toll that exhaustion and stress were taking on the people. And because He understood, God provided a means of healing for their weakness. It was called the "holy Sabbath," and it was a day of complete rest from their normal routine (Exod. 16:23). This weekly breather was designed to give the Israelites valuable time to nourish their souls through contemplation of God, relax their bodies and minds by pursuing activities that gave them pleasure, and foster deeper relationships with others.

Today we are a weary and exhausted people. Medical study after medical study speak of this and the resultant stress and burnout. The causes may differ from those of the Israelites, but the results are the same to our bodies, emotions, and spirits.

And today because of our continuing weariness, exhaustion, and stress, we too are vulnerable to attack from many sources. Stress-related diseases attack our exhausted bodies and emotional turmoil attacks our weary minds. As weariness and exhaustion sap our strength, it becomes more difficult to cling to our faith in God. Like the Israelites, we may begin to lag behind in a spiritual danger zone. It is there that we are vulnerable to the devil's attacks on our faith (1 Pet. 5:8-9).

God knows us better than we know ourselves. He knows that many of us are straining against the rest that can bring healing and protection to our bodies, minds, souls, and relationships. God knows that we feel no one could understand the responsibility we carry upon our shoulders, responsibility that makes resting impossible. But God *does* understand,

and He continues to urge us to come, rest, and be renewed. God knows that we often put off rest, thinking we will take a break as soon as a future event occurs. He whispers to us to begin our rest now, not later.

We were created to have a weekly time of rest, a time to reflect on our Savior, to participate in activities that we enjoy, and to spend time with people about whom we care. Immerse yourself in the soothing water of a Sabbath day of rest. It's for our healing and our happiness.

What a Chapter!

Deuteronomy 30–34; Psalm 36; Romans 8

Chapter 8 of Romans begins with a reassuring verse about God's forgiveness and ends with equally reassuring verses about God's love. Sandwiched between are some of the greatest promises and theological truths in Scripture. Let's look at a few of the far-ranging topics in this chapter.

Romans 8:1 is a verse of immense comfort. "So now there is no condemnation for those who belong to Christ Jesus." For someone struggling with guilt or plagued with doubt about their salvation, these are precious words.

Verses 2 through 17 tell us of the triune God and His plan for humanity. God, our *"Father*, dear Father,"* offers a plan of salvation to us "by giving his *Son* as a sacrifice for our sins." When we accept Jesus' sacrifice, our nature and the way in which we conduct ourselves will show a marked difference because we have "the power of the *Holy Spirit*" to help us turn from what displeases God. Verse 5 acts as a litmus test for our new life through Jesus: "Those who are dominated by the sinful nature think about sinful things, but those who are controlled by the Holy Spirit think about things that please the Spirit." Do we pass the test? Do our thoughts about people, plans, and desires please God? Bottom line—are we controlled by the Holy Spirit or sin?

Verses 18 through 25 assure us of the end of our great enemies—
death and decay. "All creation anticipates the day when it will join God's
children in glorious freedom from death and decay." As God's children,
we do, indeed, long for freedom from death and the other powerful
enemies we struggle against: sin, sickness, sorrow, pain, hunger, and fear.
And as God's children, we know this freedom will be our glorious reality
in Heaven. Ah, Heaven! As we begin to understand what Heaven and its
freedom will mean to us, our sense of anticipation and delight will flow
through our days on this earth.

But these verses go beyond the "glorious freedom" that will be ours
in Heaven. They look ahead to the time when Jesus Christ fulfills His
promise to return from Heaven, with the believers who have died, to
this beaten-down earth to establish a final home for all believers—the
glorious new earth! (See Isaiah 65:17 and Revelation 21.) Paul tells us "all
creation anticipates the day when it will join God's children" in liberation.
While we do not have the ability to completely understand what the new
earth will mean to all creation, it does not stretch our imagination much
to think that "freedom from death and decay" could extend to all of God's
original creation: animals, birds, fish, plant life…even polluted soil, water,
and air. The new earth is going to be the best of what God has already
created on earth but endlessly magnified over and over.

Romans 8 verses 17 through 25 and 35 through 37 also acknowledge
that on this side of eternity there will be pain and suffering because of
sin. We are going to be knocked down and know sorrow. We are going
to exhaust our resources, and we are going to plead with God to end our
own and others' misery. But verses 26 and 27 offer comfort and reason
for hope, "And the Holy Spirit helps us in our distress. For we don't even
know what we should pray for, nor how we should pray. But the Holy
Spirit prays for us…. And the Father who knows all hearts knows what
the Spirit is saying, for the Spirit pleads for us believers in harmony with
God's own will." When we can no longer go on, when our strength is
drained, and our hope is gone, we have the promise that the Holy Spirit
will pray for us to the Father. Who better to pray for us?

Verse 28 is one of the most quoted scriptural promises: "And we
know that God causes everything to work together for the good of those
who love God and are called according to his purpose for them." There
are conditions to be met to activate this promise—we must love God and

be about His purpose for us. But once these conditions are met, there are many testimonies to the truth of this promise.

And finally, verses 31 through 39 soar with the imagery of God's love for us. Paul ends that passage by writing, "And I am convinced that nothing can ever separate us from his love. Death can't, and life can't. The angels can't, and the demons can't. Our fears for today, our worries about tomorrow, and even the powers of hell can't keep God's love away. Whether we are high above the sky or in the deepest ocean, nothing in all creation will ever be able to separate us from the love of God that is revealed in Christ Jesus our Lord."

This is a significant chapter to our faith. It covers many essential points of our belief system. Verse after verse cascades over us with words of comfort, reassurance, support, unending love, Jesus' sacrifice for us, the promise of eternal life, and the call to live consistently and obediently through the Holy Spirit.

What a chapter!

WEEK 42

Good Advice

Joshua 1–5; Psalm 37; Romans 9

"The godly offer good counsel; they know what is right from wrong. They fill their hearts with God's law, so they will never slip from his path" (Ps. 37:30-31).

Our days are filled with decisions—some minor, some monumental. As we make decisions, we sometimes need advice—another's viewpoint for a "gut check" on a thought or contemplated action, or a fresh perspective on a situation. Advice may either confirm our thoughts and actions or challenge our ideas and plans. When opinions can vary so much, how can we be sure we have chosen wise counsel?

The decisive factor between good and bad counsel is, of course, the person chosen to give the counsel. When we truly seek good advice, there are criteria that can separate the so-so or even faulty guidance from good counsel. Psalm 37 declares, "The godly offer good counsel."

Do you want good counsel? Then seek a godly person. These short verses do not leave us in the dark regarding how we will identify godly persons, for "they fill their hearts with God's law" (Ps. 37:31). By knowing God's guidance as found in Scripture, good counselors will "know what is right from wrong" (v. 30).

Good counselors back up their knowledge of what is right by doing what is right. Psalm 37:31 tells us that good counselors act in such a way that they "never slip" from the path God desires for His people to travel. Consistency in behavior gives weight to a counselor's advice, brings respect, and allows his or her life to serve as an example. Do you want the best combination for a counselor? Then find someone who desires to please God, who knows His words, and who practices what he or she knows.

Even with the firmest intentions, though, we stumble and even slip from God's perfect path. No human is sinless. Good counselors will keep their focus on God's grace and use experiences from their own needed course corrections to help others with similar struggles.

The other side of the coin of needing advice is being asked to give guidance on a matter of importance to another person. These verses have something to say to each person who is a counselor rather than the person being counseled. God, whose knowledge and wisdom is so infinitely superior to ours, has revealed portions of this wisdom in His words to us. As we "fill our hearts with God's laws," we begin to understand that our own thoughts and beliefs change based on what we know of Him. And as we put what we have learned into practice, we may find that our counsel is sought more often.

In Christ, and in His Word, are all the truths, principles, and answers for good counseling.

WEEK 43

Going in Circles

Joshua 6–9; Romans 10–12

Hours stretched into days…so many days. Waiting. Waiting for something that would make sense out of this situation. Somewhere during the hours and days, the wait had started to feel endless. How could this possibly be God's plan for them?

The Israelites were ready to move forward, conquer, and possess. They had hundreds of thousands of battle-ready troops. They had tasted victory and were eager to finish the job, complete their wanderings, and establish their homes.

And here they were—stalled outside the important city of Jericho. Seven days ago, Joshua had given them an unusual battle plan. These hundreds of thousands of fighting men were not to draw their swords. They were not to charge the city. Instead, a detail of armed guards would precede seven priests, who would be blowing rams' horns. These seven priests would lead other priests, who would carry the Ark of the Covenant. The entire remaining army was to follow. And where had they headed? Around the city…in one big circle.

Before starting their march, there had been one additional command for the vast army. "'Do not shout; do not even talk,' Joshua commanded. 'Not a single word from any of you until I tell you to shout. Then shout!'" (Josh. 6:10).

Silently they began to march. There were no voices raised in question of this strange battle plan, there were no discussions of its merits, there were no shouts of encouragement ringing through the lines. Only the sound of the rams' horns drifted through the air. During that first day's march, the troop's anticipation of hearing the command, "Shout!" could almost be felt. They had faith that extraordinary things were going to happen when they shouted.

Extraordinary things were going to happen, but not on this first day. There was one important point to the battle plan God had given Joshua that he did not share with his army. Yes, they were going to march around the city as Joshua had told them, but they were going to march around the city *for seven days,* and *then* Jericho's wall was coming down. These confident troops did not realize that there was more to the battle plan than they knew.

When no command to "Shout!" came that first day, the troops returned to their base camp. During that first night, how many of them began to have seeds of doubt as to the wisdom of this plan?

The next day, the troops were up early and ready to go to battle. A new day awaited them, and surely it would be different from the last. But it wasn't. It was exactly the same…as was the next day…and the next… and the next. And with each day, did their doubts increase and their questions multiply?

They wanted to be conquerors, not followers. They were ready to be forceful, not silent. But they were completely obedient, when it wasn't easy to be obedient. They followed, trusting Joshua and trusting God, when it didn't make any sense to do so. And on the seventh day, their obedience and trust were rewarded.

On the seventh day, they silently marched around Jericho as they had for the prior six days. We can almost feel the army starting to pull back as they completed the first circle. Six days of experience had taught them that they were going to head back to camp for the day, a little more dispirited than the day before and the day before that.

But what's this? They continued to march! Twice around, three times around, four, five, six, seven times around Jericho! You probably know how the story ends, but they didn't. We can imagine anticipation is growing with each circle made, but *would* it have been? As each silent circle was completed, was anticipation increasing or were confusion, questions and even resentment on the rise? To the army, it looked the same as when they started seven days ago. They were still marching silently in circles, and it may have felt like God had forgotten them. And then, finally, the longed-for command, "Shout!" (Josh. 6:15-16).

And as they shouted, the great walls of that fortified city crumbled before their disbelieving eyes. In that moment, their questions were answered. In that moment, they understood that obedience and trust were more important than their ability to understand. In that moment, they realized that the power and wisdom of God far surpassed their own; for they weren't entering the city already fatigued from a long battle to conquer the wall. They were entering the city fresh for the fight, and they were completely victorious.

This is one of many Scriptures given as an example for our own Jericho marches—situations in our lives that we wish were different. We may feel that we are going in circles without any explanation from God. We may question why something frustrating and painful is happening if God loves us. We may feel betrayed.

But if we are wise, we too will come to accept the reality that often we cannot understand God's plans or methods for our lives. We will know that our obedience and trust are what is important.

How wise will we choose to be on our next Jericho march?

WEEK 44

Details, Details

Joshua 10–15; Psalm 38

Land surveying can be a big responsibility. Successful surveying requires meticulous attention to detail to eliminate problems for present and future generations.

Israel was in the midst of a large land redistribution that, perhaps, called for the greatest survey ever undertaken. To parcel out the vast tracts of land between the twelve family-tribes of Israel required intimate knowledge of the territory. The boundaries of each tribe's land had to be crystal clear to avoid discord throughout the nation. Future peace depended on the details of the moment.

And so Joshua began the process of dividing the land. The details of the division were evident from the start. We are told of the land given to the tribe of Judah: "the southern boundary began at the south bay of the Dead Sea, ran south of Scorpion Pass into the wilderness of Zin and went south of Kadesh-barnea to Hezron. Then it went up to…" (Josh. 15:2-3). For the next nine verses we are given the detailed layout of the land for this one tribe. And in case this level of detail was not sufficient to do away with all questions on the land boundaries, more than one hundred specific towns and villages within Judah's designated land were named.

Details layered upon details, to ensure the accuracy of the territory given to the tribe of Judah. One down…and eleven tribes to go. As you read, did you start to feel your head spinning from all the details? Maybe you couldn't take it anymore and glossed over most of it, for it is often hard to keep attentive at such a detailed level.

But interrelated to this detail is one thing that makes this land division important: the surveyor. Now Joshua was the distributor of information, but he was not the decision-maker. The land had to be divided by someone who thoroughly knew it, and that someone was God who is, without a doubt, the greatest surveyor of all time. After all, if you are the land's Creator, surveying has to come easily.

God has many attributes. Can there be any question that one of these attributes is that He cares about the smallest of details? We have seen depth of detail before with God's instructions for the construction of the Tent of Meeting, and we see it again in the details of the land distribution.

Now, it is true that we may not care a whole lot about the details of the Israelite land distribution, but God cared. We may not care about many of the details in the lives of others or even about many of the details in our own lives, but God cares. And when it comes to the details of life that do matter to us, it is reassuring to belong to the God who cares for us at a detailed level.

David certainly understood the interest and involvement that God has for His children. David writes, "You know what I long for, Lord; you hear my every sigh" (Ps. 38:9). Even our every sigh—whether caused by joy, frustration, pain, or sorrow—is heard by God who knows, down to the tiniest detail, what we long for and who knows what we need.

Yes, our God is the God of the biggest picture *and* the smallest detail of this universe. And our hearts can rest and trust in that knowledge.

WEEK 45

Twenty-One Days and Counting

Joshua 16–20; Romans 13–14

A Kansas City church had a challenge for its congregation. Could its parishioners go for twenty-one days without participating in gossip or being critical? Why did the church specify twenty-one days? Because research says it takes twenty-one days to create a new habit.

Not surprisingly, the people struggled to meet the goal. After four months, only twelve of the two hundred participants had been successful for twenty-one days in a row.

Criticism and gossip are widespread and insidious habits that often walk hand in hand. They hurt, and we know they do. We've experienced the hurt. They can have a painful, if temporary, effect upon us, or they can have permanently devastating consequences that overtake and cripple our thoughts and actions.

Believers in Christ are called to love others as Christ loves us, and yet too often it may be hard to distinguish Christians from unbelievers on the issues of criticism and gossip. It's so easy to find fault in others' actions, abilities, or looks. Our criticism may be as subtle as a raised eyebrow, the twist of the mouth, or a few ill-chosen words. Or it may be a full-blown attack…or anything in-between. The words may be directed at the person or, worse yet, to everyone but the person being criticized. Our criticisms of others may not even be voiced to anyone but held quietly in our thoughts, where they harm us.

Romans 14:4 asks the question, "Who are you to condemn God's servants?" Condemn is another word for criticize, express disapproval, put down, or verbally attack. The verse is not addressing loving, private discussions urging a fellow believer to turn from a sinful action. Scripture commonly calls this loving admonishment or concern—an entirely different matter.

Romans 14:10 repeats the question, "So why do you condemn another Christian?" Good question. There are a number of answers, but none of them is a noble one. Christians who criticize fellow believers open the door to hurt and dissension.

Perhaps the saddest note of all regarding criticism of others by believers is that it virtually shuts down their witness for Jesus Christ, because unkind criticism reeks of hypocrisy. Jesus says to love others—coldhearted criticism says the opposite.

Romans 14:10 continues with another question: "Why do you look down on another Christian?" God understood that when we criticize another person we may feel superior to that person—"looking down" on him or her. We criticize others while ignoring our own capacity for making mistakes and holding them to our standards, not God's.

Romans 14:10 concludes with a warning: "Remember, each of us will stand personally before the judgment seat of God." That warning should make us stop and think before engaging in any of these hurtful habits.

Let's strive each day to get our thoughts, our words, our body language, and our actions into the critical-free zone. Do it through prayer. Do it with the Holy Spirit's help. Do it by being held accountable by someone. But do it. How many twenty-one-day stretches can we accumulate during the rest of our lives?

WEEK 46

The End of Turmoil

Joshua 21–24; Judges 1; Psalm 39; Romans 15

"And the Lord gave them rest on every side, just as he had solemnly promised their ancestors…" (Josh. 21:44).

It may be easy for us to skip over what it meant to the Israelites to have "rest on every side." But to the Israelites it was a true gift, for they knew too well what it was like to be without it.

Decades had passed with almost constant turmoil for these people and rest had always been beyond their reach. They had wandered for years in a hostile desert environment, dealing with the dangers that came with an untamed, stark land. They had spent additional years in warfare, which resulted in more casualties and disrupted lives.

But now they were at "rest on every side" because "none of their enemies could stand against them" (Josh. 21:44). They were not at rest because their enemies had ceased to exist or because every hardship had disappeared. Their rest came because their enemies lost the power to disrupt their lives. It was God's gift to them.

Try to imagine the contrast between the rest given to these people and the life that they had known for so long. What must it have been like for them to get up in the morning rested? To look forward to the coming day with anticipation, knowing no battles had to be fought? To sit in their homes with their families, knowing their painful wanderings and deprivations were over?

We all have enemies that we struggle against. They may be of our own making, based on our poor choices, as the desert years were for the Israelites. Or our enemies may simply be the result of living in a world filled with circumstances that bring us pain, make us fearful of what lies beyond our sight, and create the memories that haunt us. What enemy do you need rest from today?

No matter what, or who, your enemies are, God can give you rest. It may be beyond your ability to believe or understand, but rest is possible through God and His promises.

Ask God for rest. To receive this gift, be willing to change what God shows you should be changed. And be assured that, with God's help, rest is available for the weary body, mind, and soul.

WEEK 47

A Slippery Slope

Judges 2–6; Romans 16; Mark 1

"Together with the Ammonites and Amalekites, Eglon attacked Israel and took possession of Jericho" (Judg. 3:13).

Not Jericho! It couldn't be. This important city had unmatched significance in the history of the Israelite nation as the site of one of their greatest military victories and spiritual high points. This was a city steeped in the meaning of the Israelites' special relationship with the living and true God.

And now it was lost. What in the world had happened during the intervening years since the Israelites had conquered this city?

What happened is that the people of Israel became complacent. And their complacency led to problems that were about to derail them. Not only were they in the midst of being challenged by human enemies, but they had been tested by God to determine the strength of their relationship with Him and had failed the test.

The test question had been clear-cut. Had the Israelites remained true and steadfast in their relationship to the Lord God, or had they been influenced by the sinful culture around them, abandoning the way of life that God had designed to bring them joy and peace? The results of the test were heartrending, for "they abandoned the Lord, the God of their ancestors, who had brought them out of Egypt" (Judg. 2:12).

This colossal failure began subtly as they grew more and more at ease with the sin that was around them. At the outset, the Israelites tested the water of the sin in their culture but recognized the danger and pulled back, knowing that it was critical for them to live in complete obedience to God. They pulled back, but they did not take the steps needed to eliminate the sin or protect themselves from it. As time passed, they were drawn to testing the water again and again and again until they could no longer identify the danger. They had desensitized themselves to the sin. And finally, they abandoned the Lord and brought misery upon themselves.

Does this sound like something we are experiencing today? Our spiritual highs can be quickly followed by spiritual lows. We may fail spiritual tests designed by God for our good. We may deliberately abandon godly principles to follow our own agenda. As we stand in the midst of our mistakes and our pain, we look back over our shoulder and ask, "How? How could I have come to this point?"

It is an age-old story. Like the Israelites, we find it amazingly easy to become complacent in our commitment to Jesus Christ rather than remain eager followers. It is amazingly easy to participate in aspects of our culture that go against godly principles rather than leading others through these cultural minefields to Christ. It is amazingly easy to become lax in our obedience. Like the Israelites, we find it easy to keep testing the waters of disobedience until we are in over our heads and sinking fast.

Loving the Lord our God with all our heart, mind, soul, and strength requires us to decide to live this way each and every day. It requires determination and discipline on our part. But it also requires something more. Our spiritual determination, discipline, and endurance must be built on the foundation of the strength of Jesus Christ. We can't have a passionate relationship with God on our own. We can't remain faithful and obedient on our own. We can't pass spiritual tests on our own. But Romans 16:25 tells us how we can do these things, and more, for it says, "*God* is able to make you strong, just as the Good News says."

As always, it is God and His words to us that make the difference.

WEEK 48

A Loathsome Tax Collector

Judges 7–10; Psalms 40–41; Mark 2

Green fertile land contrasts with blue water, gentle waves lap at the shoreline. Small wooden fishing boats come in and go out. Sea birds call overhead while waiting for fish scraps. On the horizon beyond the lake, mountains begin to rise. And on the west bank of the Sea of Galilee, lies the small town of Capernaum.

Although small, Capernaum was accustomed to much activity because Via Maris, a major road, ran right through the town. This key travel route stretched from the important land of Egypt to the equally important Syrian city of Damascus. Many merchants traveling between these two prominent trade centers stopped by Capernaum's fishing area to buy dried fish to exchange for the silks and spices of the lands to which they were headed.

Capernaum was a busy town for another reason as well. It was a border town located inside the Roman province of Galilee and adjacent to the province of Gaulanitis. Where there were borders, there were duties and tolls; where there were duties and tolls, there were tax collectors' booths…and Matthew was a tax collector.

In the Roman world of tax collecting there were hierarchies, and Matthew was on the bottom rung. He was one of the on-the-ground officials responsible for collecting taxes from both the merchant caravans as they traveled through the town and from the local fishermen. Sitting in his tax collector's booth, he was loathed by travelers and locals alike.

There were other tax collectors scattered around this important commercial area to ensure the people-to-people contact necessary to collect the taxes. These fellow tax collectors were part of Matthew's social circle.

As usual, Matthew was in his tax collection booth near the lake transacting business. Nearby, in the town proper, Jesus had been in a house teaching all day. The house was filled to the walls with people pushing, pushing, and pushing to allow one more person in to see and be near Jesus. The air of the house was stifling due to many bodies sharing space meant for only a few. But Jesus continued teaching, and the people continued listening.

Suddenly, dust began to float through the still air, followed by bits of mud, straw, and other debris. Even Jesus' words couldn't hold the crowd's attention any longer, as they began to cough, sneeze, and rub their eyes. A mat holding a paralyzed man appeared from above their heads. Jesus quickly acknowledged the man's need for spiritual and physical healing, and then forgave and healed him. As the astounded and rejoicing group observed this miracle, Jesus felt the need to be away from the hot and dirty air of the house and went out to the lake.

But as Jesus "walked along, he saw Levi [also known as Matthew] son of Alphaeus sitting at his tax-collection booth. 'Come, be my disciple,' Jesus said to him…" (Mark 2:14). There was something about Jesus that Matthew had never experienced before. "Come, be my disciple" penetrated Matthew's thoughts and then his heart and then his actions. "So Levi got up and followed him" (v. 14).

"Come be my disciple," Jesus says to us, as He said to Matthew. Come now, not later. Come, not holding back possessions or occupations or independence, but come with all that you have and all that you are.

Come, as Matthew did, telling your friends and family about your relationship with God (Mark 2:15).

Come be His disciple.

WEEK 49

We Need You!

Judges 11–14; Psalms 42–43; Mark 3

"But Jephthah said to them, 'Aren't you the ones who hated me and drove me from my father's house…?'" (Judg. 11:7).

Ancestral land was important in ancient Israel. People didn't leave their land, for it had been assigned by God to each tribe from their beginning days in Canaan. To be driven from your "father's house," or family's land, by your family members was rejection in the most real sense of the word.

Jephthah had been forced from his homeland of Gilead in Israel for something that was totally beyond his ability to control or change: his birth mother was a prostitute. He had been chased away by those who had judged him and found him lacking. He had been chased away even though he was known to be a great warrior and could have helped his fellow citizens during turbulent times of war against the mighty Ammonites.

The men Jephthah now addressed were the same people who had driven him from his land and brought sorrow to him by their actions. Jephthah had a logical question for them: "Why do you come to me now when you're in trouble?" (Judg. 11:7).

"'Because we need you,' they replied" (Judg. 11:8). To their credit, they were honest. They weren't making it on their own, and they were looking for someone who might be able to save them. "If you will lead us in battle against the Ammonites, we will make you ruler over all the people of Gilead" (Judg. 11:8).

With this statement, they acknowledged they had been wrong to push Jephthah away. They had come to realize he was the person they should follow. In their request for his leadership and his rule over their lives, they had come to a place where they could admit to themselves, and Jephthah, that they had been wrong and had sinned against him. In so doing, they humbled themselves from their previous position of supposed superiority. And Jephthah responded to their need and delivered them.

Sound familiar? It is the story over and over again of the Israelites' relationship with God. The God they should have followed was pushed aside—out of their thoughts and lives. When disasters and hard times came, as they always do, there was no one to lead them through. With the insight that difficulties brought came their reassessment, honesty, humility, and, finally, the admission, "We need You."

It is the age-old story of humanity's relationship with God. Life goes forward, and we go forward with it. As life rolls along, we sometimes allow other things to push God from our thoughts and our day-to-day lives. But then adversity strikes and we flounder without our Leader. It is then, more than ever, that we have the opportunity to stop, honestly reassess our relationship with God, and remember our need for closeness with our Creator, Savior, and Sustainer.

God hears even the most quietly whispered, "I need You."

Week 50

Two Rescues

Judges 15–18; Mark 4–6

Jesus was tired. He had spent the entire day, until evening, teaching a large crowd. This day had used up much of His physical and mental strength. It was no easy task to stay in one spot all day, speaking for many hours to make the lessons clear to people who had little knowledge of the subject matter. What would have been difficult one-on-one became exhausting when expanded to include many.

The need to rest was real, and Jesus suggested to His disciples that they take the boat, from which they had been teaching the crowd, to the other side of the lake. Jesus was so exhausted that He fell asleep "at the back of the boat with His head on a cushion" and never awoke when a "fierce storm arose" and "high waves began to break into the boat until it was nearly full of water" (Mark 4:37-38). As Jesus lay sleeping, the water lapping around Him in the boat did not awaken Him, but the disciples' frantic shouting that they were about to drown did. Jesus awoke and "rebuked the wind and said to the water, 'Quiet down!' Suddenly the wind stopped and there was a great calm" (Mark 4:39).

They were safe again, but Jesus was not rested. Would He be able to rest when they landed on the other side of the lake, the Gentile side? Gentiles were not so interested in this Jewish teacher, but the demons possessing a man were. "Just as Jesus was climbing from the boat, a man possessed by an evil spirit ran out from a cemetery to meet him" (Mark 5:2).

Let's not gloss over this man who came to meet Jesus. The demons that controlled him had brought about great suffering and isolation for the man. He had no home, for he lived in a cemetery, a place people usually avoided then as they do today. He had no protection from the dangerous storms that swept in from the lake, and he would have struggled to find food to eat. He was tormented emotionally and physically as he spent his days and nights wandering "among the tombs and in the hills, screaming and hitting himself with stones" (Mark 5:5).

Unclothed, bruised, bleeding, and battered, he was isolated by his dangerous behavior from anyone who would be tempted to show him mercy and kindness. He was a true danger to others as well as to himself, and his human contact came through frequent attempts to chain him. But he was physically strong and snapped the chains meant to control him, further isolating him from meaningful human contact. Day after day, his misery continued and deepened.

Jesus could have turned away. He was exhausted, and this man was abhorrent in many ways. But Jesus did not turn away; He turned toward the man and delivered him from the evil spirits that controlled his life.

News traveled fast even in those times, and "a crowd soon gathered around Jesus, but they were frightened when they saw the man who had been demon possessed, for he was sitting there fully clothed and perfectly sane" (Mark 5:15). Think about that. The man was so changed that it frightened the crowd. They weren't frightened because his condition had worsened but because he had been so amazingly changed for the better! The contrast was too great; they couldn't trust what their own eyes and ears were telling them.

But the man knew. He was permanently changed. He knew he had been delivered, unmistakably saved, from evil. He knew that he wanted to stay in close and intimate contact with this Man who had given him so much, and as Jesus got back into the boat to leave, the healed man "begged to go, too" (Mark 5:18).

But it wasn't yet time for this man and his Savior to remain together. The man had been given a great gift, and with that gift came a great responsibility. "Jesus said, 'No, go home to your friends, and tell them what wonderful things the Lord has done for you and how merciful he has been.' So the man started off…" (Mark 5:19-20).

Let us not be mistaken about how much we share with the man from this story. We may not suffer from the extreme effects of demonic control, but sin robs us of much of the good that God originally intended for us. We, too, are lost until we meet Jesus and are rescued.

And once rescued, we too will be able to recognize the great gift we have been given, astound others by being forever changed for the better, and tell them "what wonderful things the Lord has done and how merciful he has been" to us.

Week 51

Gaining Insight

Judges 19–21; Ruth 1–2; Psalm 44; Mark 7

Four hundred thousand troops stood before their leaders, and their leaders stood before God asking, "'Which tribe should lead the attack against the people of Benjamin?' The Lord answered, 'Judah is to go first'" (Judg. 20:18). And so Judah led the fight, "But Benjamin's warriors, who were defending the town, came out and killed twenty-two thousand Israelites in the field that day" (v. 21).

The Israelites had sought God's will, obeyed Him, and lost thousands of their fighting men. How could they make sense of what happened when logic would say that seeking God and obeying Him should lead to victories over life's battles? Instead, following God's commands had resulted in the death of many fathers, sons, and brothers.

The Israelites may have been stunned by their losses after obeying God, but they didn't turn away. They came to God again and "wept in the presence of the Lord until evening. Then they asked the Lord, 'Should we fight against our relatives from Benjamin again?' And the Lord said, 'Go out and fight against them'" (Judg. 20:23).

They had sought God again, asked for His guidance, and were given it. The result was that "the men of Benjamin killed another eighteen thousand Israelites, all of whom were experienced with a sword" (Judg. 20:25). Forty thousand Israelites were now dead.

The Israelites stood in the battlefield surrounded by this staggering and unexpected second loss. They could have chosen to see the brutal evidence all around them as a reason to turn from God and to question His goodness and care for them.

But they did not. Instead, "all the Israelites went up to Bethel and wept in the presence of the Lord and fasted until evening. They also brought burnt offerings and peace offerings to the Lord. And the Israelites went up seeking direction from the Lord" (Judg. 20:26-27).

For the third time God gave them explicit instructions. For the third time the Israelites obeyed these instructions in spite of the outcome of the prior two battles. And in the third battle God gave them victory.

Why did the third time bring victory when there had been harsh defeat at the first two battles? And how does a battle that happened thousands of years ago apply to our lives today? There are at least two aspects to these battles worth exploring: the surprising outcomes and the Israelites' response.

What was the Israelites' response to what many would interpret as a failure on God's part to protect and deliver them from real hardship? Were they confused and did they wonder if they had misunderstood what God wanted? Probably. Were they angry with God that their continued obedience had led to disaster rather than victory? Did their hearts tell them they deserved better than this from God? Did they question why? Maybe.

But the one thing that is clearly stated is that as the situation worsened, their seeking of God intensified. They progressed from the leaders asking the question of what to do before the first battle, to the leaders weeping before God prior to the second, to all of Israel weeping, praying, fasting, and offering sacrifices to the Lord so that there would be no sin on their part separating them from God prior to the third battle. These weren't quick, on-the-fly prayers for guidance but a fervent seeking of what God wanted. Their losses, their plans and hopes for the future that were now forever changed, and even their confusion turned them *toward* God—*not away* from Him.

And what was the outcome? They finally had victory, but there had been a cost. But with that cost came spiritual learning and spiritual endurance. They were a changed people, and the change could not have happened if victory had come easily and at the beginning. They were a changed people because life did not progress the way they felt it should, and it caused them to stop and seek God more deeply. They were a changed people who no longer had a halfhearted relationship with God.

We each carry heartaches, face battles, experience pain, and know fear and uncertainty. Do we base our relationship with God on how fair we think God is being during these times? Do we feel that if circumstances aren't going the way we expect that we have been cheated or abandoned by God? Are we tempted to adopt the attitude that God let us down and so we'll run things our way for now? If so, we are going to have a weak and dissatisfying relationship with God.

It was not easy for the Israelites, and it will not be easy for us. But we can choose a different way to respond to our worst blows by recognizing that we are not as wise as God and therefore we may not always be capable of understanding the bitter twists and turns of our lives. We must *decide* we will trust God's guidance in spite of troubling circumstances. We must *choose* to believe that on the other side of current hardships God has something of value for us—whether it is to bring us into closer relationship with Him, to learn a valuable spiritual insight, to cast off sin to which we have been clinging, or to simply trust Him because He is God.

Week 52

Bypassed

Ruth 3–4; 1 Samuel 1–3; Psalm 45; Mark 8

"Now in those days messages from the Lord were very rare.... The Lord called a third time, and once more Samuel jumped up and ran to Eli. 'Here I am,' he said. 'What do you need?' Then Eli realized it was the Lord who was calling the boy" (1 Sam. 3:1,8).

What must that realization have cost Eli? Eli was the high priest, handpicked by God. He was God's chief representative to the people, but God had not called to Eli, the high priest. Eli was an adult, but God had not called to the adult. God, whose presence was rarely made known during Eli's time, had called three times to the young boy, Samuel. As Eli lay upon his bed that night, what questions and emotions raced through his mind?

This was a situation that may have been humiliating to Eli. He had served as high priest for many years of his adult life, and he was now an old man, but God had not called to him. God had called to an inexperienced youth.

This was a situation that could have led Eli to be jealous or resentful of Samuel. Eli had spent his entire life in service to God; he had tried to do his best, but it seemed that his best was not good enough.

Why did God bypass him in favor of speaking to a boy? In the depths of that night, Eli knew that God calling Samuel was linked to another time that God had bypassed Eli to speak to someone else. That someone was a prophet, sent by God, with a warning to Eli. God's message had been to the point. Eli needed to discipline his sons, for they had committed atrocious sins. If they continued in this sin, God was going to remove the priesthood from Eli's descendants. Not only would the members of his family no longer be priests, they would die before their time. And while they lived, they would have lives of sadness and grief.

During the night, Eli may have longed to assert control. He could have tried to insert himself between God and Samuel. He could have tried to take back what many would consider his right as high priest. He could have tried to bargain with God.

But Eli did not. Eli told Samuel, "Go and lie down again, and if someone calls again, say, 'Yes, Lord, your servant is listening'" (1 Sam. 3:9). God did call Samuel again that night and He gave him the message that the time had come when God's judgment of Eli and his family would begin.

When Eli sent Samuel back to bed, he knew that God would call to Samuel again that night. The next morning Eli asked Samuel what God had said to him. Because of the seriousness of the message Samuel did not want to tell Eli, but he finally did.

It had been a long night and a hard morning for Eli. Upon hearing Samuel's message, Eli responded, "It is the Lord's will. Let him do what he thinks best" (1 Sam. 3:18). Eli's words were not words of bitterness or resignation but the words of someone who understood the fairness and love of God.

Eli was being disciplined because God had given him clear direction of what He wanted from Eli regarding his sons, and Eli had ignored God. Although the punishment was painful, Eli put aside reactions toward God that are frequent responses during times of discipline. He did not try to cast blame for his part onto someone else. He did not try to bargain down his punishment. He did not resent God's discipline. Most importantly, Eli continued to trust in God in spite of the discipline he was experiencing.

At some time in our lives we are going to face both of the situations that Eli experienced that night so long ago. Eli's first hurdle to overcome was being overlooked. There will come a time when we feel jealous because someone else is given attention that we feel we deserve. There will come a time when we feel resentful when someone is praised and our sincere efforts are ignored. There will come a time when we feel the deep sting of having been judged and found lacking. To react in humility the way Eli did takes prayer and determination. Eli put aside normal reactions in favor of obedience to God.

But Eli had not always been obedient, and his disobedience had led to his second hurdle of the night: the judgment and discipline of God. When judgment came, Eli trusted in God's mercy and wisdom. How many of us suffering from the consequences of our sin could join with Eli in saying, "Let Him do what He thinks best"?

It is possible for us to come closer and closer to Eli's responses of humility and trust. But it takes a desire on our part to do so, and it takes God's help. There is no question that God's help is available to us. Are we available to God?

Help Me Not to Doubt

1 Samuel 4–8; Mark 9–10

"The father instantly replied, 'I do believe, but help me not to doubt!'" (Mark 9:24).

This sentence has to be one of the most honest and important conversations recorded in the Bible. It is honest in its contradiction. And it is important for its honesty.

The father declared that he believed, and his story gives us proof that indeed he did believe that Jesus had something to offer him— healing for his son who was possessed and tortured by an evil spirit. His belief made him speak up from the anonymity of a large crowd to approach Jesus with his request. The crowd included religious teachers, an influential group hostile to Jesus but important to this man's culture. Even so, his belief that Jesus could help his son led him to make himself conspicuous in front of the religious teachers and many others. Yes, he believed.

And yet, I'm sure, this father also knew of ill people who had come near to Jesus but who had not been healed. As he came forward from the crowd, did this father's mind race back to any of those people and do a quick comparison to his son's situation? Did doubts begin to awaken as he told the story of how Jesus' disciples could not help him? Was he torn between his belief and the realities of this world of which his logic reminded him?

Yes, he was. As the evil spirit showed its control of the boy, he concluded his answers to Jesus' questions about his beloved son's condition with a plea to "have mercy on us and help us. Do something if you can" (Mark 9:22).

His actions said *belief* but his words said *doubt*. He was a torn man. And Jesus knew this. Jesus answered, "What do you mean, 'If I can?' Anything is possible if a person believes" (Mark 9:23).

And then, instantly, from the father came these beautifully honest words, "I do believe, but help me not to doubt!" (Mark 9:24). Jesus answered this man's entreaty with the help he needed to overcome his doubt. And then Jesus healed his son.

In spite of his confidence in Jesus, this man had doubts that He could heal his son. What are *our* doubts in regard to God? Do we sometimes doubt God's existence? Do we ever wonder if Jesus is who He said He was? Do we have reservations about the Holy Spirit's power or desire to help us live a life pleasing to God? Are we uncertain whether God will honor His promises? Do we question God's grace, mercy, forgiveness, love…the list is long, if we are truthful.

We are human and therefore susceptible to doubt. Doubt is one of our great enemies for it exploits our vulnerability and erodes our trust in God. If we are honest, we can admit the many times we come to God with our mind and emotions warring between doubt and belief. And even more harmful are the times when do we not go to God because of this internal clash.

"Help me not to doubt" is a prayer that may need to be on our lips often, especially on days when our focus is on troublesome situations rather than God. This needs to be our prayer when our faith falters. This needs to be our prayer because we do not possess the ability to overcome our doubts on our own.

Lord, help me not to doubt.

WEEK 54

Be Still and Know That I Am God

1 Samuel 9–12; Psalms 46–47; Mark 11

"Be still, and know that I am God!" (Ps. 46:10).

It was late autumn. I was sitting in the dark crying. Four months earlier I had injured my back in a horseback riding accident. Since that time, the pain, intermingled with loss of feeling in my right leg, had brought me low. Because there was no surgery available that would help, I was going to have to learn to live with it.

How could I? The pain and numbness overwhelmed me; my life was completely changed and not for the better. I sobbed to God to help me. To heal me. To change these circumstances. I cried so much that I was spent and sat there limply. And then I heard, "Be still, and know that I am God." I held my breath and looked around in the dark. I knew that I hadn't heard an audible voice, and yet it was as if I had, for the words were distinct and specific. In that moment I knew it was God, even though it would be a few more years before I was aware that these words were an actual Bible verse.

I became still, both physically and emotionally, and waited expectantly. But both the night and God were silent.

During the next few weeks, "Be still and know that I am God" kept returning to my mind. These words from God were the beginning of a new journey for me. My pain wasn't changing, and the numbness wasn't going away; but I was changing. My thoughts turned more to God and less to how miserable I felt. Anxiety was being replaced by calmness. Eventually I was able to say to God that even though I still desired to be healed, I was now asking for help to cope with the injury and help to trust Him in this situation. This change in how I thought didn't occur because of who I am but because of who God is.

Samuel told the Israelites, "Now stand here quietly before the Lord as I remind you of all the great things the Lord has done for you and your ancestors" (1 Sam. 12:7). As we stand quietly before the Lord, we are able to remember the great things He has done and be reminded that He can be trusted. As for me, God has done great things for me in the intervening years. The pain that caused me to cry out on that autumn night has drawn me to God in a way that would have been impossible without it. Feeling has returned to my leg most of the time, but my *physical* walk differs from what it was before the injury, as my *spiritual* walk now differs, for I have come to know that God is God.

I still catch myself succumbing to worry and concern when life situations seem overwhelming. The list of issues can grow long, and that old familiar feeling of anxiety starts to creep in. It is then that I realize once more that I need to be still and remember that God knows what is best for me as He has in the past, as He does right now, and as He will in the future.

Do We Care?

1 Samuel 13–17; Mark 12–13

"Samuel never went to meet with Saul again, but he mourned constantly for him" (1 Sam. 15:35). Samuel mourned for Saul. Not for a brief time, but constantly. In fact, Samuel grieved so long that "finally, the Lord said to Samuel, 'You have mourned long enough for Saul'" (1 Sam. 16:1).

Why did Samuel grieve so deeply for Saul? Because Saul had flagrantly and deliberately disobeyed God—not once, but twice; and when confronted with his sin, he had made excuses for it rather than acknowledge his need for true reconciliation with God.

Saul's unremorseful attitude required God's judgment, and God "rejected him as king of Israel" (1 Sam. 16:1). "The Lord said to Samuel, 'I am sorry that I ever made Saul king, for he has not been loyal to me and has again refused to obey me.' Samuel was so deeply moved when he heard this that he cried out to the Lord all night" (1 Sam. 15:10-11).

Samuel's long period of mourning began with his all-night (not merely several minutes) pleading with God for Saul. Samuel grieved for Saul the person, not for Saul the king, and Samuel grieved over the loss of the potential for good and for God that Saul had squandered.

Samuel understood the earthly and eternal consequences of Saul's defiance of God, and his grief for Saul was real. Samuel was broken by it. It consumed him so fully that God had to tell Samuel to turn his attention elsewhere.

How about the "Sauls" who are part of *our* lives? Do we mourn for someone who is in the midst of obvious sin or outright rejection of God? Do we have an awareness of the horror of being in rebellion against God? Do we seek to intervene with God for that person?

Samuel was not self-absorbed; he was concerned for others and for their relationship with the Lord. May God help us to be like Samuel, who was so deeply moved by another's sin and rebellion against God, that he did not tire easily when interceding for that person with God.

And may we resolve with God's help to not be like Saul, the other major character in this story. Saul chose what *he* wanted to do rather than what *God* wanted for him. And after his poor choices, he only went through the motions of being contrite rather than having a true change of heart. How tragic it would be to have a legacy like that of Saul, who caused the Lord much sorrow by his behavior.

It is easier to be a Saul than a Samuel. It is better to be a Samuel than a Saul. May we, with God's help, choose the better path.

WEEK 56

We're Here for an Inspection

1 Samuel 18–22; Psalm 48; Mark 14

"Go, inspect the city of Jerusalem. Walk around and count the many towers. Take note of the fortified walls, and tour all the citadels..." (Ps. 48:12-13).

Times have changed since this Psalm was written. Living in a city with many towers, fortified walls, and numerous citadels does not mean much to our time and place, but these things had great significance for the people in whose era this Psalm was written.

A city's fortified walls, citadels, and towers were solid, steadfast, and secure. The walls and citadels could be counted on to provide safety and protection to those who depended on them, while lookout towers warned the city's inhabitants of approaching danger allowing time to prepare a strong defense.

Day and night these unchanging symbols of safety provided comfort and encouragement to the people and boosted their courage. During times of peace, they increased the people's sense of well-being and confidence. During times of war, the worst of times, these easily observed signs of protection endowed the citizens with strength that was greater than their own, for their enemies had to breach the city's defenses before they could touch the people. They could outlast the enemy as long as the walls withstood the onslaught.

The psalmist told the people to "Go inspect" the fortifications surrounding Jerusalem, for he knew they could stand up to a thorough examination. He didn't want the people to take his word for the protection that surrounded them. He knew that for maximum impact the people needed to prove to themselves the strength of these structures by seeing them, counting them, and touching them. He knew that when the people had put the walls and towers and citadels to the test they would know without question that they were real and that they were trustworthy. And then their hearts could be at peace.

After the people were fully assured by what they knew to be true, the psalmist declares that the solidness, steadfastness, strength, safety, protection, warning of danger, encouragement, and endurance provided by these defenses "is what God is like" (Ps. 48:14).

God is all of these things to His children. It is God's steadfastness and unchanging nature that can bring us a sense of well-being. It is His strength and encouragement that we need during our times of unrest. It is His early warnings of spiritual danger that we need to heed. It is His endurance we need to finish our walk with Christ in this life. It is His presence that we need surrounding us.

The walls and towers and citadels differ from God in one important way. These defenses looked like they would endure forever, but they did not. But God does, for "He is our God forever and ever, and he will be our guide until we die" (Ps. 48:14).

Through both our days of peace and our days of turmoil, God will be our strength, security, and encouragement as long as we believe and trust Him the way the inhabitants of Jerusalem believed and trusted their towers, walls, and citadels.

He is our wall. He is our tower. He is our citadel. For He is our God.

Week 57

Single-Minded Purpose

1 Samuel 23–26; Psalm 49; Mark 15–16

If there is one thing that can be said for Saul, it is that he had a purpose in life, a purpose to which he was fully committed. Saul's purpose in life was to find David and kill him.

Saul was determined in his purpose. "Saul hunted him day after day…" (1 Sam. 23:14).

Saul was tenacious in his purpose. "Saul kept after him…" (1 Sam. 23:25).

Saul was resolved to accomplish his purpose. "…I'll track him down, even if I have to search every hiding place in Judah!" (1 Sam. 23:23).

Saul didn't waver in his intent. He wasn't easily distracted from the goal. Hardship and obstacles meant little to him. His dedication to the objective would have been admirable except for one problem. His objective was wrong, and it was sinful. All of Saul's potential had come down to one single-minded, all-consuming, ungodly pursuit. Where did this one pursuit lead Saul and those for whom he had responsibility?

It led Saul to waste the valuable resource of his time. He spent countless hours doing what he should not have done. Each moment spent searching for David was time that could have been spent in pursuits pleasing to God and beneficial to others.

It led Saul to waste his talent. Saul was a gifted individual, but his God-given talents were devoted to doing what was wrong.

It led Saul to turn away from his true purpose in life. As king, Saul was given the responsibility to wisely lead and protect the Israelite nation. Saul took his focus off the true Israelite enemy, the Philistines, and turned it against David, someone who should have been his ally. While Saul spent most of his time, energy, and resources to attack a fellow Israelite, the Philistines had the opening they needed to bring trouble to the nation; for, sure enough, "an urgent message reached Saul that the Philistines were raiding Israel again" (1 Sam. 23:27). Saul's misdirection of purpose put innocent people in harm's way.

It eventually led to Saul's own downfall and death, as well as the death of his sons. Saul's valuable time ran out, and he no longer had the opportunity to turn away from his wicked, personal goal toward God's worthy goal for him. Perhaps a greater tragedy is that time also ran out for his sons; for they, too, suffered the consequences of Saul's sinful pursuit.

Saul wasn't wrong in his drive to accomplish a goal. It was the goal itself that was wrong. We can only begin to imagine the good that he could have accomplished if he had been captivated by God's goals and turned his determination toward doing what God desired.

How about us? What is our purpose in life? What are our major goals? What has our attention? On what do we spend our time and talent? Where are our thoughts directed? Are we allied with the right people?

God has a purpose for each of our lives, and we have been created uniquely and lovingly to fulfill that special purpose. God wants us, like Saul, to be single-minded in our purpose, but He wants our purpose to flow out of our love for Him and for our neighbor (Mark 12:30-31).

Great things happen when we are determined, tenacious, and resolved to love God and others.

WEEK 58

Share the Burden

1 Samuel 27–31; 1 Corinthians 1–2

"When David and his men saw the ruins and realized what had happened to their families, they wept until they could weep no more" (1 Sam. 30:3-4).

How could David and his followers handle any more pain and loss? They were already suffering, for they were refugees in a foreign land. They were far away from their rightful homes and their extended families. They lived among their enemies, the Philistines—a harsh fact that required them to be always on guard.

And yet they had carved out a temporary home, Ziklag, in the land of the Philistines, and they were comforted by the presence of their wives and children. Or, at least, they had been comforted until the day when all had been destroyed by the Amalekites, who "…had made a raid into the Negev and had burned Ziklag to the ground. They had carried off the women and children and everyone else" (1 Sam. 30:1-2).

And now these warriors "wept until they could weep no more." The burden was too great. The pain was too intense. The present was too dismal. The future was too meaningless. It seemed as if there was nothing but sorrow for David and his men.

And so it is today. Tragedy and misery surround us. Individuals stagger under the weight of illness, loss, and pain. Families and entire groups of people experience the shattering effects of natural or man-made disasters. Millions weep in despair until they can weep no more.

Do we weep with them?

Each of us carries burdens of which others may not be aware. Suffering is part of each of our lives. And yet are we also able to step outside of our own issues and become aware of others in great distress? We probably won't have to look hard or long to find those for whom we can have compassion in their suffering.

It is good for us to care deeply enough to be hurt by what hurts others. That kind of caring is indicative of loving others, and love like that will drive us to do what we can to help those we know and even those we have never met; for true caring does not leave off where our personal acquaintance ends. But what can we do?

We can give of ourselves. Sometimes a listening ear, a written note, or a human touch can lighten the load and bring comfort. Time is a precious commodity in today's hectic world. It is precious to those who give it away to others, and it is precious to those who receive this simplest but most personal gift.

We can give of our talents and different skills. We often take our own skills for granted, since they may be almost second-nature to us. But to those lacking our skill set, what we know and can do may be exactly what is needed.

We can give of our resources. With true struggles often come severe financial hardships. In the midst of horrendous setbacks, people often must cope with trying to supply their most basic needs. How much are we willing to sacrifice financially to step into the gap for them?

We can pray. Have you ever faced times so difficult that you were overwhelmed, and yet you felt strengthened by God's presence? It may be that someone was praying for you.

We can serve as a reminder of God's love and strength. God can give hope when there is no hope. Let us not take for granted the truth that when there is nothing left, there is God. And when nothing else is left to block our view, we will find God sufficient to meet our physical, emotional, and spiritual needs. David is a prime example of this, for there was nothing left after his family was taken; "but David found strength in the Lord his God" (1 Sam. 30:6). And so can we, and so can others.

The story ends when David and his men are able to rescue their families and recover all that had been taken from them through the help of an Egyptian slave. May we be as willing as this Egyptian slave to take action when we become aware of others' essential needs.

Who can tell exactly how much our acts of service, sacrifice, and caring will mean to others and to God?

Thankfulness Takes Practice

2 Samuel 1–5, Psalm 50; 1 Corinthians 3

There was something that God wanted from the Israelites, and there was something that He did *not* want.

"I want no more bulls from your barns; I want no more goats from your pens. I don't need the bulls you sacrifice; I don't need the blood of goats" (Ps. 50:9,13). Wait a minute here! This made no sense.

Every Israelite made animal sacrifices. These animals were vital to the Israelites' relationship with God, for they were symbolic of the Israelites' need to be forgiven of the sins that separated them from God and God's forgiveness of those sins. God not wanting sacrifices sounded like a total contradiction to everything they practiced and everything that made them God's special people.

If God didn't want these things, what did He want? God said, "What I want *instead* is your true thanks to God; I want you to fulfill your vows to the Most High" (Ps. 50:14). Thankfulness and faithfulness were what God desired.

God wanted the Israelites to be faithful to their vows. Oh, yes, *those* vows. The vows where they had promised that God would be their only God, that they would obey Him, and that they would trust Him. The animals being sacrificed couldn't make the people believe that God was the one and only true God, and they couldn't cause the people to turn from their way of living to God's way of living. Only the people themselves could decide those things and be faithful to those decisions.

There was one other important thing the animals being sacrificed couldn't do. They could not make the people thankful to God.

God wanted the Israelites to be thankful for what they had. He wanted them to be thankful that He had provided a way for them to be acceptable to Him in His holiness—a blessing that was not to be taken lightly or for granted. Did they have shelter, food, clothing, and a way to provide for themselves and their families? Were they loved by someone? Did they have health, sight, hearing, and speech? Did they live in peace? They should be thankful.

God wanted the Israelites to be thankful for what they did not have. Were there sins for which God was withholding His judgment? They should be thankful for the opportunity to turn away from these sins and back toward God. Were there diseases, poverty, natural disasters, or wars that had not affected them? They should be thankful for protection from these hardships.

Being thankful for the good things we have and the bad things we don't have is the first and simplest level of thanks. Many have the luxury of taking life's basics for granted. Do we consider them as our rightful due or give thanks that God is so openhanded with us? It is ironic that as blessings increase, pride sometimes also increases, and thankfulness decreases.

The next level of thankfulness can be the most difficult, for it involves trusting that current hardship will result in future good. "Trust me in your times of trouble, and I will rescue you, and you will give me glory" (Ps. 50:15). Can we give God glory, or thanks, when we are faced with something that we wish was different? God wanted the Israelites to be thankful for who He was and not what their circumstances may have been. Were there times of trouble and sorrow? Were there circumstances beyond their control and beyond their ability to understand? They should be thankful because God was trustworthy, even when the situation held no apparent reason to trust or be thankful.

Can we give God thanks when something we consider essential to our lives and happiness is removed? Can we give thanks when we struggle with the lack of basic needs, poor health, weariness, broken relationships, death, fear, or even the silence of God? Can we be thankful for what we can learn and how we can be shaped to be more like Jesus by circumstances that we wish would go away?

Yes, we can! It will not be easy and it will not occur naturally. Thankfulness takes practice. If we aren't in the habit of practicing thankfulness for all that is good in our lives, being thankful will seem impractical or even false when times are tough. We hear about thankfulness in the difficult times so often that we begin to tune it out and dismiss it. But God says of those hard times, "Giving thanks is a sacrifice that truly honors me" (Ps. 50:23). Genuine thankfulness in the midst of distress reflects a trust in God that is rock solid, and any troubled heart giving thanks can testify to the sacrifice it is.

True thankfulness helps us to recall what God has done for us. It helps us remember God's holiness, power, and goodness. It increases our trust and draws us closer to God. And in an ever-widening circle, our increased trust in God leads to increased thankfulness, which leads to increased trust; and the circle keeps growing.

Thankfulness and trust. Once we are in that circle, we will never want to live any other way.

WEEK 60

A Nudge Out of the Blue

2 Samuel 6–10; 1 Corinthians 4–5

"One day David began wondering if anyone in Saul's family was still alive, for he had promised Jonathan that he would show kindness to them" (2 Sam. 9:1).

Out of the blue, David began wondering about a promise he had made many years before. David could have easily brushed off this thought and continued on with what he had been doing. But he didn't.

Instead, David stopped what he was doing and took immediate action by summoning Ziba, a longtime servant of Saul's family who could answer the question, "Is anyone still alive from Saul's family?" (2 Sam. 9:3). When David discovered that one of Jonathan's sons, Mephibosheth, was still alive, he promptly began fulfilling his promise to Jonathan.

Mephibosheth rightfully feared for his life when summoned to King David. After all, he and his young son, Mica, were the only direct heirs of Saul. With their deaths, there would be no one to assert a claim to Saul's throne.

Little did Mephibosheth know how much his life was about to change, for David did have much in mind for him—much good. David restored Mephibosheth's ancestral lands, established Ziba and his family as caretakers for this land, brought Mephibosheth and Mica to live with him in his lavish palace, and treated Mephibosheth as though he was one of David's own sons. When David put his quest to find Saul's heirs into motion, he knew he would do these things. What he did not know was that Jonathan's son was crippled in both feet.

Think about that. Mephibosheth had been dealt much hardship. Not only had his family's reign and power ended tragically but he was also crippled in both feet. Up to the time he was summoned by David, he had no way to support himself because of his injured body and the loss of his family's land to provide income. In those days, that would have been a guarantee of poverty and the likelihood of being shunned by most people.

Because of David's sensitivity to what could have been a fleeting thought, Mephibosheth was lifted from having nothing to being like the son of a powerful king. He and his family were blessed beyond their ability to imagine. And the blessings didn't stop with Mephibosheth but rolled forward to Ziba and his family, who would live on some of the best land of Israel and prosper as the land prospered.

After all those years, what brought Saul's family and David's promise to mind? No doubt it was the quiet voice of the Holy Spirit.

And the Holy Spirit continues to commune with believers in the same way today. How often, like David, do you think of an action that you were supposed to take but did not complete? How often have you remembered someone who hasn't entered your thoughts in a long time? How often do you realize, with a jolt, that you have done something that was not pleasing to God? In the life of the believer this may be the Holy Spirit's leading.

We need to be like David when we are prompted by the Holy Spirit. We need to listen and take action. At the remembrance of someone, we can pray for them and let them know we are praying and thinking of them. At the remembrance of an unfilled promise or action, we can set the wheels in motion to fulfill it. At the realization of something that is not pleasing to God, we can seek forgiveness from God and make amends with anyone wronged.

Many lives were affected and blessed when David acted on the Holy Spirit's prompting. The Holy Spirit wants to make us a blessing to others as well. The Holy Spirit wants to bring about change through us.

The gentle, quiet voice of God's Spirit is there for us to hear.

WEEK 61

Wanting What We Want

2 Samuel 11–15; Psalm 51; 1 Corinthians 6

God said David was "a man after my own heart, for he will do everything I want him to" (Acts 13:22).

David is often remembered as a man who wanted to do, and who did, God's will. But he is also remembered for the spiritual low point of his life, a time when he set about doing something that he knew would displease God. In this one glaring instance, David wanted what *he* wanted more than he wanted God, and he was willing to forsake God's presence, blessing, and direction to pursue it.

David wanted and took Bathsheba, another man's wife. He plotted, lied, and murdered until he accomplished his goal. He ignored God, but God did not ignore David for we are told that "the Lord was very displeased with what David had done" (2 Sam. 11:27).

Rarely do God's followers deliberately go against the Lord without word spreading. It was no different for David. God's prophet, Nathan, had heard. Nathan didn't talk with others about what David had done. Instead, he went directly to David and to the heart of the matter when he asked, "Why, then, have you despised the word of the Lord and done this horrible deed?" (2 Sam. 12:9).

"Why?" was a good question. David had been given so much by God, but he wanted what God had not given him. God reminded David of all that he had been given, and it was a heady list: the kingdom of Israel, protection from David's enemies, a palace, wives.... And if that was not enough, if there had been anything lacking to meet David's needs, God told David, "I would have given you much, much more" (2 Sam. 12:8). God had no desire to withhold anything that was good from David. It was David who had been mistaken about what was good for him.

After Nathan delivered God's rebuke, David again became a man after God's own heart, for he immediately confessed his wrongdoing and sought God's forgiveness. He decisively and purposely turned away from the sin of choosing his own path and came back onto God's path.

David experienced the deep joy of sin forgiven. He was forgiven, but the consequences could not be undone.

Wrong choices affect not only those who sin but also innocent others as well as God's reputation. Because of David's immoral choices, he and Bathsheba had to live with the memories and shame of their sin. They also had to live with its immediate and long-term consequences: the death of their first child, the murder of members of David's family, and the rebellion of David's own household against him as king and father. These were severe and far-reaching consequences.

But there was another consequence that grieved David's heart the most: his sin had "given the enemies of the Lord great opportunity to despise and blaspheme him [God]" (2 Sam. 12:14). When you truly love the Lord, as David did, knowing that you willfully brought dishonor to His name is an incredibly painful thing.

David's story plays out over and over again through the ages in many different ways. We believers are God's children, but we continue to want what we know is in conflict with what God desires for us. We ignore our consciences, and we ignore God. We plot and lie to ourselves. We act as if God has the worst in mind for us rather than the best. We forfeit what God has for us and settle for much less. And then, too often, we are selective in our memories, ignoring our own actions and blaming God rather than ourselves when the consequences come.

And when all is said and done, when we have turned from our sin and back toward God, the consequence that may bring the greatest sorrow is the dishonor we have brought to God. It is a hurtful thing to give others reason to judge God by *our* wrongful actions. Years of consistent living may be needed to overcome the perception of hypocrisy brought about by those actions. Yes, we have been forgiven and made whole through Jesus, and our hearts rejoice with thankfulness for being forgiven. But we must live in the shadow of the consequences of those sins.

Life has enough natural difficulties without stacking our own sinful choices on the pile. As we contemplate an action that we know is dishonoring to God, we need to practice turning away from it. Yes, it is easier said than done, but it is most assuredly easier than living with the consequences. The sooner we start stepping away, the easier it is. The sooner we stop dwelling on our sinful desire, the easier it is. The sooner we stop trying to have it both our way and God's way, the easier it is.

Be thankful in remembering the good things that God has brought into your life, and believe that He will continue to bring good things to you. Be resolute in not selling God short and in not believing that you can choose more wisely than He does for your life. Be unyielding in saying *yes* to God and *no* to sin.

Be dedicated to being a person after God's own heart.

Week 62

Freedom

2 Samuel 16–18; Psalms 52–54; 1 Corinthians 7

"The Lord has now set you free from the awful power of sin" (1 Cor. 7:22). This is such a simple sentence, but these thirteen words present several important truths.

The first truth is a sad one. Sin is awful and brutally oppresses us. It either brings misery immediately or brings it eventually. There never comes a time when we can ignore sin; for though it can be subtle, it is always destructive. Who hasn't felt the bitter sting of the consequences of sin—our own and others?

The second truth is also sad. Sin is a powerful force and so pervasive that we have to think hard to even begin to imagine our existence on earth without its awful influence. Even when we recognize it, even when we desire to escape from it and know the potential pain of sin, it remains a lethal force in our lives.

But the third truth gives us reason to be hopeful. Jesus Christ our Lord liberates us from sin and its power. Jesus, nothing else, frees us, and we are free because of His loving sacrifice.

And the final truth turns our hope into joy. At the moment in which we believe that Christ's sacrifice has made us acceptable to God we are "free from the awful power of sin"—not sometime in the future but *now*. Yes, we become free at that exact moment.

But if we are free, why does sin still exert so much power and control over us? Why don't we *feel* free of sin's power? Could it be that *being* free and *acting* free are not the same thing? We don't instinctively know how to act free of sin, and because of this we often don't feel free.

Whenever I think of the difference between being free and acting free, I am reminded of my visit to Africa. While traveling through the countryside, our group came upon several armed men in uniform standing together. The Africans traveling with us immediately tensed with fear, told us to keep our eyes averted, our heads down, and not to draw attention to ourselves. This was not a natural reaction for me. My experiences with authority figures was different than theirs. If the others hadn't told me to do these things, it would never have entered my thoughts or my actions. But for them there was no other way to react, no other appropriate way to respond. Even if they had suddenly been granted the type of freedom I knew, their immediate reactions would not have differed, for their experience had taken root in their thought process. They would technically be free, but their reactions and thoughts would take time to change.

And so it is with us and sin's power. When freedom becomes a reality, we don't quite know what to do with that freedom. Freedom from sin isn't innate to our understanding. Our world is so influenced by sin's destruction, and we have lived so long with this awful domination, that we have to learn step-by-step what freedom from sin truly means. It takes a lifetime to shed all of our old feelings and old ways of acting. Situations we face after we are free can continue to trigger reactions or thoughts ingrained in us while we were not free.

We are works in progress. It takes time and practice to become accustomed to our freedom and for our mindset and reactions to be transformed. And for those times when we feel shaky in our freedom, we can call upon Jesus for help. He will answer our call.

Rejoice! For we are "now set free from the awful power of sin." Praise God for an astounding gift!

WEEK 63

Why Me?

2 Samuel 19–23; 1 Corinthians 8–9

"But we know that there is only one God, the Father, who created everything, and *we exist for him*" (1 Cor. 8:6). We exist because God, who created everything, created us. But why did God specifically create each of us?

Probably sometime in your life you have wondered about this same thing. Why were you put on this earth? Why you? You may *still* wonder about these things.

This verse in First Corinthians 8 makes the answer to those questions completely clear. "We exist for him." We are uniquely crafted by God, and each person is unlike any other of God's creations. We have similarities, but even identical twins are not completely identical. God wanted us, and so we were created. But why create us at all?

David tells us part of the answer to that question. Speaking of God, he said, "he delights in me" (2 Sam. 22:20). Like David, we exist because our existence can bring God pleasure. As with any devoted parent, God loves His children and takes delight in them. Now stop and think about that. We delight Him!

Can you picture it? No matter what our chronological age when we begin our journey with God, we all start at the same place of infancy in the Lord. Like a child, our spiritual steps may be bold as we set out in exploration of our new world, or our steps may falter as we fall down while learning to walk. But each step we take to draw closer to God brings Him delight.

Each time we talk with God through prayer or seek to know Him better by studying His word to us in the Bible, we bring Him delight. Each time we trust Him in a difficult situation, we bring Him delight. Each time we choose God's way rather than our way, we bring Him delight. And even for those times when we stray from His path but return, confessing our sins, we bring Him delight in our return. Yes, we are created for Him—for the genuine delight He takes in each of us.

But a person without a purpose is a bored and restless person, and that leads to another part of the answer to our question about the reason for our existence. God has given us an essential purpose; for here on earth, God is partially made known to others through our lives. People come to know God's attributes and greatness with each word we share about Him. They come to know Christ's love through each loving action we take. They come to know the power and comfort of prayer as we pray for them. They come to know the difference that Jesus makes in a life when they observe the difference He has made in our lives.

Our lives have a purpose, and it is an important one. Because of our unique set of abilities, characteristics, backgrounds, and contacts, each of us has opportunities to help someone know more about Christ. This may be a person with whom others may never be able to make the same connection that you can make. Whom has God entrusted to you?

In this life we juggle many worthy goals and purposes. But as "we exist for him," the desire to make Jesus known to others can become part of all our other goals and purposes. Without that desire, we will instinctively sense a missing piece to our purpose. When Paul wrote, "I run straight to the goal with purpose in every step," he grasped how every other goal and purpose could be coupled with life's *main* goal of helping others know Christ (1 Cor. 9:26).

Why were we the ones created? We'll understand it more clearly when we are finally in Heaven and experiencing some of God's delight with us. For now, we have the remarkable blessing of living purposeful lives representing our Savior to others.

Something's Not Right Here

2 Samuel 24; 1 Kings 1–4; Psalm 55; 1 Corinthians 10

"But after he had taken the census, David's conscience began to bother him" (2 Sam. 24:10).

Does your conscience ever kick in and, out-of-the-blue, you have a sense that something isn't quite right? Maybe it's a little nagging feeling that keeps popping up even though you may not be able to immediately identify the cause. Or maybe it hits you like a ton of bricks, and there is no doubt what is troubling your conscience and, therefore, you. Regardless how it gets our attention, David gave us a perfect example of how to handle a bothersome conscience.

To his credit, David's conscience began to bother him after he had taken the census, not before. While contemplating and conducting the census, he was unaware of his sinful motivation for taking it. He was in that state of oblivion we all inhabit at times.

David started out oblivious, but that didn't stop his conscience from pinpointing a problem. As soon as his conscience began to bother him, David sought to discover the cause. This brings up the first important point about David's conscience. He trusted it. David knew God's laws and could test his conscience against this knowledge. He knew that his conscience was not overly sensitive, pointing out wrong where none existed, just as he knew that it was not insensitive to actual wrong.

David didn't ignore his conscience or try to rationalize that there was no reason for it to be bothering him. He understood that his censoring conscience acted as a direct communication line with the Holy Spirit. His conscience was a gift from God, pointing out a sin that needed to be dealt with.

We aren't told how David determined what was bothering his conscience, but there may be times when the cause of an awakened conscience is not immediately known. At these times a prayer asking for understanding and knowledge of what has activated our conscience may be needed.

It wasn't long before David realized the cause of his bothered conscience. It was the census—not necessarily the physical act of taking it but the underlying reasons behind it. David had become proud of the extent of his kingdom and the number of people under his rule. He forgot that the people and possessions had been put under his rule because God desired it, not because of David's abilities. And in a faulty, but too common reaction, rather than relying on God, David began to rely on the power and possessions given to him by God. With misplaced trust, David depended on the sheer number of fighting men available to protect his power and possessions. He had come to the place where he discounted the many times in the past when God had provided and protected those things. As soon as David realized his wrong motives, he turned away from his pride and self-reliance, confessed his sin, and asked for forgiveness.

David was correct to immediately seek forgiveness. But seeking forgiveness, and receiving it, does not negate the consequences of our sin, nor does it relieve us of taking action to minimize its consequences. David's action in this situation was to choose which consequence he and the nation of Israel would suffer. David chose, and the entire nation suffered through a deadly plague. David's personal punishment included seeing the devastation that fell on 70,000 people and knowing that it was due to his sin. How long did that gut-wrenching knowledge linger with David? How long does our own pain linger when we know that our actions have caused others to suffer? Consequences can be costly.

As there can be for us, in the end there was reconciliation between David and God. David was restored to his intimate relationship with God, but this could not have happened without David heeding that bothersome conscience.

One of the primary reasons our conscience exists is to keep us in alignment with God's will for our lives. Imagine the increase in chaos and woe on this earth if we did not have consciences to help guide our thoughts and actions. When the Holy Spirit is part of our lives, there is going to be a nudge to our conscience when we have done something displeasing to God. Quiet, or not so quiet, reminders from our conscience let us know that, as believers, we have some soul searching to do, probably some forgiveness to seek, and most likely some action to take.

A healthy conscience is an important gift from God. When your conscience knocks, open the door wide and answer the call.

WEEK 65

People Building

1 Kings 5–9; 1 Corinthians 11–12

"As you know, there is no one among us who can cut timber like you Sidonians!" (1 Kings 5:6).

The most important building project in Israel's history was underway. A permanent tabernacle was being built to honor God's presence and to unite the people in worship. The tabernacle, or temple, was going to be both immense and beautiful. Many supplies and much talented labor would be needed over the seven years it would take to complete the project. Timber was one of those supplies.

King Solomon led the building project. As the plans got underway, Solomon wrote a letter to another powerful king, Hiram of Tyre, who ruled over the Sidonians. The letter was a request for Hiram to supply the giant cedar and cypress beams and paneling that would be needed to construct the temple. The timber was essential to the project; no timber, no tabernacle. Solomon ended the letter with a fact. No one cut timber like the Sidonians.

It was a fact. But it was much more than that. It was recognition of a talent of the Sidonians, and Solomon did not hesitate to acknowledge it. By his recognition, Solomon inferred his appreciation for that talent, and then he went one step further. He asked Hiram to "Let my men work alongside yours…" (1 Kings 5:6). With the Sidonians leading the way, there was assurance that the beams and paneling would be properly crafted and by working alongside them, the Israelites could learn from their expertise.

With Solomon's encouraging words being passed from tree cutter to tree cutter, do you think the Sidonians took greater pleasure in doing what they naturally did so well? Hiram seemed to, for we are told that "When Hiram received Solomon's message, he was very pleased and said, 'Praise the Lord for giving David a wise son to be king of the great nation of Israel'" (1 Kings 5:7). Hiram wasn't resentful that Solomon asked for valuable cedar timber or massive amounts of labor. He was pleased and praised God for Solomon's wisdom.

Sidonians were good foresters. But Sidonians are not alone in being special. God makes each of us unique—with different physical abilities, emotional responses, intelligence levels, outlooks, and talents (1 Cor. 12:1-11). One quick look at nature proves that variety is a major characteristic of all that God creates. The differences in nature are vast, but each difference enhances and is important in supporting the whole, just as the Sidonians' talent supported the whole temple.

Each person possesses something in his or her nature that is worthy of being recognized and is needed for God's work to be supported and completed. With some people, these positive characteristics are easy to identify. With others, it may require more time and deeper digging. But the things worthy of recognition are there.

Do encouragement and recognition for others flow as naturally from us as it did from Solomon for the Sidonians? Or do unfair criticism, faultfinding, and nitpicking come too easily? Words can wound or words can build up. Words can help people see their God-given worth or turn their eyes from God as they seek to recover from an encounter with another.

Recognition and encouragement are a powerful duo. As Christians, directed to love others, we need to consistently practice using these tools. Look around. Find something in another that deserves genuine recognition, and then be an encourager. Solomon's building plan for the temple included the Sidonians. God's building plan for others includes us!

Making Sense of Trying Times

1 Kings 10–13; Psalms 56–57; 1 Corinthians 13

Have you noticed how often the Bible talks about sorrow, suffering, and fear? In both the Old Testament and the New Testament it is a frequent theme. Why do so many passages return again and again to this subject?

Could it be because the Bible deals in realistic life situations? And it is a reality that we often deal with sorrow, suffering, fear, or a combination of these because our lives bear the consequences of a world harmed by sin. The Bible comes back to these struggles repeatedly because these struggles come repeatedly into our lives.

This week our reading addressed fear: "But when I am afraid, I put my trust in you" (Ps. 56:3).

It addressed sorrow: "You keep track of all my sorrows. You have collected all my tears in your bottle. You have recorded each one in your book" (Ps. 56:8).

And suffering: "Have mercy on me, O God, have mercy! I look to you for protection. I will hide beneath the shadow of your wings until this violent storm is past. …I am weary from distress" (Ps. 57:1,6).

But the overriding theme this week, as in prior weeks, is God's help during times of difficulty. He is the answer when life is overwhelming: "I put my trust in you." He is the answer when it seems too hard or confusing to take the next step: "I will hide beneath the shadow of your wings until this violent storm is past." He is the answer when we are broken down by sorrow and pain and want comfort: "You have collected all my tears in your bottle."

Yes, life can hold hardship and heartache. It can be confusing and overwhelming. But, God is God, and God is with us, and God is love. Only God can take the bad times of our lives and make them into something good for us.

Often the pain, suffering, and sorrow do not make sense at the time we are experiencing them. They may not even make sense looking back over the years, but eventually they will; for we are promised that although "now we see things imperfectly as in a poor mirror, then we will see everything with perfect clarity. All that I know now is partial and incomplete, but then I will know everything completely, just as God knows me now" (1 Cor. 13:12).

We often look at our circumstances and miss seeing the lessons being learned, the growth that is happening, and the trust in God being developed. Trying to make sense of all that happens in our lives now is like looking at ourselves in mirrors that purposely distort the way we look. The image is suggestive of reality but grossly misrepresents it.

It is similar to how the world looks to those of us with vision problems. Without correction, our eyes see, but not clearly. It takes lens correction or surgery before we have a possibility to see with "perfect clarity." With perfect clarity we can see the sharper image, the truer colors, the brighter light, the more realistic depth. Without the correction, the world is duller, flatter, darker, distorted. If we had no sight correction, we wouldn't know that what we saw naturally was distorted. It would be our only reality. In the same way, our life situations are distorted by what we do not know, and what we do know now "is partial and incomplete."

But someday we will see our lives on earth clearly and completely. We will know "as God knows us now." God not only sees us as we are, but He also sees the person we are becoming. God sees how the often painful forces in our lives can be used for our good to shape us into someone more complete.

Yes, the Bible comes back to the hard times again and again, as we do. But some day, some glorious day, those hard times will be forever behind us, and we will know and understand. And until that time, we can cling to God, who cares about our sorrows; we can hide under the shadow of His protective wing, and we can trust when we are afraid.

It may not be easy to do so. It may not seem natural or logical to do so. But God is wiser than our logic, our natural inclinations, and our knowledge. God knows us better than we know ourselves.

God is our truest reason for hope in our times of fear, sorrow, and suffering.

WEEK 67

Then and Now

1 Kings 14–17; Psalm 58; 1 Corinthians 14–15

"But whatever I am now, it is all because God poured out his special favor on me—and not without results" (1 Cor.15:10). Each phrase of this sentence from Paul to the Corinthian church reverberates with assurance or challenge. While Paul was speaking of himself, his thoughts apply to all children of God. Let's break it down.

"But whatever I am now…" These words imply that something about us has changed from the past. "Now" we are different from what we were before. How are we different? And when did this change occur?

"Now" divides time into two distinct periods separated by a specific point in time. That specific point was when we consciously came into a relationship with God. It was then that we were renewed and set free from our past. In God's sight, what we were before we said "yes" to Jesus no longer matters. All of that was *then* and we are living in the *now* of our relationship with Him. We are different people. *This is our assurance.*

But "now" also implies an ongoing period of time. Whatever Paul was the week, month, or year before in his obedience to, trust in, and love for Jesus Christ was not what he was at the present moment. What is important is not only what we are, but what we are becoming since we came into a relationship with Christ. Are we moving forward with Jesus? *This is our challenge.*

Paul changed and we change "because God poured out his special favor on" each of us. We do not receive a mere trickle of mediocre kindness from any ordinary benefactor. We are absolutely drenched in God's special favor.

God's special favor provided the way for us to be acceptable to Him through Jesus Christ and gives us the guidance of the Holy Spirit. God's special favor conquered our great enemy—death—and gives us a future in heaven. God's special favor gives us talents and skills for our use right now. These special favors, and many others, are poured out to each believer—no exceptions. *This is our assurance.*

When we have been so completely changed, our lives should not be "without results." "So, my dear brothers and sisters, be strong and steady, always enthusiastic about the Lord's work, for you know that nothing you do for the Lord is ever useless" (1 Cor. 15:58). One important aspect of "the Lord's work" involves telling others about Jesus Christ so they can have the freedom, joy, and assurance that we do. *This is our challenge.*

Paul's single statement captured some of the major assurances and challenges of a life in alignment with God. Live in that assurance! And be determined in meeting the challenges, for therein lies a satisfaction that is otherwise unattainable in this life.

Week 68

Showdown at Mount Carmel

1 Kings 18–21; Psalm 59; 1 Corinthians 16; 2 Corinthians 1

"But Elijah said, 'I swear by the Lord Almighty, in whose presence I stand, that I will present myself to Ahab today'" (1 Kings 18:15).

Ahab was king of Israel when kings had a great deal of power. It was said of Ahab that he "did what was evil in the Lord's sight, even more than any of the kings before him" (1 Kings 16:30). Now that took some doing because there were some incredibly evil and disobedient kings prior to Ahab.

Elijah, the prophet, was God's messenger. Not surprisingly, there was much conflict between Ahab and Elijah because Elijah consistently pointed out Ahab's shortcomings in the eyes of God. In fact, Ahab despised Elijah.

It had been three years since Elijah last met with Ahab. At that time, Elijah warned that God was sending a drought in punishment for Ahab's and the nation's sins. The drought devastated the land, the people, and the animals. As usual, Ahab ignored the clearly stated reason for the drought and blamed the devastation on Elijah, the messenger. The day that Elijah came to present himself to Ahab was the day God was going to end the drought; but first, there was going to be a confrontation.

Now an ordinary human being who knew that he was going head-to-head with an angry and powerful king might think twice before acting. But Elijah was not ordinary. Elijah knew he stood in *God's presence.*

When Elijah and Ahab came face-to-face, Ahab set the tone. "So it's you, is it—Israel's troublemaker?" (1 Kings 18:17). Elijah simply replied that it was Ahab and his family who had made trouble for Israel by their disobedience to God and worship of Baal. Elijah's courage to speak the truth was not foolishness. He had *spiritual power* because he knew "in whose presence" he stood.

But there was a more important issue to settle that day, and Elijah was there to settle it. He told Ahab, "'Bring all the people of Israel to Mount Carmel, with all 450 prophets of Baal.' Then Elijah stood in front of them and said, 'How long are you going to waver between two opinions? If the Lord is God, follow him! But if Baal is God, then follow him!'" (1 Kings 18:19,21). Elijah was a *spiritual witness* because he knew "in whose presence" he stood.

And then the showdown began! The priests of Baal cut a bull "into pieces and lay it on the wood of their altar, but without setting fire to it…. Then they called on the name of Baal all morning, shouting, 'O Baal, answer us!' But there was no reply of any kind. Then they danced wildly around the altar. So they shouted louder, and following their normal custom, they cut themselves with knives and swords until the blood gushed out. They raved all afternoon until the time of the evening sacrifice, but still there was no reply, no voice, no answer" (1 Kings 18:23,26,28-29).

"Then Elijah called to the people, 'Come over here!'" (1 Kings 18:30). The crowd drew near to the Lord's altar where Elijah stood. They watched as he rebuilt the altar, dug a ditch around it, piled wood on top, and prepared a bull to be burned as a sacrifice. As Elijah stepped back from his work, he directed that four jars be filled with water and poured over the bull, wood, and altar. He gave the same instructions three times until "water ran around the altar and even overflowed the trench" (1 Kings 18:35). To the onlookers it must have seemed as if Elijah was setting himself up for spectacular failure. After all, they had spent the entire day waiting for the prophets of Baal to succeed under much easier conditions. Elijah had *spiritual backbone* that led to faithful obedience regardless of the situation because he knew "in whose presence" he stood.

Elijah walked up to the soaked altar and began to pray. He boldly asked God to prove that He was truly God, able to do what Baal could not. In the moments from Elijah's prayer until God's answer, we can almost sense the various responses of the crowd—hope, disbelief, indifference, and curiosity. But Elijah was *sure and confident* in God because he knew "in whose presence" he stood.

"Immediately the fire of the Lord flashed down from heaven and burned up the young bull, the wood, the stones, and the dust. It even licked up all the water in the ditch! And when the people saw it, they fell on their faces and cried out, 'The Lord is God! The Lord is God!'" (1 Kings 18:38-39).

There were spiritual results and renewal for many because Elijah was fully aware "*in whose presence*" he stood. But there was a path to follow before this renewal could happen. As long as Elijah remembered in whose presence he stood, he was given encouragement and strength by God as needed. When Elijah did not remember in whose presence he stood, he faltered, but that is a story for another time.

We, too, stand in the presence of God, and because of that presence, spiritual power and results are available to us. The questions are: to what degree are we aware of God's presence, and how does that awareness affect our actions, thoughts, and outlook?

WEEK 69

So They Went on Together

1 Kings 22; 2 Kings 1–3; Psalms 60–61; 2 Corinthians 2

Elijah and Elisha were walking together on the dusty road. Elijah was God's principal prophet of that time, and Elisha was his student. The day had begun as many others for the two companions but everything was about to change. Elijah's days on earth were about to end dramatically and spectacularly because "the Lord was about to take Elijah up to heaven in a whirlwind" (2 Kings 2:1).

Elijah knew this and "said to Elisha, 'Stay here, for the Lord has told me to go to Bethel.' But Elisha replied, 'As surely as the Lord lives and you yourself live, I will never leave you!' So they went on together to Bethel" (2 Kings 2:2).

"So they went on together"—side by side, as they had since Elisha became Elijah's student. As they approached Bethel, they were met by a group of God's prophets who lived there. The prophets drew Elisha aside "and asked him, 'Did you know that the Lord is going to take your master away from you today?'" (2 Kings 2:3). Picture the group clustered around Elisha as they passed on this important news they had received straight from God!

"'Quiet!' Elisha answered. 'Of course I know it'" (2 Kings 2:3). Yes, Elisha knew. He was fully aware that a time of grieving was approaching—the time he and his trusted friend, mentor, and teacher would be parted. Elisha knew the path ahead held uncertainty and sorrow, but he also knew he would not leave Elijah and they would end this day together... here in Bethel.

But there was a change in plans. God had told Elijah to go to Bethel; Elijah did, and Elisha had followed. With the Bethel prophets gathered around, God redirected Elijah. Elijah was now headed to Jericho.

"Then Elijah said to Elisha, 'Stay here, for the Lord has told me to go to Jericho.'" As he did a few hours before on the way to Bethel, Elijah offered Elisha a reprieve from experiencing the grief that was to come. "But Elisha replied again, 'As surely as the Lord lives and you yourself live, I will never leave you.' So they went together to Jericho" (2 Kings 2:4). Elisha was loyal to Elijah and did not take the easy way out, even though it was offered a second time.

So once again "they went on together." As Elijah and Elisha entered Jericho, the scene from their approach to Bethel was repeated. It was now the Jericho prophets who met them, eager to share their knowledge with Elisha of Elijah's last day on earth. Repeating what he had told the Bethel prophets, Elisha also ordered these prophets to be "Quiet!" He already knew what they knew (2 Kings 2:5). With all these voices offering man's insight and knowledge, was it getting harder to hear what God was saying?

If it was, Elijah was able to overcome the distraction and hear God's redirection once more, for he "said to Elisha, 'Stay here, for the Lord has told me to go to the Jordan River.' But again Elisha replied, 'As surely as the Lord lives and you yourself live, I will never leave you.' So they went on together" (2 Kings 2:6).

And at the Jordan River, God met Elijah and took him home to Heaven.

Elisha met the test of continual changes, distraction, coming sorrow, and upheaval to his life. This testing did not shake his loyalty to his own calling or to Elijah. Three times Elisha could have been distracted by others offering counsel, knowledge, and truth. Three times Elisha was given the opportunity to turn aside and avoid this painful parting. But Elisha was faithful. Elisha said to Elijah, "I will never leave you." And he didn't. So they went on together—together through whatever life brought to them.

Jesus says to us, "I will never leave you" (Heb. 13:5). And He doesn't. Like Elisha, we determine if we stay where we are in our faith or go on together with Christ through whatever life brings to us.

WEEK 70

At That Very Moment

2 Kings 4–8; 2 Corinthians 3–4

The wealthy Woman from Shunem recognized that Elisha was a holy man of God. She respected Elisha, wanted to do something to show her respect, and had the material means to help him. So "she invited him to eat some food. From then on, whenever he passed that way, he would stop there to eat" (2 Kings 4:8). As she came to know Elisha better, she desired to do more to help him, so she made "a little room for him…a place to stay" whenever he came by (v. 10).

The Woman from Shunem met Elisha's needs for food, shelter, rest, and friendship. But this was not a one-sided friendship. There came a time when Elisha met one of the deepest needs of the Woman from Shunem by bringing her son back to life after his sudden death.

This miraculous event was not the end of the contact between Elisha and the Woman from Shunem. Sometime later, Elisha told her to take her family and leave Israel because God was going to send a famine. The Woman from Shunem listened and moved to the land of the Philistines during the seven years of famine. Although this woman was wealthy, she trusted Elisha and left most of her wealth behind when she abandoned her dwelling place, her land, and the income that the land produced.

"After the famine ended she returned to the land of Israel, and she went to see the king about getting back her house and land. As she came in, the king was talking with Gehazi, the servant of the man of God [Elisha]. The king had just said, 'Tell me some stories about the great things Elisha has done.' And Gehazi was telling the king about the time Elisha had brought a boy back to life. At that very moment, the mother of the boy walked in to make her appeal to the king" (2 Kings 8:3-5).

Now many people would consider this to be an amazing coincidence. The Woman from Shunem had been away from her home in Israel for seven years. On the same day she decides to go to the king to seek his help in reclaiming her land and home that had been taken from her without compensation, the king is in the mood to hear some good stories. It was up to Gehazi to pick which story to tell from the many examples he could give. He was in the midst of the Woman from Shunem's story at the "very moment" she entered the king's presence.

But her good fortune didn't end with Gehazi's story. "'Look, my lord the king!' Gehazi exclaimed. 'Here is the woman now, and this is her son—the very one Elisha brought back to life!'" (2 Kings 8:5). The Woman from Shunem hadn't come alone; she had brought her son along! It's hard to believe such a lucky string of coincidences.

The king of Israel could barely believe it either. "'Is this true?' the king asked her. And she told him that it was. So he directed one of his officials to see to it that everything she had lost was restored to her, including the value of any crops that had been harvested during her absence" (2 Kings 8:6).

What were the odds? Slim to none. And yet it happened in perfect sequence and perfect timing.

Of course, we know it was not coincidence, nor was it luck. It was God. The Woman from Shunem had been obedient to what Elisha, the man of God, had told her, leaving everything behind; and now she needed help. And God was there. We can see God's hand in the people who came together, the king's question, Gehazi's answer, and the timing. In fact, it happened so naturally and so perfectly that it almost becomes easy to miss God's care and loving attention to each small detail in this woman's life.

God is still at work today in His children's lives. Be alert! Don't miss God's loving attention to the smallest details of your life. Coincidence is a word used incorrectly to explain the reality of God's quiet involvement in our lives.

Week 71

One of "Those" Days

2 Kings 9–12; Psalms 62–63; 2 Corinthians 5

Some days it isn't easy being a follower of Jesus Christ. Now granted, there are days when it does feel easy, when things couldn't seem more perfect in our relationship with Jesus or with others. But then there are "those" days…including the kind of day that one of God's prophets had in Second Kings 9.

This unnamed prophet had been summoned by Elisha to do an important job: anointing Jehu as the next king of Israel. We aren't told, but I imagine the unnamed prophet had been picked because he was faithful to God, up to the task, and obedient. In other words, we can probably conclude that he was doing everything "right" as far as his relationship with God went. But his faithfulness did not ensure that life would move along smoothly. Let's take a look at this unnamed prophet's day.

First he was told by Elisha how to accomplish the task. "Get ready to go to Ramoth-gilead. Take this vial of olive oil with you, and find Jehu. Call him into a back room away from his friends, and pour the oil over his head. Say to him, 'This is what the Lord says: I anoint you to be the king over Israel'" (2 Kings 9:1-3). Well now, that doesn't sound so hard. Except for possible travel issues, doing what God directed sounded straightforward. But there was one more directive from Elisha for the unnamed prophet: "Then open the door and run for your life!" (v. 3).

Being forewarned about an event doesn't always translate into peace of mind. If, up to this point, there had been any misconception in the prophet's mind that obedience to God and faith in Him would assure a smooth and trouble-free life, that erroneous belief was cleared up with Elisha's words of warning.

Do you think these words of warning caused the prophet to consider going in the opposite direction of Ramoth-gilead? Did he fear this day would be his last on earth? Did he wonder if serving the Lord and obeying him was worth walking into certain trouble? Did he feel let down by God, who seemed to be rewarding his obedience with life-threatening danger?

Maybe so, but the prophet did what he was asked to do. He went to Jehu, drew him aside from his fellow army officers, anointed him as the next king of Israel, gave him direction from God, and then "opened the door and ran" (2 Kings 9:4-10).

Now remember that the unnamed prophet did exactly what he had been told to do by Elisha and ultimately by God. Nevertheless, he must have been an amusing sight running from the house as fast as he could. In fact, he made quite an impression on Jehu's fellow army officers, for when Jehu went back, "one of them asked him, 'What did that crazy fellow want? Is everything all right?'" (2 Kings 9:11).

Didn't God care about how strange the prophet looked or that he was mocked for obeying God? How would this prophet have an impact on any of these people in the future when he had appeared so foolish in their eyes?

Even Jehu who knew that the prophet had been sent by God to him with an important message added his own words of ridicule, for he answered his companions by saying, "You know the way such a man babbles on" (2 Kings 9:11).

That was the icing on the cake. Not only did Jehu mock the prophet but all people like the prophet. Other believers were lumped together in general disdain.

These types of circumstances and results do not make sense to us. We struggle with the concept that we can be obedient and faithful to God and still encounter resistance, hardship, and contempt from others—*our* "run for your life" moments. We struggle with the concept that, as we reach out in Christ's love, we may be met with scorn and ridicule—*our* "what did that crazy fellow want" moments. We struggle with the concept that we are judged by other Christians' actions—*our* "you know the way such a man babbles" moments. Results like the unnamed prophet experienced go against our instinctive belief that, if we do the right thing, we will be protected by God, appreciated by others, and rewarded for it.

For the times when being a Christian is not easy, we have Jesus' time on earth as an example of how to cope and how to react. Who was more disliked, more persecuted, more mocked, or considered more delusional than Jesus? And what was Jesus' reaction? He drew closer to the Father through prayer, He continued in His obedience to God, He forgave those who caused His suffering, and He continued to love.

Jesus knew the reasons for *His* persecution, mocking, and death. Although we may not know the reasons when we face ridicule or opposition for being God's followers, we have been shown by Jesus how to respond.

Draw closer to the Father. Pray. Continue in obedience and trust. Forgive. Love. And some day, in God's timing, the reasons for the hard times will become clear to us.

Week 72

Caution! Slippery Conditions

2 Kings 13–16; Psalms 64–65; 2 Corinthians 6

"Ahaz was twenty years old when he became king…. He did not do what was pleasing in the sight of the Lord his God, even sacrificing his own son in the fire. He imitated the detestable practices of the pagan nations the Lord had driven from the land ahead of the Israelites" (2 Kings 16:2-3).

How far Israel had fallen! They were no longer a people united but a people divided into two nations, warring against each other. They were no longer a people who followed God and served as examples to others but a people who could not be distinguished from their sinful neighbors. And now Ahaz, the king of the southern Israelite territory, had copied "the detestable practices of the pagan nations" and killed his own child to honor a man-made god.

Because we tend to rank sins, Ahaz's act appears to be the vilest to us. But in reality every step taken away from God by each Israelite was equally as horrid as Ahaz's brazen act of human sacrifice. For by not turning *away* from their sin, the Israelites began to *tolerate* more sin in their lives in an escalating descent away from God and toward evil. It seems inconceivable that these people could have come to this point after knowing God and receiving so many of His blessings.

It is almost inconceivable…unless we understand our own propensity to slip away from God's direction. Here are five steps that lead us away from God.

1. We lose sight of the fact that God loves us and desires what is best for us. If this is not a core belief of ours, then our faith in God's goodness will be shaken when we experience hard times. And when our faith is under attack, we tend to trust God less and start trusting in something smaller and weaker than Him.

2. We stop being thankful for what God has done for us. Ingratitude breeds discontent, and discontent leads to searching for something to fulfill what we feel is missing from our lives.

3. We allow God to become less than first in our lives. Our thoughts of God, our times of prayer, our study of the Bible, and our desire to please Him diminish. We become willing to compromise our beliefs, principles, and obedience as God recedes from our thoughts and daily routines.

4. We become vulnerable to the influence of evil, as we begin to desire what *we* want more than what *God* wants for us. Without God's control over our tendency to selfishness, our focus zeroes in on pleasing ourselves, and we search for something to satisfy what only God can satisfy in our lives.

5. And finally, we stop being determined about turning away from sin. We no longer care that what we are doing is wrong.

The Israelites were certainly not the only example of people in close relationship with God who turned away from Him—bringing sorrow to themselves, to God, and to others. If only they were. But example after example in the Bible tells the same story. It can too easily be our story as well.

But the story doesn't need to end with final rejection of God. David, who committed grievous sins, also knew the joy of forgiveness. He, along with all who have turned away from their sin toward God, declares, "Though our hearts are filled with sins, you forgive them all" (Ps. 65:3).

We can get back on track and stay there by practicing the opposite of what makes us vulnerable to sin in the first place. Trust God's promises of His care and love for us regardless of our circumstances. Be grateful to God. Keep God first in our lives. Desire what God wants for us. Be resolute in our determination to turn away from what tempts us to sin.

Those are actions we will never regret and actions that will lead to the joy of hearing God say about us, "I will be their God, and they will be my people" (2 Cor. 6:16).

WEEK 73

Mysterious Influence

2 Kings 17–21; 2 Corinthians 7–8

"Hezekiah son of Ahaz began to rule over Judah…" (2 Kings 18:1). "Hezekiah son of Ahaz." Those few words carry with them certain expectations. Hezekiah was the son of one of Judah's most wicked kings, Ahaz. Led by Ahaz's example, the Israelites drew away from God; worshiped man-made idols, ignored God's commands, and even sacrificed their own children to their man-made gods (2 Kings 16).

Hezekiah was a son who escaped being a human sacrifice of his father's, but he had lived for twenty-five years under Ahaz's influence and the influence of the multitudes who followed in Ahaz's footsteps. Twenty-five years was a long time to be exposed to continual disobedience to God and the pursuit of evil. Twenty-five years of being surrounded by a culture that abandoned God takes a toll on a person's thoughts and actions. This had been Hezekiah's life.

And now Hezekiah was king. Would the old saying "like father, like son" be true for Hezekiah and for his kingdom? Would Hezekiah have the same values as his family and the nation of Judah?

Hezekiah would not. We are told that "He did what was pleasing in the Lord's sight, just as his ancestor David had done. Hezekiah trusted in the Lord, the God of Israel. He remained faithful to the Lord in everything, and he carefully obeyed all the commands the Lord had given Moses" (2 Kings 18:3,5-6).

Stop and think for a moment of how great a contrast there was between Ahaz, the father, and Hezekiah, the son. Think how unlikely it was that Hezekiah would become both the man and the king that he became. How did Hezekiah come to learn about the true God of Israel and to shake off the wicked influences of his upbringing and culture?

There can only be one way other than direct intervention by God. Someone showed Hezekiah a different way to live, serving as an example of a life controlled by God. Someone talked to Hezekiah about a true relationship with God. Someone's life, when combined with the power of God, had a greater influence on Hezekiah than the ungodly lifestyle that surrounded him. Scripture is silent on who this person (or persons) was. It may have been Isaiah the prophet, another prophet, a relative, a friend.

The person who spoke to Hezekiah and led him in the way of the Lord is unnamed, but his or her influence was great. That person was an important instrument used by God not only in Hezekiah's own life but in the life of the nation of Judah. Because of this unnamed person, Hezekiah chose to follow and obey God. And because Hezekiah followed God, it was said of him, "There was never another king like him in the land of Judah, either before or after his time" (2 Kings 18:5).

Yes, this person is unnamed in history, but his or her name and obedience are known by God. This person may not have had an inkling of how far his or her godly influence would spread as Hezekiah was shown another way to live; but God knew. Paul describes similar believers of his day as "splendid examples of those who bring glory to Christ" (2 Cor. 8:23).

Like Hezekiah's mentor, we can be "splendid examples" of someone who brings glory and honor to Christ by sharing our lives in Jesus with others. We were given a great gift when someone told us about the good news of Jesus Christ. We were given a great gift when someone modeled to us a life influenced by Christ.

Live as a splendid example of Christ, offering those same gifts to others.

Week 74

Direct Access

2 Kings 22–25; Psalms 66–67; 2 Corinthians 9

"Go to the Temple and speak to the Lord for me and for the people and for all of Judah. Ask him about the words written in this scroll that has been found..." (2 Kings 22:13).

The scroll that Hilkiah, the priest, found in the Lord's Temple at Jerusalem was no ordinary scroll. It was a scroll that contained words given to Moses by God. Hilkiah had found none other than the Book of the Law, God's blueprint to Israel for leading a life pleasing to Him and beneficial to them. This important scroll had been discarded long ago as evil king after evil king ruled Judah, the southern kingdom of Israel. As the kings and the people turned further and further away from God, the scroll was forgotten.

Now the scroll was no longer lost nor forgotten. It had been read to Josiah, the current king of Judah. Josiah was unique for this era because he was a king who desired to serve the Lord. It is said of Josiah that "never before had there been a king like Josiah, who turned to the Lord with all his heart and soul and strength..." (2 Kings 23:25).

Finding the Book of the Law and hearing it read should have been a time of great joy. Josiah wanted to please God, and with this scroll in hand, he and the people didn't have to wonder how to do that, for they now had a detailed document telling them what they needed to know. But Josiah was not rejoicing. He was deeply troubled, for he realized that the people of Judah were doing exactly what God had told them not to do, and their punishment would be severe.

This is what caused Josiah to ask the priest to speak to the Lord for him. Josiah needed to understand completely the troublesome words of judgment contained in the scroll.

Surely if there was a person who could come directly to God to speak of matters weighing on his heart, it was Josiah. The fact that he did not do so is striking. Why did Josiah ask Hilkiah to go to the Temple and speak to the Lord for him? Why didn't Josiah speak to God directly?

"Go to the Temple and speak to the Lord for me" vividly tells the difference between Josiah's times and ours. In Josiah's time, God's presence dwelt among the people, as it does today, but with one significant difference. God's presence resided usually in one specific place, the Temple in Jerusalem. And in the Temple a heavy curtain created a barrier between God's presence and those who came to the Temple.

There was only one time each year when someone was allowed to pass by that curtain to enter the Holy of Holies, and the high priest was that someone. To breach the curtain at any other time meant death; open access to the presence of God did not exist. This was forever changed, however, at the moment of Jesus' death, as Christ ripped open the Temple curtain from top to bottom. By His sacrifice, Jesus offered us the great gift of direct access to God at any time and at any place.

Think about that! We have unlimited access to God at any time and at any place—to ask anything, to say what is on our hearts, to seek direction. We do not need to go through a third party. We have a direct relationship with our Lord.

God answered Josiah's questions through the prophetess Huldah. God may still answer our questions through another. But God is as likely to directly answer the heart that seeks Him and His will through the quiet voice of the Holy Spirit who now resides in each believer.

Josiah needed a middle man to approach God, but God heard Josiah pray as He has always heard those who talk with Him from the beginning of creation. "So I have indeed heard you, says the Lord" (2 Kings 22:19).

God is with us through prayer and His Word. We can call on Him at any time and in any place—gifts for us to savor time and time again.

Boundaries that Matter

1 Chronicles 1–6; 2 Corinthians 10

"Our goal is to stay within the boundaries of God's plan for us" (2 Cor. 10:13).

God has a plan for us, and it is a good plan. It is custom-made for each of us, and we are made for it. It is a plan that incorporates our unique abilities, personalities, experiences, and knowledge. It is a plan that begins unfolding on the day of our birth and is lifelong in its duration.

It is a plan that allows each of our lives to have impact and significance. Our impact may be quiet and influential to only a small group of people, or it may be easily evident to large groups. Either way, we can be certain that our lives will be important to those for whom God plans it to be.

But the secret to a life of great impact is staying "within the boundaries" of God's plan. Each step outside of God's plan for our lives weakens our impact. Paul understood this and had a worthy goal. He didn't want to run ahead of God's plan for him with undisciplined enthusiasm or lag behind in defeat. He didn't want to waver from side to side in uncertainty. He didn't want to step outside the plan, overcome by life's temptations and trials. No, Paul wanted to stay "within the boundaries of God's plan."

This week we read through multiple lists of individuals' names (1 Chron. 1–6). These people were picked from a vast group, and their stories are of lives lived within and outside of God's plan. While we may not know anything about some of these names, the author of First Chronicles surely did, as did his contemporaries…as did God. Although many of those included on the lists have not stood the test of time when it comes to human remembrance, this does not diminish their influence for either good or bad, depending on their response to staying within the boundaries of God's plan for them.

Our names are also part of a genealogy. Years from now, we may be remembered or we may be forgotten by those living at that time. But for those whom our lives are to influence, let us live within the boundaries of God's plan, so that memories of our stories will evoke the thought that we were people who pleased God and loved others. That is as worthy a goal for us as it was for Paul.

The day will come, as we live within the boundaries of God's plan for us, that we will see Jesus face-to-face and hear Him say, "Well done, good and faithful servant." What a beautiful benediction those words will be to our life here on earth.

WEEK 76

The Answer to Adversity

1 Chronicles 7–11; Psalm 68; 2 Corinthians 11

The apostle Paul did not have an easy life after becoming a follower of Jesus Christ. In Second Corinthians 11:23-27, Paul tells of his physical and emotional suffering. These are real stories of a real man whose life was in continual pain and danger, a life with great stress. It is sobering if we stop and actually think about what Paul tells us of his life.

Paul was despised by others. He was betrayed by people with whom he identified—his fellow Jews. He faced danger from those who claimed to be followers of Christ but were not. And his life was imperiled by hostile Gentiles.

He was robbed. He was stoned and suffered such intensive injuries that he was believed to be dead by those stoning him. On at least eight different occasions, he was whipped on his bare back and shoulders with leather straps or rods, nearly to the point of death. Many times, after being whipped, he was not gently nursed back to health but jailed. And to be jailed in Paul's time often meant being in a dark, underground dungeon where prisoners were malnourished, treated cruelly, and lived in squalid conditions—if they survived.

Paul's hardships came not only at the hands of people but through the fury of nature. He told of being caught in flooded rivers and of being shipwrecked three times on different ocean journeys, once spending an entire night and day adrift at sea.

Whether on land or at sea, Paul faced physical discomfort. Many times he was exhausted, hungry, thirsty, and cold. His life was marred by pain, weakness, and sorrow.

Paul didn't make it through these continual brutal setbacks because he was stronger than most of us, but because he clung to God and believed—genuinely believed—that all of these things were working for his good and the good of others. It is not hard to imagine Paul repeating the words of Psalm 68:19 as he faced each hardship, "Praise the Lord; praise God our savior! For each day he carries us in his arms." Paul was comforted by God each day, and his joy in his relationship with Jesus Christ overcame the pain of his horrendous difficulties.

Even today there are those who face hardships that are as terrible and as real as Paul's. Imprisonment, torture, and even death are realities for many people around the world because they are followers of Jesus Christ. If we begin to grasp the horrifying situations in which they live, we will be energized to pray for these Christians.

Pray for their faithfulness to God; pray for their witness, courage, safety, and healing; and pray for their families. Pray that they will be able to forgive those who cause them harm. And pray that they will know the reality that God carries them each day in His arms.

The message of Psalm 68:19 is for us, too. Although we may not be coping with the type of brutality that Paul faced and other Christians face today, we may be carrying heavy burdens of unrelenting stress, pain, fear, grief, weariness, or uncertainty. We'd like to lay our load down and be refreshed with renewed hope. Remember God is near us, and He is willing to carry us in His arms if we will reach out to Him to be held.

WEEK 77

Nature Has Its Say

1 Chronicles 12–16; 2 Corinthians 12–13

Twice this week nature played a noteworthy role in our reading, and both times God's creation was acting in ways that probably seem unnatural to us.

In the first example, trees were chosen to give direction and guidance to a human being. David and his troops were going into battle against the mighty Philistine army. David sought direction from God on how to proceed, and God answered, "Do not attack them straight on. Instead, circle around behind them and attack them near the balsam trees. When you hear a sound like marching feet in the tops of the balsam trees, attack! That will be the signal that God is moving ahead of you to strike down the Philistines" (1 Chron. 14:14-15).

God used trees—objects of nature that we typically think of as having no ability to communicate—to lead David and his troops into a victorious battle. David listened to what the trees had to say even though it meant looking at God's creation differently.

This experience must have had great impact on David and how he viewed the world that surrounded him. At a later date, when the Ark of God was brought to Jerusalem with unparalleled rejoicing, David painted a picture of nature having emotion and recognizing the astounding presence of God. He said, "Let the sea and everything in it shout his praise! Let the fields and their crops burst forth with joy! Let the trees of the forest rustle with praise before the Lord!" (1 Chron. 16:32-33).

These words were not written by someone who saw nature as unknowing or voiceless. These words almost explode with fervor and enthusiasm, acknowledging nature's relationship with its Creator. These words tell of living items praising God in their language—a language certainly different from our own but one able to communicate nevertheless.

Have you recognized their declarations? Have you stood in a field of wild flowers and heard the whispers of God's provision and care? Have you stood in a forest and heard the gentle creak of the tree trunks and the rustle of their leaves singing out God's wisdom as wind moves against them? Have you stood at the edge of the ocean and heard the roar of the sea, beside a lake and heard the lap of its wave, or beside a brook and heard the rippling of its current as each repeats its praise for God's greatness?

Scripture urges us to "each day proclaim the good news that he saves. Tell everyone about the amazing things he does" (1 Chron. 16:23-24). Normally, this would be thought of as a directive to humans, but it seems that God's other creations do proclaim the goodness and love of their Creator each day. Let's join their choir.

WEEK 78

To the Rescue!

1 Chronicles 17–21; Psalm 69; Galatians 1

"'If the Arameans are too strong for me, then come over and help me,' Joab told his brother. 'And if the Ammonites are too strong for you, I will help you'" (1 Chron. 19:12).

Joab was King David's cousin and his army commander. Joab did not hold this position because of family ties for he was a courageous and fierce warrior. And commander of the army was no idle position because David and the nation of Israel were often at war against strong enemies, as they were now.

This battle was somewhat different from others, for "Joab saw that he would have to fight on two fronts" (1 Chron. 19:10). Joab would face the Arameans on one front, and he would send his brother Abishai, another courageous and fierce warrior, to face the Ammonites on the other front.

Joab and Abishai were both skillful, both dedicated to the cause, and both proven in battle time and time again. But the outcome of this battle was not assured, for they faced enemies who were also skillful and proven in battle. Joab understood that sometimes dedication, knowledge, and skill were not enough to win battles. Circumstances could tip the balance against even the strongest and most prepared person and create a need for someone else to come to the rescue, a time to "come over and help me." Joab anticipated that this battle might be one of those times for either his brother or himself, and so they made their plans.

Joab and Abishai feared being overwhelmed by human enemies. This might also be the case for us at some time, but it is more likely that we will face different enemies with the potential to overwhelm us. Enemies such as disease, physical limitations or pain, depression, grief, weariness, or diminished trust in God may plague us. It is important for us to turn toward God during these times, but it is also important to have a fellow human, whose wisdom and love we trust, to "come over and help" us face our battle. Such a relationship can help rescue us during our times of need, just as a lack of support can contribute to our defeat.

But Joab and Abishai's relationship did not move in only one direction. Yes, they were willing to accept the other's help; pride would not stand in the way of admitting they needed the other. But they were also willing to give the other help. There is little doubt that what each was doing in his own battlefront was important and not easily altered. For one to come to the other's aid called for an entirely different focus, a realignment of effort, and a temporary abandonment of his own goals. None of this would be easy to do, but each was willing to do so, if needed.

Are *we* willing to move in both directions, not only to seek help, but to give it? As it was true for Joab and Abishai, being available to come over and help does not always make for an easy life. Flexibility may be required. Priorities may have to change. Interruptions to plans we have made may abound as we accommodate another's needs. "Come over and help" relationships are not trivial relationships but ones that operate at a deeper level.

Battles are won together just as they were for Joab and Abishai. May God enable us to put aside our pride when we need to ask others for help and to put aside our plans when we are the ones needed.

Worthwhile Work

1 Chronicles 22–27; Galatians 2

"All of the Levites who were thirty years old or older were counted, and the total came to thirty-eight thousand. Then David said, 'Twenty-four thousand of them will supervise the work at the Temple of the Lord. Six thousand are to serve as officials and judges. Four thousand will work as gatekeepers, and another four thousand will praise the Lord with the musical instruments'" (1 Chron. 23:3-5).

There were many tasks to keep the Temple of the Lord functioning properly and to assure that the religious life of Israel aligned with God's commands for worshiping Him. Thirty-eight thousand people were assigned specific tasks by King David to accomplish these two goals.

Thirty-eight thousand is a startlingly large number! But even that number did not account for all the Temple workers, for it did not include the "Levites *twenty* years old or older," the people who were supervised by those "*thirty* years old or older" (1 Chron. 23:27). Thirty-eight thousand people…and many more! What does the magnitude of that number say about the work of the Levites?

It shows that the work of the Temple was considered vital to the well-being of the nation. The people accomplishing the work were respected for their service.

They were also respected because they were talented. God had given this sizeable group of people specific skills to be used in their work. As they used these God-given talents and skills, their work would have been pleasing to them and to God.

Finding equally skilled workers to replace those leaving service would not have been a problem either. Thirty-eight thousand people working with people younger than thirty allowed the next generation to be well trained. And there would be much to learn, for any activity requiring that many people would have numerous variations and unexpected situations. Mind-numbing boredom would not have been a problem.

And neither would weariness, for a group of people this large allowed for adequate rotation of staff to prevent the discouragement of overwork.

In these verses and chapters we glimpse God's thoughts regarding work. Work—the way it was intended to be—brings pleasure, is alive with learning, and gives purpose to our lives.

But from the days of Adam, our work has often been tainted by the effects of sin. Work situations are often a far cry from God's ideals. Rather than fulfillment and satisfaction, weariness, discouragement, confusion, and frustration may reign in our working environments. Or we may be unemployed and longing for the security of a job or uncertain about the stability of our employment. If any of these describe your current work situation, talk to God about it. He hears and cares.

And if your work and workplace are similar to the Levites, enjoy this special gift and remember to pray for others to have the same blessing.

Week 80

Always Welcomed

1 Chronicles 28–29; 2 Chronicles 1–2; Psalms 70–71; Galatians 3

There is something special about being warmly and sincerely welcomed. It only takes a few moments, but what a difference it makes. Do you know this type of welcome? It's the kind where there is no mistaking that your presence is wanted and your companionship is valued. It's the kind of welcome where you can relax and be yourself because you are accepted just as you are.

But welcomes come in many varieties. Even in the most loving of human relationships, we may not always *feel* welcomed. Although relationships may be genuine, circumstances may make welcomes distracted, even careless. The cause of a lukewarm welcome may have nothing to do with us and everything to do with the circumstances of others—circumstances that cause them to be more focused on their own situations than on our presence. But the result is the same; we don't feel appreciated when we are inattentively welcomed.

On the other hand, there may be times when we feel we do not *deserve* to be welcomed—times when we know our behavior doesn't warrant a warm welcome because our actions have caused pain to others.

Then there are the times when welcomes are a mere formality. Caring isn't usually part of these types of welcomes, for they rely more on manners than on relationships and may matter little to our feeling of well-being.

And then there is the welcome that *isn't*. Times when we feel minimized, excluded, or ignored are painful. We may first experience this type of reception as a child; unfortunately, however, such experiences do not stop happening as we become adults. These situations cut deeply into our emotions, sometimes leaving wounds that are slow to heal.

David knew all of these types of greetings, but he also knew a place where he would always be assured of a genuine and loving welcome. David said to God with confidence, "Be to me a protecting rock of safety, where I am always welcome" (Ps. 71:3). And God does not only welcome the giants of faith like David. We, too, are always welcomed by God.

How do we wrap our minds around the great gift of being always welcomed by God? Who of us has ever experienced being always welcomed in any relationship? It is almost humanly impossible to consistently offer a loving welcome to another. But God offers us the gift of being always welcome. We are welcomed, wanted, valued, and prized each time we go to God.

Even if we go to God hundreds of times a day, His welcome will always be as loving and genuine as the first time. He desires our presence as much as the first time. Each time we come, God welcomes us with arms wide open regardless of what brings us to Him. Even for times we do not feel we deserve a loving welcome, "always" means *always* when we are being welcomed by God.

God's love has changed us. And part of that love is being always welcomed by Him. Can we pass this gift on to others? It may be that a warm and loving welcome is special, at least in part, because it is a rare occurrence in the multitude of human relationships we have.

As we practice loving others in the way Jesus loves us, we can follow God's example of being always welcoming. Just as that makes a difference in our lives, it will make a difference in others' as our welcomes show they are wanted and valued. That is life-changing love. As we give thanks to God for always welcoming us, we can ask His help in being genuinely welcoming people.

A Glorious Presence

2 Chronicles 3–7; Galatians 4–5

It was a big day for Israel, one of the biggest—a day of passionate, joyful, loud celebration. It was the day that the newly built Temple of the Lord was being dedicated in Jerusalem. After this day, Israel would no longer worship God in a tent. They would now come to this building, which reflected the greatness and glory of God. A huge crowd extended out from the Temple. On this day, as on all days, the priests stood in their customary places in front of the worshipers. And then something extraordinary happened.

"At that moment a cloud filled the Temple of the Lord. The priests could not continue their work because the glorious presence of the Lord filled the Temple of God. The priests could not even enter the Temple of the Lord" (2 Chron. 5:13-14; 7:2).

Even though the priests' lives were dedicated to serving the Lord, they were stopped in their tracks by the actual *presence* of God. They felt it. They saw it. They experienced it. God's presence was too awe-inspiring for them to continue in their normal daily activities. It was "glorious" because it was God!

But God was not evident only to the priests, for "when all the *people* of Israel saw the fire coming down and the glorious presence of the Lord filling the Temple, they fell face down on the ground and worshiped and praised the Lord, saying, 'He is so good! His faithful love endures forever!'" (2 Chron. 7:3).

The priests along with the people instantly fell to the ground in worship, for they experienced the tremendous power of God. They instinctively knew they were in the presence of a vastly superior being. And they instinctively knew one other thing from being in the presence of the Lord—they knew the Lord "is so good" and that "His faithful love endures forever!" They knew that as surely as if it were something solid that could be touched because God's presence communicated that truth to them as they lay humbly upon the ground.

God's "glorious presence" did not appear by coincidence on the day the Temple was dedicated. Preparation for this day had been ongoing for many years. During those years the nation and its people had been focused on God—gathering the building materials, making the plans, constructing the building, and training the priests and other caretakers of the Temple. On the day that the Temple was dedicated, the nation was completely focused on God, praising Him. With their focus and their praises rising, the glorious presence of the Lord came to them.

And at that moment the Israelites knew without any doubt that God was God and far beyond human understanding. How we cheat ourselves when we forget what the Israelites knew with certainty that day. We bring God down to our logic, our abilities, and our core beliefs, and then we struggle with doubt in the small god we have created. But God is too "glorious" to be fully explained by our own experiences, thoughts, and knowledge.

Someday we will actually be in the Lord's glorious presence and then, and only then, will we begin to grasp the complete power, majesty, and awesomeness of the one and only true God. And until then, catching even a glimpse of God's "glorious presence" changes how we think and how we act today.

God came to the Israelites because their focus and worship were steadfastly fixed on Him, not only on the day the Temple was dedicated but for many days before that. May we each share this same steadfast focus and experience life-changing glimpses of God's presence through His Word, through prayer, through our times of worship, and by our obedience and eagerness to do God's will.

A Major Make-Over

2 Chronicles 8–12; Psalm 72; Galatians 6

"Solomon now turned his attention to rebuilding the towns that King Hiram had given him, and he settled Israelites in them" (2 Chron. 8:2).

The towns given to Solomon by King Hiram had seen better days. They were broken down and in need of help, but in spite of this Solomon saw value in them.

So Solomon "turned his attention" to them. He set out to repair and rebuild the towns. Solomon didn't just use the remaining material, trying to get by with what was left. The old material was the starting point, but he made something better out of it by introducing additional materials. The old and the new came together and became something different, something finer, stronger and more beautiful—if Solomon's other building projects serve as examples.

Building projects eventually come to an end, and so did this one. The building effort immediately made the towns more desirable to others, but that desirability also made the towns vulnerable because they were defenseless. They needed life in them to make them complete. Solomon recognized this, and so "he settled Israelites in them." These Israelites would not only protect what had been rebuilt against foreign invasion but improve upon what had been changed.

Solomon's story resembles how Jesus came to rebuild our lives. Jesus knew we needed to be rebuilt from the soul on out. He knew that without Him we were broken and in need of help. He saw our value when neither we nor others could see it.

But unlike Solomon's rebuilding plans, Jesus did not have to turn His attention to us, for His attention has always been, and always will be, on us. As soon as we allow it, God is prepared to start rebuilding our lives, using only the best materials. We are rebuilt on the lifeblood and body of Jesus Christ.

But like Hiram's towns, humans need to be protected from what will harm us—including our great spiritual enemies, Satan and his demons.

God, in His wisdom, recognizes that we cannot be left vulnerable like an empty town, and so He sends a new resident into His children's lives—the Holy Spirit. The Spirit dwells within us and among us—offering us comfort, guidance, encouragement, companionship, and protection.

There is one other application we can make from Solomon's rebuilding project and that pertains to our relationship with others. Who in our path needs help rebuilding their lives? Who needs our knowledge, skills, empathy, or our relationship with Jesus to help regain their spiritual, physical, or emotional strength? As we look around us, we see the opportunities are endless. Paul recognized the universality of these opportunities when he wrote, "Share each other's troubles and problems, and in this way obey the law of Christ" (Gal. 6:2).

Will we turn our attention to those who need us? It is often easier to ignore the ruins and not put in the effort to help rebuild a broken life, but then something valuable is lost just as it would have been if Solomon had not rebuilt Hiram's towns. Just as it would be if Jesus was not rebuilding us.

And that leads to the final important difference between Solomon and Jesus' rebuilding projects. Solomon's came to an end. Jesus' rebuilding plan is ongoing. It begins when we turn toward Him as our Savior and continues throughout our lives as the Spirit helps us be more like Jesus.

Are we on schedule with Jesus' rebuilding plan for our lives? Or have we forced unnecessary construction delays? Jesus' rebuilding plan is worthy of our attention, commitment, and gratitude.

WEEK 83

Weed Whacking

2 Chronicles 13–17; Ephesians 1–2

"He was committed to the ways of the Lord. He knocked down the pagan shrines and destroyed the Asherah poles" (2 Chron. 17:6).

Not again! Those pagan shrines and Asherah poles were like weeds, difficult to eliminate and multiplying quickly.

Jehoshaphat, a man committed to following the Lord, was now king of Judah, the southern Israel nation. He knew, if left unchecked, these idols would choke the life out of the people's relationship with God by moving their focus from Him.

So here was Jehoshaphat, destroying idols left and right. The question is how could there be any idols for him to destroy? Hadn't Jehoshaphat's father, King Asa, "removed all the idols in the land of Judah and Benjamin and in the towns he had captured" (2 Chron. 15:8)? Hadn't Asa made his dedication to the cause clear when he removed his own grandmother from her position as queen mother because she made an Asherah pole? Hadn't the people "entered into a covenant to seek the Lord, the God of their ancestors, with all their heart and soul" (2 Chron. 15:12)? After that, how could any idols remain for Jehoshaphat to destroy?

The answer is simple, yet sad. During Asa's purge of the Asherah poles and pagan shrines, they "were not completely removed from Israel" (2 Chron. 15:17). Many shrines and Asherah poles were destroyed, but a few were not; and those few opened the way for others.

Asa and the Israelites knew these idols were wrong and a danger to them. The steps they took to destroy the idols prove that they knew. The problem was that while they were willing to take care of *most* of the issue, they were also willing to not take care of *all* of it. They settled for better than it had been and called it good enough. But the remaining poles and shrines were waiting to trip them up again and again.

Asa wanted to rid the nation of its sin of worshiping idols, but he lacked the strength and endurance to complete the mission. Because these shrines were not dealt with completely, they lived on to cause problems for another day and in another place.

There are parallels here for our own lives. We do not have Asherah poles or pagan shrines, but sins not dealt with will grow like weeds. If we are not thorough in our determination to get rid of these sins, they will trip us up, subtly weaken the good in our lives, and eventually choke the life and joy out of our relationship with Jesus. We need to be intolerant of sin's influence in our lives and aware of what it steals from us.

We lack adequate strength to deal with sin's constant bombardment without help from the Lord, but "the eyes of the Lord search the whole earth in order to strengthen those whose hearts are fully committed to Him" (2 Chron. 16:9). The Lord's eyes are searching for those who call to Him for help in fighting the weeds of sin that spring up like Asherah poles, and it is His strength that can help us to be outstanding weed whackers.

So let's rev up those weed whackers and keep them humming!

Waiting for Tomorrow

2 Chronicles 18–22; Psalm 73; Ephesians 3

It was news that made brave men alarmed, even frightened. A vast army from Edom was on the march; their destination was Judah; their goal was conquest. They had the manpower and the equipment to do exactly that, and their march would lead to suffering, destruction, death, possibly even annihilation for the people of Judah.

King Jehoshaphat knew he and his nation were vastly outnumbered and could not win this battle. In his hopeless situation, he asked the Lord for help and ordered that the nation observe a fast, gather in Jerusalem, and seek God along with him.

With the men, women, and children of the nation surrounding him, King Jehoshaphat wisely called to God. Getting right to the heart of the matter, he prayed, "O our God, won't you stop them? We are powerless against this mighty army that is about to attack us. We do not know what to do, but we are looking to you for help" (2 Chron. 20:12).

God heard this cry for help and, in the presence of all the people, sent His answer. Through the voice of Jahaziel, son of Zechariah, God said, "Do not be afraid! Don't be discouraged by this mighty army, for the battle is not yours, but God's. Tomorrow march out against them…. But you will not even need to fight. Take your positions; then stand still and watch the Lord's victory" (2 Chron. 20:15-17). King Jehoshaphat may have been outnumbered, but he was not outgunned!

God had made a promise that "tomorrow" there would be victory. But there was the remainder of this day before tomorrow dawned. There were many hours to test a person's faith and trust. Each man, woman, and child had heard what God had promised, but as the hours slipped by, what were their thoughts, and what were their fears? As family groups gathered together for the evening, they would have discussed little else but what they had experienced during this day in the presence of the Lord and what they would experience during the next.

Some of these people would have been rejoicing, fully confident in God's promises. Their confidence would have been built on their remembrances of other promises made by God and their recognition that every promise ever made by Him had been kept. They may have wondered *how* God would accomplish what He said He would do, but they would have already been praising Him for the victory.

Others would also have remembered promises made by God and even recognized that the promises had been kept. As they reviewed the day, they, too, would have wondered how God would accomplish this thing He said He would do, but doubt would have crept into their thoughts. Although God had honored His promises before, this time was different, this time they were involved! They would be people torn between head and heart belief, one moment doubtful and one moment believing.

Still others would judge God by their own beliefs of who He was. They would cut God down to their size and find Him lacking for such an impossible victory. Yes, they had heard the voice, they knew the stories of other promises kept and other miracles performed, but to them it was hearsay, and what they would be facing in the morning was real—alarmingly real. They would be a people relying on themselves, burdened by what lay ahead. No comfort awaited them during the night.

The night passed, and early the next morning the army of Judah gathered for battle: those who trusted in God's promise completely, those who were torn, those who did not believe. Jehoshaphat, knowing there were different levels of trust and belief, challenged the people: "Believe in the Lord your God, and you will be able to stand firm" (2 Chron. 20:20). Then Jehoshaphat rallied the people further with additional reminders of God's power and faithfulness by "appointing singers to walk ahead of the army, singing to the Lord and praising him for his holy splendor" and faithful love (2 Chron. 20:21).

As they sang, the army of Judah advanced toward the enemy. Those weak in belief gathered strength from those with more. Doubt did not stop those with little faith, their participation not differing from those with great faith. In obedience they moved forward.

When they arrived at the lookout point they saw the battle was already over. God had kept His promise, as He always does, for at the exact moment the singing and praise had begun, God caused Judah's enemies to destroy each other. As God's army gazed out over the wilderness from the lookout point, there was no enemy to fight, for they were already dead.

There are plenty of battles in our lives, battles taking many different forms and time spans. God has given us many promises applicable to the battles we face. We have God's promises, and we have even seen some of God's promises fulfilled. This knowledge can give us great faith, but at some point in our various battles, we are going to experience reactions similar to each of the groups of Judah.

When we are confident and believe strongly in God's promises, may we remember to *lead* those who are not. When we are shaken and doubting God's promises, may we remember to *follow* those who are not. But whether confident or doubting, may we remember to *obediently* follow God, for He is faithful in all His promises.

"Take your positions…and watch the Lord's victory" (2 Chron. 20:17).

WEEK 85

Don't Shoot the Messenger

2 Chronicles 23–27; Ephesians 4–5

"Follow God's example in everything you do, because you are his dear children. And do not bring sorrow to God's Holy Spirit by the way you live" (Eph. 5:1; 4:30).

There are times when there is no doubt in our mind that what we are doing or thinking is wrong and bringing sorrow to God. At other times, we may truly be blind to the wrongness of our actions. Whether aware or not, sometimes we need someone to bring us up short. This was true for two kings of Judah.

The first king, Amaziah, was a man who "did what was pleasing in the Lord's sight, but not wholeheartedly" (2 Chron. 25:2). In spite of Amaziah's halfheartedness, God honored him and gave him victory in a battle against Judah's enemy, the Edomites. There was no mistaking God's help in this battle, but astonishingly enough, Amaziah celebrated by worshiping idols taken from the dead Edomites. Amaziah was fully aware this was wrong; he did it anyway.

"This made the Lord very angry, and he sent a prophet to ask, 'Why have you worshiped gods who could not even save their own people from you?'" (2 Chron. 25:15). Good question. Before the prophet could finish his message, "the king interrupted him and said, 'Since when have I asked your advice? Be quiet now before I have you killed!'" (2 Chron. 25:16).

By his reaction, we see evidence of other issues with Amaziah besides the obvious sin of worshiping an idol. He had become blind to his sin of pride that caused him to be unwilling to hear the truth or listen to instruction.

Before leaving, the prophet finished his warning. Through the prophet's words, Amaziah was given a chance to see how wrong his actions were, a chance to ask God's forgiveness, and a chance to change his ways. But Amaziah refused to listen, and God's punishment led to the plunder of Jerusalem, Amaziah's capture in war, and his eventual assassination. Amaziah's unwillingness to hear God—through another's voice—brought hardship to many.

Amaziah's son, Uzziah, became the next king. Doing what was pleasing in the Lord's sight, being favored by God, and then growing proud seemed to run in this family. As God blessed Uzziah with more lands, more power, and more wealth, his pride led him to intentionally disobey God "by entering the sanctuary of the Lord's Temple and personally burning incense on the altar" (2 Chron. 26:16).

Again, God sent someone to point out the obvious sin. "Azariah the high priest went in after him with eighty other priests of the Lord, all brave men. They confronted King Uzziah and said, 'It is not for you, Uzziah, to burn incense to the Lord. That is the work of the priests alone who are set apart for this work. Get out of the sanctuary, for you have sinned'" (2 Chron. 26:17-18).

Pigheadedness, as well as pride, also seemed to run in this family, for "Uzziah was furious and refused to set down the incense burner he was holding. But as he was standing there leprosy suddenly broke out on his forehead. King Uzziah had leprosy until the day he died. He lived in isolation" (2 Chron. 26:19,21).

It took courage for the unnamed prophet and Azariah to confront these two kings about their wrong actions. Their hope was to bring reconciliation between God and the kings, but what they received was anger and disdain.

Both Amaziah and Uzziah are examples of people who allowed their pride to keep them from hearing and heeding a message given for their own good. These messages weren't from people who were constantly negative and critical. These messages were from people who came to address a specific action. Hearing it was difficult, but ignoring it was truly catastrophic.

Has God sent someone to show us how to be more pleasing to Him or to point out where we are wrong? It is probably easy enough to identify those times, since these types of interactions are often initially irritating to us, as they were to Amaziah and Uzziah. It is a rare and humble human being who is open and immediately willing to hear what he or she is doing wrong. But if we begin to understand the consequences from which these messengers are trying to save us, our reaction should be one of thankfulness to them and to God. By being attentive to someone brave and caring enough to point out where we have gone wrong, we can gain wisdom we would not otherwise have.

Are there situations where we should be the messenger? If so, after much prayer, present the message in a loving way. Be willing to go through the discomfort of giving the message with the hope it will help to draw the person closer to God. This was Paul's goal for the Ephesians when he wrote, "throw off your old evil nature and your former way of life. Instead, there must be a spiritual renewal of your thoughts and attitudes. You must display a new nature because you are a new person, created in God's likeness—righteous, holy and true" (Eph. 4:22-24).

It is a lifelong journey to become righteous, holy, and true; and in our lifetime we will sometimes need to hear we have gotten off-track, just as sometimes we may need to be the voice giving that message. Neither telling nor hearing is easy, but each is necessary as we continue in our journey of becoming people whose actions—and reactions—are guided only by God.

A Courageous Confrontation

2 Chronicles 28–32; Psalm 74; Ephesians 6

It was a large group being forced toward Samaria, the capital city of the northern kingdom of Israel. Bystanders along the way couldn't help but be amazed by this massive throng of 200,000 women and children. And what a sight they would have been. All of them were hungry, thirsty, and now homeless; many grieved for their husbands, fathers, and brothers; some were naked; and far too many were injured, ill, or near physical collapse from the forced march. These women and children were the spoils of war.

This mass of humanity, pushed along by the army of Israel, were the citizens of Judah, the southern kingdom. Their extreme suffering was one of the results of the sin of Ahaz, the king of Judah. Ahaz had purposely turned away from God, and now he had been defeated in battle by Israel.

But God had not intended for Israel to punish Judah to these cruel extremes. "In a single day, Israel's king killed 120,000 of Judah's troops… captured 200,000 women and children…and took tremendous amounts of plunder" (2 Chron. 28:5-8). These women and children were the people now being marched to Samaria.

There was a man amidst the bystanders who looked, saw the suffering, and could not be silent. One man. This man, a prophet named Oded, stood before the army of Israel as they returned home and challenged their actions. He said, "The Lord, the God of your ancestors, was angry with Judah and let you defeat them. But you have gone too far, killing them without mercy. And now you are planning to make slaves of these people.... What about your own sins against the Lord your God? Listen to me and return these captives you have taken" (2 Chron. 28:9-11).

One man saw this horrible injustice and could not let it go. One man's words and courage persuaded four other leaders of Israel—Azariah, Berekiah, Jehizkiah, and Amasa, and together they "confronted the men returning from battle. 'You must not bring the prisoners here!' they declared. 'We cannot afford to add to our sins and guilt'" (2 Chron. 28:12-13).

These five men's ethical stand completely changed the direction of what was happening. "The warriors released the prisoners and handed over the plunder. Then the leaders came forward and distributed clothes from the plunder to the prisoners who were naked. They gave them food and drink and dressed their wounds. They put those who were weak on donkeys and took all the prisoners back to their own land. Then they returned to Samaria" (2 Chron. 28:14-15).

Five men in the vast crowd had the courage to stand up for what was right and against what was clearly wrong. Five men were willing to risk their lives by confronting an army, heady from a great military victory, with its moral and spiritual failings. These men could easily have lost their lives by standing for what was right. But that danger did not stop them. And what a difference their stand made to 200,000 people.

We need to stand for what God stands for: mercy and justice. Moral and spiritual failings that cause great suffering are still happening today. They are happening to individuals and to large groups of people. They are happening both locally and globally.

We need to be involved in matters of mercy and justice. If you are not aware of issues of injustice and abuse, pray for connections to such knowledge. God will reveal ways for each of us to make a difference as we represent God here on earth—standing up for what is good, true, and right, and standing against what is not.

Be one of the five.

WEEK 87

Under New Management

2 Chronicles 33–36; Psalms 75–76; Luke 1

Once again, Judah, the southern kingdom of Israel, was ruled by a man whose life was marked by sin. Manasseh should have been an example to his people of a person in close relationship with God. Instead he was an example of a ruler who had no respect for or belief in God whatsoever.

Manasseh's sins were many. He worshiped the stars, Baal, and Asherah rather than God. He built altars to these false gods and then gave his own sons as burnt offerings. He trusted mediums, psychics, and witchcraft for answers rather than God. And the people of Judah followed where Manasseh led them. No discernible difference existed between them and the exceedingly evil cultures of the surrounding nations.

But God offered mercy. In spite of the enormous rejection by Manasseh and the people of Judah, God "spoke to Manasseh and his people" (2 Chron. 33:10). God would not judge and punish Manasseh and Judah without giving them a chance to change.

As in previous times, the king and the people ignored the warnings and disregarded the messenger.

As a result of rejecting God's mercy and warnings, Manasseh and Judah were punished. The Assyrian armies took Manasseh prisoner. "They put a ring through his nose, bound him in bronze chains, and led him away to Babylon" (2 Chron. 33:11). It may be easy to skim over what happened, but the pain and humiliation were real to Manasseh, for the Assyrians were exceptionally cruel and fierce conquerors.

Now it is often during times of hardship that God truly has our attention. Our hard times aren't always because we are being punished, but when they are, we can either stubbornly cling to our sinful choices or we can turn toward God. Manasseh, who had been one of the wickedest men who ever lived, made the wise choice. He "sought the Lord his God and cried out humbly. And when he prayed, the Lord listened to him and was moved by his request for help" (2 Chron. 33:12-13).

Manasseh humbly called out to God to save him, and the Lord reinstated him as king of Judah. Notice that before rescuing Manasseh, God did not make him prove his intent for an ongoing relationship with God. God simply saved him. But Manasseh was a different person, for he "had finally realized that the Lord alone is God!" (2 Chron. 33:13) Manasseh was restored to his kingdom in Jerusalem, but more importantly, he began his relationship with God.

Manasseh did not only move from unbelief to belief; he became a devoted follower of the Lord and encouraged the people of Judah to do the same. What he did before, he no longer did. He no longer worshiped false gods but destroyed the altars built to them and restored the Lord's Temple. Manasseh's change proved that he was a new person with a new outlook and a new agenda. It was evident who had control of Manasseh's life. Manasseh was under new management.

There is a difference between trusting Jesus as our Savior and trusting Jesus as our Lord. There is cause for celebration when we trust Jesus as our Savior and are rescued from our sin and made acceptable to God. But, like Manasseh, we should go a step further and let Jesus also be our leader, the one in charge of our lives. Is God only your Savior, or is He also your Leader?

When we no longer limit Jesus to the role of our Savior but allow Him to be our Lord as well, His impact will infuse every part of our lives. Following Jesus changes what we do, what we think, and who we are. It did for Manasseh and it will for us too.

Passionate Persistence

Ezra 1–5; Luke 2–3

The Israelites were no longer a nation. Years of warfare, first with Assyria and then Babylon, had led to the death or deportation of the Israelites from both the northern and southern kingdoms of Israel. The land that had been given to them by God had been taken over by others.

But now the Israelites' captors, the Assyrians and the Babylonians, had in turn been conquered by Persia. And a new day was dawning for the Israelites. King Cyrus of Persia declared, "The Lord, the God of heaven, has given me all the kingdoms of the earth. He has appointed me to build him a Temple at Jerusalem. All of you who are his people may return to Jerusalem" (Ezra 1:2-3).

Hundreds upon hundreds of thousands of Israelites had been exiled, and now they and their descendants were free to return to Jerusalem. But freedom to return did not translate into action for many of the Israelites. They had carved out acceptable lives in their exiled lands, the journey back to Jerusalem would be dangerous, the work of building the Temple difficult, and they would be strangers in their homeland. Only fifty thousand were passionate enough about being "his people" to return to Jerusalem to rebuild the Temple where God's presence had been.

But those fifty thousand were dedicated. They arrived in the Jerusalem area, settled in, and got to work. Rebuilding the Temple wasn't easy work, for the Israelites "were afraid of the local residents" (Ezra 3:3).

The Israelites probably had reason to be afraid of the nonlocals, as well, but it was the local residents who had the greatest power to make their lives difficult, affect their safety, and rob them of their peace of mind. Those fifty thousand people had legitimate reasons to be afraid, but they moved ahead doing what they had been asked to do by God through King Cyrus. Their desire to please and obey God overcame their fear.

The Israelites' steadfast faith and actions had an energizing effect on the local residents. "Then the local residents tried to discourage and frighten the people of Judah to keep them from their work. They bribed agents to work against them and to frustrate their aims. This went on during the entire reign of King Cyrus of Persia and lasted until King Darius of Persia took the throne" (Ezra 4:4-5).

Darius took the throne thirty-seven years after Cyrus began his rule! There is no doubt that the local resistance slowed the Israelites' efforts over those thirty-seven years, but it did not stop them. The Israelites did what they could while the opportunity existed.

Finally, the local resistance won. The Israelites stopped building but not before the altar had been completed and the foundation of the Temple re-laid.

Fear of the "local residents" can feel familiar. As one of "his people," Jesus has told us to go and tell others about our faith. Often it is the thought of doing this with our neighbors, co-workers, community contacts, and friends that causes us to fear our own local residents. We fear we might be considered radical, out-of-touch, or ridiculous. We fear we may be rejected or disliked. We fear we may cause conflict or not have the answers to questions that arise. These fears are real, but they should not control our actions.

What should control our actions is dedication in doing what Jesus has told us to do by sharing with others the story of what He has done for us. Sometimes our words are welcomed, and sometimes they are not. We may be forced to stop if others do not want to hear. But it is important for us to keep trying for those willing to hear. The Israelites faced resistance but kept rebuilding until they were forced to stop. By that time they had laid the Temple's foundation, which would be built upon by others. In telling our stories, we are laying the foundation that God can, and will, build upon.

Hundreds of years after the fifty thousand Israelites faithfully rebuilt the Temple's foundation, Mary and Joseph took Jesus to be dedicated at that same Temple, now magnificently rebuilt upon that foundation. While there, they were met by a godly man, Simeon, who told them, "…this child will be rejected by many in Israel, and it will be their undoing. But he will be the greatest joy to many others" (Luke 2:34).

When Jesus is important in our lives and we are aware of His presence, our telling others will become important and, eventually, natural to us. Fear or no fear, we can share this "greatest joy" with others, for we know what it has meant to us.

WEEK 89

The Searchers

Ezra 6–10; Psalm 77; Luke 4

As Jesus began His formal ministry, He traveled to the small villages that dotted Galilee, teaching about God and the people's relationship with Him. In one town, Capernaum, Jesus not only taught the people but healed those who were sick. Leaving Capernaum, He traveled to the town of His childhood—Nazareth.

Of course, news of Jesus' teachings and healings in Capernaum traveled along with Him to Nazareth. The crowd in Nazareth logically would have expected the same for their town. As the people gathered at the synagogue to hear Jesus teach, they were impressed by Him. "All who were there spoke well of him and were amazed by the gracious words that fell from his lips" (Luke 4:22).

But in a matter of minutes, Jesus' message did not seem nearly as gracious to the crowd. They became furious when Jesus implied that their skepticism about His being sent by God would cause them to lose not only God's blessing but keep Jesus from doing the kinds of miracles He had done in Capernaum. "Jumping up, they mobbed him and took him to the edge of the hill on which the city was built. They intended to push him over the cliff, but he slipped away through the crowd and left them" (Luke 4:29-30). Thus ended Jesus' interaction with the townspeople of Nazareth.

Jesus returned to Capernaum where people throughout the region came to hear the wisdom of His teachings and to experience the healing of the sick or those tortured by demonic power. Jesus stayed in Capernaum for a time because of the receptiveness of the people. Before departing the area, Jesus needed a time of rest and preparation for the next part of His ministry. He went into the wilderness where the crowds were unlikely to follow because of the harshness and difficulty of that place.

But the people of Capernaum had experienced the power, kindness, and wisdom of God through Jesus. When Jesus couldn't be found in

Capernaum, "the crowds searched everywhere for him" until they found Him (Luke 4:42). The severity of searching in the wilderness didn't stop them, for they had found that the troubles in their lives—and there were many—were bearable while they were with Jesus.

Jesus has told us to seek and we shall find. Luke 4 tells of two different crowds and two different searches. The crowds of Capernaum "searched everywhere" for Jesus. The crowds of Nazareth searched for something less than Jesus and the truth that He brought, something to fit their own expectations.

What are *we* searching for, and *where* are we willing to search? If we are searching for Jesus during our good times *and* our wilderness times, we will find Him, for He desires to be found. If we are searching for Jesus only during specific times in our lives—such as difficult times—we will shortchange ourselves. If we are searching for something other than Jesus, we may or may not find it, but we will ultimately be disappointed by the inferior imitations for which we have settled.

When the crowds of Capernaum finally found Jesus, "they begged him not to leave them" (Luke 4:42). Jesus had made that much of a difference in their lives. Their minds were open to what He had to say to them, their hearts were open to what He asked of them, and their souls had experienced the life-changing reality of Jesus as Lord.

Lord, help us to be like the crowds of Capernaum, willing to search for the real You.

Hard Times and Long Waits

Nehemiah 1–4; Psalm 78; Luke 5–6

Artaxerxes ruled the Persian Empire, the dominate world power of his time, and was the most powerful person on earth. Nehemiah was an important servant of King Artaxerxes; he was the king's cup-bearer. Wherever Artaxerxes was, Nehemiah would be nearby.

At the moment, they were at the winter palace in the capital city, the fortress of Susa. It was late November in Susa, a pleasant time of rains and lower temperatures after the scorching dry summer months. Although Nehemiah lived in Persia, his heart dwelt in Judah, home of Jerusalem and God's Temple.

Nehemiah must have been grateful for the good things in his life— peace, prosperity, relative freedom, and a sense of accomplishment in his work. This late November day was an especially happy one for Nehemiah. His brother, along with other men, had arrived from Judah for a visit, and they would have news of Jerusalem.

Nehemiah could barely contain his excitement. Upon seeing the group, he asked almost immediately about "how things were going in Jerusalem. They said, 'Things are not going well for those who returned to the province of Judah. They are in great trouble and disgrace. The wall of Jerusalem has been torn down, and the gates have been burned'" (Neh. 1:3).

And with those words, Nehemiah's world came crashing down. No walls and no gates meant that the city and its residents were completely vulnerable to their enemies, and they had plenty of those. Nehemiah wept and mourned for days. His spirit was broken; he was overwhelmed, for there was no easy answer for his homeland and its people, whom he loved.

In the midst of this crushing sorrow, Nehemiah prayed, "O Lord, God of heaven, the great and awesome God who keeps his covenant of unfailing love with those who love him and obey his commands, listen to my prayer!" (Neh. 1:5-6). Nehemiah hurt to the depth of his soul, but he recognized one great truth. God, who possesses all power, loved him, would hear, and would help.

Nehemiah didn't know *how* God would solve this situation, or *when*, but he believed God could and would. He bolstered his confidence by recalling God's promise to the Israelites that "even if you are exiled to the ends of the earth, I will bring you back to the place I have chosen for my name to be honored" (Neh. 1:9).

Nehemiah prayed for days. Knowing that he did not have the ability to change this situation on his own, he made plans to do what he could. Those plans included talking to King Artaxerxes. He prayed again, asking God to "please grant me success now as I go to ask the king for a great favor. Put it into his heart to be kind to me" (Neh. 1:11).

His prayer for the king's kindness was no idle request. Although Nehemiah would have been in the king's presence each day as his cup-bearer, as a servant, he could not speak without an invitation from the king. So Nehemiah waited for his opportunity to approach the king. And then he waited and waited some more. Six months later Nehemiah was still waiting, still praying, and still downcast by the knowledge that things were only worsening in Jerusalem. Nehemiah's plan took patience and trust in God's timing.

Finally the day came for which Nehemiah had waited. Artaxerxes asked, "Why are you so sad? You look like a man with deep troubles" (Neh. 2:2). Those words, even if quietly spoken, would have resounded in that room, for to show sorrow before the king was the equivalent of putting your life on the line. And now that Nehemiah was being given the exact thing for which he had prayed, he was frightened. But after a lifetime of trusting God, Nehemiah did what came naturally to him when he was frightened: he silently prayed for help in choosing his words, just as he had prayed for God's help to provide the opportunity.

Nehemiah answered the king. Silent tension ricocheted in the room as everyone waited for Artaxerxes' reaction. And then the king spoke, "Well, how can I help you?" (Neh. 2:4). And with those words, plans were made to renew Jerusalem's security—and honor—by rebuilding her walls and gates. The long wait was over.

Have you ever felt crushed by life's circumstances? Maybe you feel like that now or recognize the likelihood of it in the future. There are many life situations where it would be unnatural *not* to feel sorrow, pain, fear, or shock.

In the midst of deep distress, we should use Nehemiah's example as a wise path to follow. We need to pray earnestly and honestly, and if our situation leaves us unable to pray, we should rest in Jesus' prayers on our behalf until we can resume praying. As we pray, we need to remember that Nehemiah was never condemned by God for mourning over what caused him distress, and neither will we be. We need to cling to the knowledge of God's love for us. We need to remember His promises pertaining to our situation. We need to do what we can, but wait—if we must—for God's timing and answers.

Waiting is hard. Waiting can be frightening as we try to cope and try to make sense of our situations. Waiting can make us impatient, angry, and feeling abandoned by God. Waiting can make it difficult to remember God's love and promises. But ultimately, waiting can be used by God to increase our trust, teach us valuable lessons, and help our faith to become stable.

Life can be hard, but God is always faithful, loving, and able to be trusted. He is truly Emmanuel—God with us—during the hard times and the long waits.

WEEK 91

Growing Awareness

Nehemiah 5–9; Luke 7–8

They were stories from different time periods and about different events. But the stories share the same problem and have the same solution.

We begin with the Israelites' story. Under Nehemiah's leadership, the wall of Jerusalem had been rebuilt in only *fifty-two days*. In those few days, the Israelites accomplished what they had been unable to do in the prior *ninety years*. For ninety years, their fear of their enemies' opposition to the wall and the indifference of some of their own people had stalled any progress. But now, with God's help, the wall was rebuilt.

Six days after the wall was completed every man, woman, and child gathered to celebrate and to hear the words God had given to their ancestors. As these words were read aloud, their celebration turned to sorrow. The people wept with remorse when they recognized they were not doing what God had told them to do as His holy people. Their spiritual leaders recognized the genuineness of the people's regret and told them they should "celebrate with great joy because they had heard God's words and understood them" (Neh. 8:12).

As they began to understand the words they had heard, their desire to know more grew. The next day, the family leaders met again with Ezra, the priests, and Levites "to go over the law in greater detail," so they could begin to implement it. Following the meeting, all the people gathered together once again for the entire week to celebrate and hear "Ezra read from the Book of the Law of God on each of the seven days" (Neh. 8:13,18). Armed with this life-changing knowledge, the people went home.

But they didn't stay home long. Two weeks later, "the people returned for another observance.... They confessed their own sins and the sins of their ancestors. The Book of the Law of the Lord their God was read aloud to them for about three hours. Then for three more hours they took turns confessing their sins and worshiping the Lord their God" (Neh. 9:1-3). They were sincere about their renewed relationship with God, and God had shown them much that needed to be dealt with.

Almost five hundred years later, Jesus was dining at the home of a religious leader named Simon. While they dined, a disgraced woman came into the room and knelt at Jesus' feet, weeping. Her tears fell on His feet; she wiped them off with her hair. Simon thought to himself, "this proves that Jesus is no prophet. If God had really sent him, he would know what kind of woman is touching him. She's a sinner!" (Luke 7:39).

"Then Jesus spoke up and answered his thoughts. 'Simon,' he said to the Pharisee, 'I have something to say to you.... I tell you her sins—and they are many—have been forgiven....' The men at the table said among themselves, 'Who does this man think he is, going around forgiving sins?'" (Luke 7:40,47,49).

Two different times and two different incidents, but both the Israelites and the disgraced woman had become aware of their failures to live as God wanted. Why were they more aware? For the ancient Israelites, their attention had turned steadfastly toward God for a month after the wall was rebuilt. They voluntarily spent much time hearing and studying God's words to them. They heard what God had to say to them, took it to heart, confessed their sins, and showed their love for God by changing the way they lived.

The disgraced woman would have had the opportunity to hear Jesus' words directly and study His life as He ministered in her city. The contrast of Jesus' life to her own would not have been lost on her as she came to understand the life God had wanted for her from the beginning of her days. She had spent enough time around Jesus to want the life He offered, to feel remorse for living in a manner opposite to that, to seek forgiveness, and to show her love.

There is one more similarity between the two stories, in that religious leaders played a big part in each—but in completely different ways. Ezra, the priests, and the Levites led the people with words and example, urging them to draw closer to God.

Simon was also a religious leader, a Pharisee, as, most likely, were his fellow diners. Jesus had "something to say" to them, but they could not hear what Jesus needed them to hear. They were blinded, looking at the disgraced woman's sin, judging her, and rejecting Jesus. They missed who Jesus was, and they missed an opportunity to see the disgraced woman in a different way. The important thing to them was that as they compared themselves to her, they looked pretty good.

The Israelites, the disgraced woman, the priests, Simon, and his fellow diners shared one thing: they were all sinners and in need of God's forgiveness. Unlike Simon and his fellow diners, the Israelites, the priests, and the disgraced woman were more attuned to God. They knew their shortcomings, and they turned to God to change them.

We, too, share the same thing with the people from this week's stories. We may think of ourselves as similar to the disgraced woman, having committed sin that causes us great shame. Or we may think of ourselves as people doing the best we can but making mistakes along the way, as probably many of the Israelites thought of themselves. We may even think of ourselves as morally superior to others, as Simon and his guests did. But the bottom line is, we have sinned, we will continue to do so, and we need God's forgiveness.

Nehemiah understood this, for he said in gratitude for God's forgiveness of his own sin and that of the Israelites, "You are a God of forgiveness, gracious and merciful, slow to become angry, and full of unfailing love and mercy" (Neh. 9:17).

Sin was the problem. Jesus was the answer. Sin is still the problem. Jesus is still the answer.

Life-Changing Joy

Nehemiah 10–13; Esther 1; Luke 9–10

There is something inviting about joy. Whether joy is evident through loud celebration or is quietly courageous and hopeful in the face of adversity, it piques our curiosity and draws us to discover the source.

The Israelites were in a loud, joyful mood. On this special day, the people were dedicating the newly rebuilt wall surrounding Jerusalem. For ninety years, the proof of their leaders' apathy and their enemies' opposition had been right before their eyes, for there had been no city wall to proclaim that Jerusalem was a city worthy of protection. For ninety years, the Israelites had coped with and been shaped by the unfair actions of others, the intimidating circumstances, their own apprehension, and their discouragement. They had not forgotten God, but their burdens turned their focus from Him, and their joy was smothered.

But Nehemiah stepped into this picture of fear and indifference, and in fifty-two days the wall was built! The circumstances did not change when Nehemiah came onto the scene. In fact they worsened, but Nehemiah helped bring the Israelites' focus back to their source of help, hope, and joy—God.

Now that the wall was complete, "the joy of the people of Jerusalem could be heard far away" (Neh. 12:43). This is not surprising because the people wanted to declare the goodness of God and the difference He had made in their lives.

And they had a plan to do exactly that. They divided into two groups and up on the wall they went, marching around Jerusalem. And they didn't merely march. They sang songs of happy thanksgiving as they were led by priests and Levites playing trumpets, cymbals, lyres, and harps. Their joy was the kind that could not be restrained, so "they played and sang loudly and clearly" (Neh. 12:42).

The people were not embarrassed or shy about their joyful proclamation of praise to the God who loved them, provided for them, and protected them. To those who heard and worshiped the same God, the marchers' joy would have increased their own joy. To those who heard but did *not* worship God, the joy of the Israelites would have drawn them to investigate, for it is hard to ignore genuine joy. And to those who were the Israelites' enemies, this loud and clear expression of joy would have been salt in the wounds. But salt is both painful and healing. Knowing full well what this joy represented, these enemies would need to decide if they would continue to dismiss God or begin to rethink their relationship with Him.

It is easy enough to display our joy in being a child of God when we feel we have something to rejoice over. But life does not hold only those things. The joy that comes with trusting God in the midst of things that cause us pain speaks loudly and clearly to our belief in God's goodness.

We see this type of joy in Jesus' life as He traveled from Galilee toward Jerusalem to His eventual death. Jesus knew what was coming: His physical suffering, the rejection by those whom He loved, His death, and His painful separation from God as our sin became a barrier between them. In spite of all of this, "Jesus was filled with the joy of the Holy Spirit" as He taught His followers and the curious crowds (Luke 10:21). Genuine joy during difficult times was not a natural reaction for Jesus, and it is not for us. But it is possible with the help of the Holy Spirit.

Joy can be more than something that triggers curiosity or is inviting. It can be life-changing if it allows us to share with others what it is about our relationship with Jesus that makes us joyful. As believers, we have been given a great gift: the possibility of experiencing joy in all circumstances. Our joy may be linked to a happy occasion like the Israelites' and shared with enthusiasm. Or it may be like Jesus' joy, existing in spite of a difficult situation and shared quietly. Either way it will be compelling.

WEEK 93

Carried to Safety

Esther 2–6; Psalm 79; Luke 11

"For when Satan, who is completely armed, guards his palace, it is safe—until someone who is stronger attacks and overpowers him, strips him of his weapons, and carries off his belongings" (Luke 11:21-22). These few words spoken by Jesus draw our attention to a subject we may not often think about. Let's reflect on these specific words concerning the battle between Jesus and Satan, for we are at the center of that war.

"For when Satan, who is completely armed..." Jesus knew Satan. He knew that Satan was real and dangerous, and so should we. Jesus knew that Satan's goal is the capture and domination of each of us. He leads a dedicated fighting force of evil spirits, employs an array of sophisticated weapons, and continually executes well-planned strategies. Satan and his troops delight in the fight and are clever and ruthless. On our own, there is no hope to outwit, outfight, or outmaneuver them. This is a sinister and powerful enemy.

"...guards his palace..." This palace is not a place of beauty, comfort, and happiness. This is a place of bondage. What makes your skin crawl with fear; what sound sets you on edge; what smell repulses you; what memory taunts? Put these together, plus more, and a picture of this palace begins to take shape. The true depth of the horror and hopelessness of existing in that palace cannot be described.

"...it is safe..." Satan regards what he has captured in warfare as his. It is safe but not in a protective or a good way. It is safe from escape. The captives will long for escape, but on their own are doomed.

There is no hope and no chance *"until someone who is stronger attacks and overpowers him [and] strips him of his weapons."* And we know that "Someone!" It is Jesus! Jesus is stronger. Jesus has overpowered, does overpower, and will overpower Satan and strip "him of his weapons." What we cannot do, Jesus can.

Why does Jesus care enough to go to battle against Satan? Jesus wants what Satan already has captured and what Satan is actively pursuing. Jesus attacks Satan so He can carry "off his belongings," for these belongings are precious to Jesus. We are the belongings Satan has cornered, confused, exhausted, or captured. For those being pursued, Jesus has come into the battle to give strength, protection, and guidance in the fight. For those who are already prisoners of Satan, Jesus stands ready to rescue and free. Pursued or imprisoned, in this life there is always hope—if we turn away from Satan the captor, to Jesus our Rescuer.

Satan's goal is to lure us to his palace through the strategy of deception and temptation. Jesus knows Satan's strategies in this war and has taught His followers a simple but effective prayer: "Don't let us yield to temptation" (Luke 11:4). In this life, we must keep walking away from the palace each day. This is the winning response to the war Satan wages against us.

Sometimes it is easy to forget about spiritual warfare because it seems that our physical lives hold enough challenges without thinking of the spiritual realm. Spiritual warfare may seem remote if we cannot draw on actual experiences of physical war to make it real. Unless we have experienced being hunted down by an enemy who wants to destroy us or make us a prisoner, it is hard to understand the true horror of these situations. But not being able to fully comprehend these things does not make them any less real and does not make our response any less critical.

After being stripped of his weapons, the only way Satan can win a battle and exert power over us is if we yield to his temptations or listen to his discouragement. For by doing so, we take the captured weapons out of Jesus Christ's loving hands and give them back to the one who is determined to destroy us.

If we stand with Christ, our war is won.

WEEK 94

When Life Turns Upside Down

Esther 7–10; Job 1; Luke 12–13

As the first chapter of Job opens, the logical thought would be, "Who wouldn't want to be Job!" Superlatives are needed to describe his life, for he had everything going for him in a big way—God's approval, material riches, and family harmony.

Job was a man who pleased God. God said Job was "the finest man in all the earth—a man of complete integrity" (Job 1:8). What would it be like to live life in such a way that God would say we were the finest people on earth? The foundation of this type of life was built upon Job's desire to stay away from evil, and God honored this desire.

Material blessings followed spiritual blessings, for Job was considered the richest person in the land of Uz. He had "seven thousand sheep, three thousand camels, five hundred teams of oxen and five hundred female donkeys" at a time when livestock was clearly a sign of wealth (Job 1:3). Not only did he have these animals, but he had the employees, land, food, water, and shelter to care and provide for them.

Job was also rich in family. At a time when large families were desired, he was the father of ten children. His grown children enjoyed each other and came together frequently for parties and celebrations. These celebrations were another sign of Job's wealth, for most people in those days labored from sunup to sundown, but Job's family had the means to live a life of ease. The rhythms of Job and his family's lives were good, very good.

This good life was something that even Satan noticed—and didn't like, since blessings and happiness aren't his trademarks. So Satan laid down a challenge to God: let him test Job's devotion.

When the testing began, Job went in a matter of minutes from a wealthy person with many possessions to a person with no material wealth remaining. In those same minutes, he suffered an even greater loss: the death of his children and his servants.

Any human would stagger under this news. Job's grief was deep and painful. Under the weight of this tremendous loss, he "fell to the ground before God" and said, "I came naked from my mother's womb, and I will be stripped of everything when I die. The Lord gave me everything I had, and the Lord has taken it away. Praise the name of the Lord!" (Job 1:20-21).

And with these words, Job becomes a noteworthy man, not because of his prior wealth, but because of his character. In the midst of almost unbelievable blows, Job showed that under all the trappings of this life, he was first and foremost a humble man, a faithful follower of God, and a thankful person.

Job was humble. He had lost all of his possessions, but by Job's words we can see that his pride had not grown with his possessions. Unlike many people, Job did not think it was solely his intelligence, skills, or labor that brought these possessions to him in the first place. He gave God the credit for giving him everything he had. Job was not a self-made man; he was a God-made man, and he recognized that great truth.

Job was faithful in his trust of God. Job had lost almost everything. The land—without Job's children, servants, and livestock—was now strangely quiet except for the sounds of grief. But these sounds of grief did not include questions on how he would survive. Job truly believed it was God who had provided for him in the past; this drastic change in his circumstances did not change his belief that God would provide for him now.

Job was thankful. Job's reputation as the "finest man in all the earth" was well-deserved. How many of us could have lived through this experience with the words, "Praise the name of the Lord!" as Job did? Bitterness, anger, confusion, shock, or self-pity would be the more natural reactions. It is easy to praise God when things are going the way we like or when something that we don't like has ended, but to praise God during such a severe trial speaks of true belief in God's goodness.

Job remained rich in the way that was most important—his devotion to God. There is much to learn from his life.

WEEK 95

Our Deepest Fears

Job 2–6; Psalm 80; Luke 14

"Then Job scraped his skin with a piece of broken pottery as he sat among the ashes" (Job 2:8). Let's take a moment to relate to the real, living, breathing, feeling person of Job rather than to Job, the character in a story.

Job is in agony. There is little if any value left in his life. His children and servants are dead; his wealth is gone. He is sitting among the ashes of what had been his life, scraping at his skin with a piece of pottery. The pottery and his life are the same—broken.

He is covered in swollen, throbbing boils and scabs—in his hair and beard, on his face and eyelids, in the folds of his skin, and between his fingers and toes. Every square inch of his skin is covered in pain. Every blink of the eye, every muscle movement, and every breath he takes sends searing pain throughout his body, making it difficult even to escape through sleep. Seeing Job frightens and repulses people.

Job, this righteous man, this man whom God called "the finest man in all the earth," (Job 1:8) is in profound suffering and has been for months. Job raises his anguished voice to ask why such bitter circumstances have been allowed into his life.

After pouring out his sorrowful confusion, Job says, "What I always feared has happened to me. What I dreaded has come to be" (Job 3:25). These words telling of Job's fears and dread are striking, for they refer to the entire period of Job's life prior to this time of testing; a period marked by his obvious blessings and his strong and sure relationship with God. We tend to think that someone possessing the material wealth and spiritual maturity of Job would have no reason to fear and therefore would not. But Job says, "What I always feared has happened." Job had feared what was now a reality: physical suffering, the loss of loved ones, the loss of wealth, reduced standing in the community, and not having God's protection from hardship.

What are *our* deepest fears? Is it death or the process of dying? Pain? Disease? Being alone or unloved? Losing those we love the most? The inability to meet our needs? Loss of control of something we think we must control? Not living up to a standard we or others have set? Or thinking that we cannot be forgiven by God or pleasing enough to Him?

God says, "Trust Me," but as our fears surface, we may find it difficult or impossible to do so. And that reality often leads Christians to struggle not only with fear but also with the feeling that God is disappointed in us because of our lack of faith and trust. But it is interesting that in this account, Job's fears did not make him unacceptable to God even though his fears suggested some lack of faith and trust in God. Job's fears existed at the same time that God considered him "the finest man in all the earth."

There are many Bible verses that address our fears, for God understands us and knows our emotional frailties. King David expressed his thoughts on his own fears when he said to God, "but when I am afraid, I put my trust in you" (Ps. 56:3).

We want to be able to echo David's words on fear and trust, but consistent, deep, unshakable trust in times when we are fearful is not always easy. As our fears begin to engulf us, our truthful prayer may be a slight variation on David's—"I am afraid, *help me* put my trust in You."

God hears those honest words, cares about our struggles, and will draw near to us.

WEEK 96

Misguided Counsel

Job 7–10; Psalms 81–82; Luke 15

Last week as we left Job, he was sitting in an ash heap in wretched physical and emotional condition from loss of wealth, family, and health. Job had been suffering for months.

For the past seven days, three of Job's closest friends have been with him. They had heard that Job had met with great disaster, but nothing prepared them for what they saw when they arrived after a long journey. Job's misery stuns and shakes them. For now, they sit silently with him in acknowledgment and support of his great suffering, as their minds search for ways to help, for words to bring comfort and hope.

Finally Job breaks the anguished silence with words filled with confusion and despair. And after seven days of contemplation, his friends are ready with answers, for they genuinely care for Job and want to see his suffering end. Eliphaz jumps in first and confidently tells Job, "Stop and think!...My experience shows that those who plant trouble and cultivate evil will harvest the same" (Job 4:7-8). His logic follows what his eyes tell him: Job is suffering; evildoers suffer; therefore Job has done evil. But Eliphaz also has words of hope for Job: "Consider the joy of those corrected by God! Do not despise the chastening of the Almighty when you sin. For though he wounds, he also bandages. He strikes, but his hands also heal" (Job 5:17-18).

Bildad agrees with Eliphaz and has come up with the solution to Job's suffering. He wants Job to confess his sin. Bildad is sure that once Job confesses the sin that caused this great punishment, God "will yet fill your mouth with laughter and your lips with shouts of joy" (Job 8:21). Job's friends long for him to be restored to his former self, and they offer hope along with what they think is the solution to Job's situation.

Job's friends were sure only good things happen to those who obey God, bad things happen only to those who sin, and God restores sinners when they confess their wrongdoing. They firmly believed their theology was on target for Job's situation, and they were anxious for Job to take their advice. There was only one thing wrong. Two out of three of their theological beliefs were wrong—even though these beliefs were widely held. And based on his recent experiences, Job knew that two out of three of these beliefs were wrong.

"Yes, I know this is all true in principle," Job answered (Job 9:2). But Job had not sinned, and he knew it. He had nothing to confess in order to be healed and restored. His friends' theology, although offered in love, did not help Job. In fact, it led to *more* suffering and pain for Job because now he had to carry the burden of his good friends' assumption that it was his moral failure that led to his circumstances.

Job's friends did many things that serve as good examples for us as we seek to comfort others. They left what they were doing to come and be with Job. When others turned away from Job, they stayed by his side. They didn't push Job but waited for seven days until he was ready to talk.

They were true friends and wanted to see his suffering end. But their advice was misguided.

There is much suffering in this world, and somewhere in the midst of that suffering, there comes a time when reassurance, rather than advice, is sought. Scripture is filled with words that can give comfort during times of sorrow. In those times, share the words of God that give hope to a downcast heart.

Death of a Dream

Job 11–14; Luke 16–18

"Gathering the twelve disciples around him, Jesus told them, 'As you know, we are going to Jerusalem. And when we get there, all the predictions of the ancient prophets concerning the Son of Man will come true. He will be handed over to the Romans to be mocked, treated shamefully, and spit upon. They will whip him and kill him, but on the third day he will rise again.' But they didn't understand a thing he said. Its significance was hidden from them, and they failed to grasp what he was talking about" (Luke 18:31-34).

Jesus clearly laid out for the disciples what was going to happen to Him. And in case there was any confusion, Jesus gave them a reference source—the ancient prophets—so they could examine the writings from long ago that spoke of the days drawing near. The disciples had all the information they needed to understand.

And yet they did not "understand a thing he said." Not one of them. Nothing fell into place, and "they failed to grasp what he was talking about." From our vantage point 2,000 years later, we wonder how it could be.

It was simply because the disciples were living in the "now" of this situation. They were in the midst of the details. Even though they had been told what the future held, their minds couldn't take it in. Each of them had cherished beliefs of what Christ's kingdom meant to them, and Jesus' words and their beliefs were clashing head-to-head. And although they had heard the promise that Jesus would rise "again on the third day," they had also heard for at least the third time that Jesus was going to die. If any part of the message was sinking in, it was the thought of Jesus' death and the death of their dreams—and that was too painful to deal with.

Similar to the disciples, the twists and turns of life can leave us reeling and overwhelmed. It becomes hard to imagine how we will make it through each day, and we cannot begin to fathom that any good could come of these crushing situations.

How we long for relief from all that plagues us. We are in good company, for we know that the disciples felt these same human emotions too. Even Jesus, contemplating His approaching suffering, death, and separation from God, longed for relief. But if we can keep our faith in God through these times, as Jesus did, we often begin to see what we could not see at first—the good that has been accomplished through the pain.

Looking back a few months after hearing Christ's crushing words, the disciples could clearly see the good that had been hidden by the broken dreams to which they clung. The fulfillment of those harrowing words resulted in a Savior, who through His resurrection had conquered both death and sin for them and for all who sought this gift.

What about us? Sometimes we look back at the times that tested us and see how God provided for us. Maybe we see how we have grown in a way that would not have been possible without our time of suffering. Or we see that our faith and trust in God have increased.

During this life there will be times we do not understand what has happened or why. The question is whether or not we can trust God even when we do not understand the bigger picture of our painful circumstances. The answer to that question is that we can—but only with God's help, for this kind of faith and trust is never simple or easy. But it is powerful, and it is life-changing.

How to Be a Friend

Job 15–19; Psalms 83–84

For weeks we have been reading of Job's severe physical, emotional, and spiritual suffering. Circumstances completely out of his control had isolated Job.

In his loneliness, he needed someone who would stand by his side. Job needed a friend. But the sad fact is that Job did not have the type of friend he needed, and his plea, "Have mercy on me, my friends, have mercy, for the hand of God has struck me," is poignant (Job 19:21). Covered with painful sores, grieving the loss of his family, stripped of his possessions, and trying to reconcile his closely held beliefs about God to the reality of what he was experiencing, Job begs his friends to show him understanding and kindness.

Why would Job have to beg for these responses when his needs were so obvious? In the midst of his intense suffering, Job found that "people jeer and laugh at me.... My friends scorn me" (Job 16:10,20). Job's friends had moved from support to scorn. And Job's neighbors and acquaintances mocked him to his face or whispered about him behind his back. How could they be so cruel?

But are we so different? As we look around our workplaces, neighborhoods, schools, social gatherings, and even our churches, isn't that how it is too often? The person who most needs a friend is ignored, becomes the brunt of gossip, or is belittled by others. Their wounds may not be as obvious as Job's, but they are nonetheless painful, and they give rise to the same sort of vulnerability and anguish.

It may be someone who is a shy newcomer. It may be someone who is unsure of him or herself, awkward, or tentative because of past rejections. It may be someone who does not have the same abilities, standard of living, customs, or background as the majority, and therefore stand out as different from everyone else. Whatever the reason, they are the people standing on the fringes of your group, silently pleading, "Have mercy on me"—be my friend.

People's rejection and scorn hurt Job so much that he said, "I pour out my tears to God" (Job 16:20). Think about that. Job should have been able to pour out his tears to his friends and even his acquaintances, for Job had much to cry about. But he was rejected. Subtle or blatant, rejection is powerfully destructive.

There seems to be something about another's vulnerability that brings out the worst in some people, but this should never be the case for followers of Jesus Christ. We are to be friends of the friendless. We are to be the ones to show acceptance to the unwanted. We are to be the ones to show mercy to the vulnerable.

Be the one who shows God's love to others.

Week 99

Listen Carefully

Job 20–23; Psalm 85; Luke 19–20

The psalmist wrote, "I listen carefully to what God the Lord is saying, for he speaks peace to his people, his faithful ones. But let them not return to their foolish ways" (Ps. 85:8). These few phrases give a good blueprint for successful living. Let's break them down and relate them to a familiar biblical character: Zacchaeus.

When we read or hear the story of Zacchaeus, some of us may find our minds going back to the children's song: "Zacchaeus was a wee, little man and a wee, little man was he. He climbed up in a sycamore tree, for the Lord he wanted to see." Zacchaeus *did* want to see the Lord, and he did indeed have to climb a tree to get a good look. But Jesus knew exactly where to look for Zacchaeus, and as He "came by, he looked up at Zacchaeus and called him by name. 'Zacchaeus!' he said. 'Quick, come down! For I must be a guest in your home today'" (Luke 19:5).

Zacchaeus listened carefully to Jesus and obeyed immediately, climbing down quickly from the tree to take "Jesus to his house in great excitement and joy" (Luke 19:6). Zacchaeus didn't think about reasons why it would be inconvenient to have Jesus come to his house for dinner. He didn't question what caused Jesus to pick him out of the crowd. He didn't weigh long-term consequences of Jesus' request or contemplate his response. He merely obeyed quickly. And most importantly, he did so in great excitement and joy.

Zacchaeus' life was filled with turmoil when he climbed that tree to see Jesus. His world was in an uproar because Israel, the land in which he lived, was occupied by Roman troops; he and his nation were not free. His personal life was filled with turmoil because people became angry at the mere thought of him being a tax collector, and Zacchaeus lived in the midst of those angry people. In fact, when the crowd heard that Jesus was going to Zacchaeus' house, of all places, they "were displeased" and grumbled that Jesus had "gone to be the guest of a notorious sinner" (Luke 19:7). Zacchaeus was no slouch when it came to living a life filled with turmoil.

The psalmist assures us that the Lord "speaks peace to his people, his faithful ones." In a world that always seems to be in turmoil and with our lives often mirroring the same, the Lord will speak peace to us, His people. Once we have experienced true turmoil, we recognize peace for the great gift that it is. But this is not a promise for the world at large. It is a promise to God's "faithful ones," those who desire to please God and to stand with Him. And Zacchaeus wanted to please God.

Jesus recognized this desire and spoke peace into Zacchaeus' life. Zacchaeus responded with authentic gratitude. "I will give half my wealth to the poor, Lord, and if I have overcharged people on their taxes, I will give them back four times as much!" (Luke 19:8). Here was a life that was radically, miraculously, wonderfully changed by Jesus because of Zacchaeus' willingness to listen and obey. Jesus summed it up when He said, "Salvation has come to this home today, for this man has shown himself to be a son of Abraham" (Luke 19:9). In an instant, Zacchaeus had become one of God's "faithful ones." His old way of life was upended, and he was a new person.

But the psalmist warns, "let them not return to their foolish ways." It is so easy to do exactly that even after experiencing the peace of God. Temptation calls to us. Life's trials weary us. Culture, which seldom aligns with godly principles, pulls us away from God and toward those things that will not bring real peace to us. And that is exactly why it is important for us to listen carefully to God rather than to other influences.

We aren't told the rest of Zacchaeus' story, but it is not difficult to imagine the pressure and ridicule he probably experienced. For those who lived as Zacchaeus had before his salvation, his actions must have seemed absolutely insane. Give half—HALF—of his wealth away! And from the remaining half, pay out four times the amount of anyone he had overcharged! The nature of his job was to overcharge, so it is safe to assume that Zacchaeus went from being a wealthy person to someone with drastically reduced assets.

It is also likely that Zacchaeus' friends were uncomfortable with his altered status and priorities. His changed life may have left them feeling bewildered or even guilty. They may have deserted him or tried to badger him into going back to his old way of life. As Zacchaeus' friends dropped away, did those who were already followers of Jesus trust him and embrace him as a fellow believer, or was he still a "notorious sinner" in their eyes? We don't know the answers to these questions, but we know it is probable that Zacchaeus faced some tough trials in his new life and strong temptations to "return to foolish ways."

Where do *we* fit in the psalmist's statement? Do we "listen carefully to what God the Lord is saying" through reading the Bible and quietly reflecting on what we've read? Do we store Scripture in our minds, so we are guided by it during times of temptations and hardships? Have we experienced God's peace? Are we "his people, his faithful ones," refusing to return to our foolish ways?

If so, then we understand the excitement and joy that Zacchaeus felt when he climbed down from that tree and listened carefully to Jesus. Salvation has come to our home, and we are blessed.

Week 100

Temptation Alert!

Job 24–28; Luke 21–22

"'Why are you sleeping?' he [Jesus] asked. 'Get up and pray. Otherwise temptation will overpower you'" (Luke 22:46). Jesus was with the disciples in the Garden of Gethsemane as He prepared for the horrendous ordeal ahead of Him: His trials, His suffering, His separation from God the Father, and His death. In the midst of this tremendously important time in His life on earth, Jesus turned His attention away from His own approaching agony and toward His disciples—to guide and warn them regarding temptation.

This strikes me as particularly significant. At this most crucial point in history, Jesus' words would have been especially meaningful, for these words were some of the last He would speak to His closest friends and followers before His death. Over the years, these disciples had learned many important truths from Jesus. Jesus could have reminded them of any one of those lessons. But He did not. Instead He warned about the danger of temptation and urged the disciples to be preemptive in prayer so they would not be overcome by it.

The disciples were exhausted, confused about the future, and not overly worried about temptation at that moment. Are *our* thoughts and reactions regarding temptation similar to the disciples? Are we naive about temptation?

It is sometimes hard to recognize that we are part of a great ongoing spiritual battle, for we are much more aware of the physical realm in which we exist than of the spiritual realm where temptations originate. Temptation was real and relevant to Jesus. It was so real that He urged His followers to pray about it often in one of the greatest examples of prayer ever recorded: "don't let us yield to temptation, but deliver us from the evil one" (Matt. 6:13).

Are we nonchalant about temptation? Do we recognize that we may be tempted but give it little thought? Temptation often begins subtly because Satan wants to deceive us into complacency. This was one of the reasons why Jesus warned us to anticipate and be prepared to defend against temptation in our lives. Satan and his followers aren't going to use flashing warning lights proclaiming, "Temptation coming!" Temptation is usually characterized by a more subtle approach.

Are we praying about temptation as directed by Jesus but choosing the wrong time to ask for help? Do our prayers begin after we're in the midst of the battle? Jesus urged us to pray much earlier in the process, for He wants us to be prepared, and not caught off guard when temptation comes. By waiting until we are in the thick of temptation to pray about it, we make it much harder to stand firm and to come out of the temptation triumphant.

Are we deceived regarding our ability to withstand temptation? We may have been a Christian for a long time and feel we are not as susceptible to temptation as someone newer to faith, but we need to think again. The disciples spent years with Jesus, but He knew their vulnerability to temptation. On one of His last days on earth, Jesus warned the disciples, and especially Simon Peter, that "Satan has asked to have all of you, to sift you like wheat. But I have pleaded in prayer for you" (Luke 22:31-32). Jesus knew that the temptations the disciples would soon face were too great for their own strength to overcome, and He pleaded to the Father for their perseverance and for faith that would not fail. This was serious stuff, so serious that Jesus set aside His own suffering to concentrate on the temptations of His disciples.

Make no mistake about it—Satan and his followers want to destroy our witness and our lives. Jesus, unlike us, truly understands the spiritual conflicts playing out in this world and wants us to be ready for battle. Our weapons are outlined in Ephesians 6, Luke 22, and Matthew 6. We are urged to "pray at all times," and to "stay alert, and be persistent in your prayers for Christians everywhere to be able to stand firm against all strategies and tricks of the devil" (Eph. 6:18,11).

Be alert! Don't take something lightly that God has taken so seriously.

Week 101

Overcoming Overwhelming Circumstances

Job 29–32; Psalms 86–87; Luke 23

The Roman authorities had a specific objective to accomplish with crucifixions. Designed to act as a deterrent to behavior not approved by Rome, they were purposely painful, gruesome, and public. But Jesus also had a specific objective to accomplish through crucifixion. By His death, Jesus willingly became the bridge between each of us and God. Luke tells us of two differing responses to Christ's crucifixion.

To understand these two responses, we need to fix a more accurate image in our minds of how Jesus looked at the time He was crucified. He was beaten so severely that He would have scarcely been recognizable. His back would have been shredded from being whipped until the skin was gone and the muscles and bones exposed. More ripped skin and profuse bleeding would have resulted from His beard being pulled out in chunks and large thorns being driven into His skull. Continued beatings from the soldiers, who were skilled at such a thing, would have resulted in grotesque bruising and swelling. Struggling to carry His crossbeam uphill, Jesus would have been dizzy, nauseous, and weak from the beating, dehydration, loss of blood, and blazing sun.

When Jesus arrived at the place of crucifixion, large spikes—not flimsy nails—were driven through His wrists, His feet, and the nerves that ran through them. Hanging by His arms with His lower body twisted would have compressed Jesus' chest cavity, making exhaling nearly impossible. To allow enough room for His lungs to exhale, Jesus would have been forced to straighten his body by pushing His battered, raw back upward against the rough wood of the cross—making each breath a painful struggle.

This is the real picture of Jesus as He hung between two criminals, also crucified, and suffering in a way that is hard to fully understand. As they hung there, the first criminal looked at Jesus and gasped out in scorn and derision, "So you're the Messiah, are you? Prove it by saving yourself—and us, too, while you're at it!" (Luke 23:39). Logically, who could blame him for the sarcasm? Was there anything about the battered and dying Jesus that would cause any person to look beyond His outward vulnerability?

There was, for the second criminal looked at Jesus dying beside him and said, "Jesus, remember me when you come into your Kingdom" (Luke 23:42). This man was able to see beyond the physical appearance of Jesus, beyond the fact that Jesus hung on a cross just as he did, and beyond the knowledge that Jesus was dying. He looked in faith and trust at something that could not be seen or even fully imagined in his present circumstances.

Like the two criminals, we may face situations that feel insurmountable, situations that seem like they will destroy us. The question becomes: of the two criminals' reactions to Jesus, which would best describe us during those times?

The first criminal demanded that Jesus prove Himself by changing the man's circumstances immediately and completely. The second criminal was open to the faith and trust that allowed him to see beyond the merciless situation he was in. And by faith and trust, he saw that there was a future, there was hope, and there was an answer to his suffering.

No further words are recorded between Jesus and the first criminal, but to the second, Jesus said, "I assure you, today you will be with me in paradise" (Luke 23:43). Could there be any greater change in circumstances than to move from a painful, humiliating death to the wonders and joys of "paradise"?

It is often when faith is hardest to come by, that we are most in need of it. With God to help us, we may be astounded at how our circumstances change or how our ability to cope changes with each small step of faith that we take. These changes may not occur at the time or in the manner in which we think they should, but surely, if there is anyone who understands and can be trusted with our wounded bodies, hearts, and minds, it is our loving and powerful Savior, for He has been wounded too.

The Messengers

Job 33–37; Luke 24; Philippians 1

"But very early on Sunday morning the women came to the tomb, taking the spices they had prepared. They found that the stone covering the entrance had been rolled aside. So they went in, but they couldn't find the body of the Lord Jesus. They were puzzled, trying to think what could have happened to it. Suddenly, two men appeared to them, clothed in dazzling robes. The women were terrified and bowed low before them. Then the men asked, 'Why are you looking in a tomb for someone who is alive? He isn't here! He has risen from the dead! Don't you remember what he told you back in Galilee, that the Son of Man must be betrayed into the hands of sinful men and be crucified, and that he would rise again the third day?' Then they remembered that he had said this" (Luke 24:1-8).

In those few minutes, these women, Mary Magdalene, Joanna, Mary the mother of James, and several others, must have felt a chaotic mix of emotions. As the women approached the tomb, they were grieving deeply over Jesus' death. Puzzlement and confusion would have mingled with their grief when they found the tomb empty. As their minds searched for possible explanations for the empty tomb, sheer terror would have overcome their confusion and puzzlement when they saw two extraordinary men in dazzling robes. By the time the two men began to speak to them, the women must have been overwhelmed by the sheer intensity of their feelings and the strangeness of the past few days.

But then the words the two men spoke began to penetrate the muddle of their many emotions, and they were able to hear the best news ever heard. "Don't you remember?" the men asked, He told you "he would rise again on the third day." And this was the third day!

Have you ever wondered why it was these women, rather than the disciples or someone else, who first heard and knew that Jesus was alive? Were they any less confused or frightened than the apostles and the others who had gathered together behind locked doors for protection from the Jewish leaders as they tried to make sense of the prior few days? Did they love Jesus any more than the others who were grieving together over Jesus' death? It is doubtful that their grief or fear differed much from how the others were feeling.

What did differ was their behavior. The women came out from behind closed doors to bring burial spices to the tomb of Jesus as an expression of their love for Him. They put their fears of the authorities and their confusion over the recent events behind them to the extent that they willingly took this first step of love. These beginning steps put them in the place where the two angels could remind them of Jesus' promises. And although these angels were startling and fearsome messengers, the women trusted them, for their message was a reminder of what Jesus had said about Himself. In the end, it was Jesus' own words that brought to them the confirmation, peace, and joy that replaced their confusion, fear, and grief.

With believing hearts, they "rushed back to tell his eleven disciples— and everyone else—what had happened" (Luke 24:9). Can you picture the scene? The women—flushed with excitement, their garments dusty and slightly askew from the mad dash back to the city—banging on the locked door so they could enter…and then trying to catch their breath as words tumbled out of their mouths. They had amazing good news, and they wanted to share it!

Now if you would ever expect a warm welcome to be given to someone telling about Jesus' resurrection, you would think it would be during this first telling. The women, after all, were telling those who knew and loved Jesus, too, and who had heard the same words from Jesus that the women had heard. Yes, it would be logical to think that the disciples would be as joyful as the women at this good news, "but the story sounded like nonsense, so they didn't believe it" (Luke 24:11).

These women knew that Jesus was alive, and they hadn't hesitated for a second to share this good news with others. But their message of hope and good news was rejected. Can you imagine the discouragement and frustration they must have felt? They were bursting with the good news, but they could not make the others believe.

However, their words did not fall completely on deaf ears, for "Peter ran to the tomb to look. Stooping, he peered in and saw the empty linen wrappings; then he went home again, wondering what had happened" (Luke 24:12). Peter had enough questions about the women's story to check further but not enough faith to believe what he had heard from them or seen with his own eyes. The empty tomb was not enough proof. Many hours later, Jesus appeared to Peter, and it was then that the disciples and the others came to believe what the women had first said was true.

It is good for us to remember the lessons we can learn from the women who were the first to go to Jesus' tomb. Their story provides us with great examples of faith and love in action in spite of fear or confusion. Their story teaches us that Jesus' resurrection is fantastic news we need to share with others, but that we may face ridicule or rejection as we reach out to others with His story. Their story also teaches us that those who do ridicule or reject Jesus' story upon first hearing it may come to believe it at a later time.

These women did what Jesus instructed His disciples to do during His last days on earth. Jesus said, "With my authority, take this message of repentance to all the nations, beginning in Jerusalem: 'There is forgiveness of sins for all who turn to me'" (Luke 24:47).

The women were messengers, as are we, and Jesus is our message of hope to the world.

WEEK 103

The Power of Intercessory Prayer

Job 38–42; Psalm 88; Philippians 2

At the start of the last chapter of the book of Job, we find Job a changed man from the person introduced in the first chapter. Job is no longer a father of living children, no longer wealthy, no longer in good health, no longer respected within his community. But in one important way Job is the same person we first met: he continues to be a humble man.

Throughout Job's horrendous ordeal, he desperately wanted to hear from God regarding why he was suffering, but God was silent. Now, however, God is no longer silent. His answer? God is to be trusted for who He is—the all-knowing, all-powerful Creator of all that exists. God is not to be evaluated by what we think He should, or should not, allow in our lives. In humility, Job replies to the Lord's chastisement by saying, "You ask, 'Who is this that questions my wisdom with such ignorance?' It is I. And I was talking about things that I did not understand.... I take back everything I said, and I sit in dust and ashes to show my repentance" (Job 42:3,6).

In the midst of one of the most intensely difficult times a human being could experience, Job recognizes his sin of not trusting God and admits that he has lost sight of God's greatness. Many people, after enduring such intense suffering and seeing no end in sight to it, would feel justified in continuing to argue why their treatment by God was unfair. Job is not one of them. Although his circumstances remain the same, Job now sees his life differently from how he saw it before hearing from God. In humility, he repents and seeks God's forgiveness, which is freely given to him.

Now the story could have ended right there, but it would have been incomplete because Job is not the only person needing to seek forgiveness. There are still his self-assured and long-winded friends. In justice and righteousness, God turns His attention to these friends, who, we can be sure, wished that they had spoken less, loved more, and known God better. God says, "I am angry with you...for you have not been right in what you said about me, as my servant Job was. Now take seven young bulls and seven rams and go to my servant Job and offer a burnt offering for yourselves. My servant Job will pray for you, and I will accept his prayer on your behalf. I will not treat you as you deserve" (Job 42:7-8).

Notice that while his friends are to bring the bulls and rams to offer for their sins, it will be Job's intercessory prayer and faith that restores his friends' relationship with God. For those of us who have loved ones and friends in need of intercessory prayer, God's acceptance of Job's prayer for his friends shows the power of such prayers.

Let's look at the path that the Lord and Job took to come to this remarkable conclusion. We have already seen that Job recognized his own sinful attitude toward God, that he had repented, and that he had received forgiveness. As Job realized his own need for forgiveness, he may also have realized he would need to forgive others who had hurt him deeply. How easy and natural it would have been for Job to hold great resentment against his friends, to allow this resentment to fester, and to refuse to pray for them. But as Job prayed for those who had hurt him, he began to extend the same forgiveness to them as he had received from God. With a clear conscience and a forgiven soul, Job could pray in close fellowship with God.

Is there any of us who does not struggle at times with the need to forgive and the reluctance to do so? We are not alone in this conflict of desires. God will help us, as Paul confirmed to the Philippians: "For God is working in you, giving you the desire to obey him and the power to do what pleases him" (Phil. 2:13).

As Job stepped forward in obedience to God, and "prayed for his friends, the Lord restored his fortunes" (Job 42:10). Again, note the sequence of events: Job's fortune was restored after he prayed for his friends, not before. If it had only been Job's wealth that was restored, he may have lived a life hampered by bitterness and resentment—things for which material goods could not compensate. Material restoration came after the more important spiritual restoration.

If there was ever an example of a life story that would justify anger and bitterness toward God and others, this was it. If there was ever a set of circumstances that would require God's help in overcoming a person's natural inclination to stop trusting Him, this was it. And if there was ever an example of a life well lived in spite of horrendous setbacks, this was it. Job was honest before God, recognized his own sin, sought God's forgiveness, forgave others, and obeyed God when it was difficult to do so.

What a life! What a story! What an example for us!

WEEK 104

Dreams

Proverbs 1–4; Psalm 89; Philippians 3–4

"You can lie down without fear and enjoy pleasant dreams" (Prov. 3:24). Dreams play a significant part in at least three stories in the Bible.

There was the story of God using a dream to warn Joseph, the father of Jesus, to take the infant Jesus and Mary and flee to Egypt before Herod could harm Jesus (Matt. 2:13-15). This dream urging action became a dream leading to salvation.

Nearly two thousand years earlier, another Joseph, the son of Jacob, was given the ability by God to explain the meaning of dreams. Joseph interpreted the dreams of Pharaoh's chief baker and his food taster, both of whom, like Joseph, were imprisoned at the time the dreams occurred (Gen. 40). These dreams, given by God, would eventually lead to outcomes of great significance for many people.

These outcomes began to unfold two years later through another dream, and this time it was Pharaoh who dreamed. His dream could not be interpreted by his magicians or wise men but was explained by Joseph. Because of this dream and his interpretation, Joseph was released from prison, became the second most powerful man in Egypt, prepared the country for seven years of famine, saved countless lives that would have been lost due to the famine, and brought reconciliation to his own family—the ancestors of the Israelite nation (Gen. 41–47). Who could doubt the importance of dreams when the results of this one were so far-reaching?

Dreams are important to us as well. Who doesn't appreciate a good night's rest, a rest with nothing preying on our minds, no worries or fears lurking, a sleep populated by untroubled dreams?

But our dreams are not always pleasant. There are times, as we lie down to rest, that a seemingly endless succession of thoughts begins running through our minds. Thoughts that we are sometimes able to control during our waking hours can wash over us as we seek sleep: "What if…." "Why won't they…." "I don't know what to do about…." "I am frightened by...." And these thoughts follow us into an uneasy sleep jarred by heart-pounding or puzzling nightmares.

It is during these times that we can call out to God for His assurance, His comfort, and His peace. We can ask God for guidance about the things that trouble us, recalling scriptural promises. And we can practice trusting God when it is not easy to do so, asking for His help for serene sleep.

There is one other type of dream we may experience—one that, while not a nightmare, is troubling nevertheless. This is the kind of dream that contains behavior, thoughts, or desires that we recognize are not pleasing to God. As in our waking hours, we have three responses to these types of dreams:

- We can allow our waking thoughts to be enticed by these dreams, opening ourselves to what we should not be thinking.
- We can deceive ourselves into thinking that because they are only dreams, they are not important and require no action.
- We can ask God to forgive our thoughts from which these dreams spring.

Let us be as wise and responsible about our hours of sleep as we should be during our hours of wakefulness. Dreaming or awake, let us ask God's help to fix our "thoughts on what is true and honorable and right" (Phil. 4:8).

WEEK 105

How Powerful Is Your God?

Proverbs 5–9; Colossians 1–2

"This same Good News that came to you is going out all over the world. It is changing lives everywhere..." (Col. 1:6). A powerful verse. That is perhaps why I so clearly recall the day when I realized I doubted some of the words of this verse. I had heard and believed the Good News, so how could I not believe that it had the power to change lives everywhere?

That was the question I struggled with that day, barely able to believe my own thoughts. A few minutes before, it had been a day like many others. While taking a walk, I had been asking God to bring the Good News to someone who needed her life to be changed. But this time as I prayed, I realized that my words were empty ones, for I doubted that God had the power to change this particular life. I had no trouble believing that God could change a life that wasn't beset with horrendous problems. But this person had dug a hole so deep there were no easy human solutions—possibly no tough solutions, either. And in that moment of truth, I faced the fact that I did not actually believe God could *drastically* change a life in deep trouble or rebellion. Stunned, I stopped walking and stood absolutely still.

As I stood there, a second important truth became evident. In that moment, I realized I had made the Creator God of the universe into a god who was small enough to fit my comprehension. I had been shrinking God down to my abilities, to my size, to my understanding, thinking that there were some things simply too hard for the Lord.

With that realization, I had to decide in what I actually believed. Did I believe in the god I had made up in my mind, a god not much different from the man-made idols of the Old Testament, or did I believe in God as the one true God—all-powerful, all-knowing, all-loving, and with the power to change lives everywhere.

Beginning to pray again, I asked God's forgiveness for believing in my image of who He was and to help me to know Him better. From that defining moment, God has answered that prayer. Through the Bible, through prayer, through others, and through hard times that have increased my trust, I have seen the awesomeness of God.

That day the Good News changed not only my life but my belief that it can change anyone's life. Now I am convinced that it is often *only* God who can change a life for the better. Colossians 1:17 tells us, "He [Jesus] existed before everything else began, and he holds all creation together."

Do we, or someone we love, need to be held together today? Each of us is part of the creation that Jesus can, does, and will hold together. Jesus can heal broken relationships, addictions, self-loathing, hatred, and wrongs that have been done to us, just as He can forgive the sins that we have committed. It doesn't matter how messed up the life, it can be renewed by God, for He is bigger than any of the things that bring us low. Whatever has rocked our world can be used by God for our good, if we allow Jesus Christ to change our allegiance, direction, reactions, thoughts, and attitudes.

Paul was one of those who had been drastically changed by Jesus Christ, and he could assure the Colossians that the Good News of Jesus Christ was "changing lives everywhere, just as it changed yours that very first day you heard and understood the truth about God's great kindness to sinners" (Col. 1:6).

What do you think of Jesus and the ability of His Good News to change lives? How powerful is your God?

Knee-Deep in Miracles

Proverbs 10–14; Psalm 90; Colossians 3

"Let us see your miracles again; let our children see your glory at work" (Ps. 90:16). Moses, who wrote Psalm 90, surely knew about miracles. He had seen them, felt them, and lived them. A walk down memory lane shows that even a few of the miracles Moses had been part of forms a mind-boggling list.

Moses' life began with a miracle, for he had been spared while other Hebrew boys were killed at birth. Not only was his life spared, but this child, born as a Hebrew slave, was raised as a member of Pharaoh's own family (Exod. 2).

Many years later after fleeing to the desert to hide after killing an Egyptian, he was called by God to be the leader of the movement to free the Hebrew slaves and mold them into the Israelite nation. One of the first miracles to occur in this process was the transformation of Moses, a man with little self-confidence and little speaking ability, into the person through whom God would perform many other miracles to accomplish His objective (Exod. 2–3).

Those miracles came swiftly in the form of overwhelming plagues of frogs, gnats, flies, locust, hail, boils, and the death of livestock. Finally, three days of total darkness and then the tragic death of the firstborn son of each Egyptian family convinced Pharaoh to do what he swore he would not do—release the Hebrew slaves (Exod. 8–12).

Not surprisingly, before long Pharaoh and his army pursued the Hebrews. As the slaves stood trapped between the Red Sea and the Egyptians, God performed one of the most famous miracles in history when He separated the waters and made a path through the sea, allowing the massive number of Hebrew slaves to pass through to the other side unharmed by the water or the Egyptians (Exod. 13–14).

As the former slaves moved toward a new homeland, there were more miracles during their desert wanderings: water from a rock, bread and quail from Heaven, physical healings, and victories over those who would harm them (Exod. 16–17).

Yes, the Israelites were knee-deep in big-time miracles during the early days of their release from Egypt. And here was Moses looking back to those numerous miracles, asking God to "let us see your miracles again." What was it about those miracles that caused Moses to long to see more, and what conclusions may we draw from them?

Miracles obviously represent the power, wisdom, and glory that can only be associated with God. Miracles are out of the realm of human ability but fully in the realm of God's ability. Could it be that Moses longed for miraculous displays of God's magnificence to encourage the Hebrew children's faith? From the psalmist's words, we will assume that these children had not experienced the miracles of the exodus from Egypt. They had to take the stories of God's power by faith rather than by sight. As we know, this is not always an easy thing to do.

Miracles are also tangible evidence of God's personal care for us—His protection, love, and provision for us. Was Moses seeking the tangible assurance miracles provide to people of their importance to God?

Did Moses ask God to "let us see your miracles again" because the Israelites' recollection of the mighty acts of God during the chaotic, early days of their journey had left them feeling as if God had forgotten them during later, calmer times?

Or was Moses actually pleading with God to allow the people to "see" the miracles that were still occurring in their lives? After all, the tangible evidence of God's guidance and protection was never out of the Israelites' sight since God's presence appeared each day as a great cloud and each night as a column of fire (Exod. 13:21-22). And forty years of shelter, food, and water for people and animals in a desert where supplies were limited was miraculous, as was a large group of people living in peace on land that was not their own. God was not absent, but had the people lost sight of His quiet miracles and ever-constant presence?

"Let us see your miracles again; let our children see your glory at work." We join our voices with Moses asking for the sheer joy of seeing God's power, wisdom, and glory through His wondrous miracles. But let us also join our voices with Moses asking for help to notice the quiet miracles of each day and God's presence always with us.

Right Words at the Right Time

Proverbs 15–18; Psalm 91; Colossians 4; 1 Thessalonians 1

"Everyone enjoys a fitting reply; it is wonderful to say the right thing at the right time!" (Prov. 15:23). How often have we thought of what we would like to have said to someone after it was too late to say it? What makes a "fitting reply" so difficult to accomplish?

Well, according to the proverb, there are two elements that must come together to have a fitting reply. We must know the right thing to say and then say it at the right time. How can we begin to consistently do this?

Proverbs 16:2 says that "the Lord examines their motives," so examining our motives is a good place for *us* to start, if we desire to have the right thing to say. Sometimes our motives are less than honorable. We may want to strike back at others when we feel defensive. We may want to build ourselves up by the words we speak—to be noted as witty, quick on our feet, or intelligent.

On the other hand, our motive may be to build up others—to be helpful, kind, encouraging, or lovingly corrective. As we grow in our relationship with God, our motive may become to represent Him in everything we say—marking us as people of integrity, honor, and love.

Second, our words must spring from the right source, if they are to be the right thing to say in any given situation. For words to be right, they must carry wisdom, knowledge, or understanding within them. These building blocks of a fitting reply can be gained through many sources such as the Bible and other teachings based on biblical principles. As we make these sources of wisdom part of our thought patterns, knowing the right thing to say will become easier, for "from a wise mind comes wise speech" (Prov. 16:23).

Finally, to find the right thing to say, we need to plug directly into our power source—God. Praying for help to keep our mouths shut and our minds open helps us develop the patience to wait until the right time has arrived to speak. And asking God for His help in choosing our words in all situations will lead us to the right thing to say when it is time to speak.

The right thing said at the right time is a worthy goal, one shared by Paul when he urged the Colossians to "let your conversation be gracious and effective so that you will have the right answer for everyone" (Col. 4:6).

And now because Proverbs 17:27 declares that "a truly wise person uses few words," it is time to end.

WEEK 108

Great Gifts

Proverbs 19–23; 1 Thessalonians 2–3

"Ears to hear and eyes to see—both are gifts from the Lord" (Prov. 20:12). Hearing and sight. We know they are gifts. We even know they are "gifts from the Lord." But that doesn't stop us from taking them for granted most times. That is, until something happens to diminish either of them, and then we quickly recognize what magnificent gifts they are.

Why is it so easy to take for granted that which we long for after it is gone? It is not only our physical senses that fall into this category but all of the gifts that we receive from God.

A list of those gifts is long: mental agility, physical mobility, health, people we love and people who love us, adequate shelter and food, clean water, and the beauty of nature—to name a few of the most obvious ones. And then there are the gifts that define God such as His forgiveness, love, protection, promises, and comfort.

The abundance of God's gifts makes it easy to be complacent about many of them. We regard them as the way things should be, what we expect. We forget how critical each is to our well-being, and we forget to be grateful.

So how do we shake off complacency and go about pursuing thankfulness until it becomes an ingrained habit? Here is one simple and yet effective way for us to recall our gifts from the Lord. Each night before going to sleep, thank God for one thing for which we have not thanked Him in the past.

An immediate side benefit of this suggestion is that practicing it sets our minds on positive things as we prepare for sleep. But an ongoing benefit is that it opens up our mind to thinking about what we have to be thankful for and expressing our thanks on a consistent basis. This practice also broadens our outlook, for it does not preclude thanking God for the things for which we have been thankful in the past but challenges us to add to that list, and to do so daily. If we follow this suggestion, it is likely that some of those "new things" for which we are thankful may not be new to our lives but merely new to our recognition of how much we appreciate them.

As we practice being thankful, we will be changed and our view of our world will be changed. The world may still be a place of hardship, disappointment, and strife, but we will begin to be able to pick out the good that is so often drowned out. Attitudes of complaining and dissatisfaction will gradually fall away as they are replaced with the by-products of thankfulness: enthusiasm, joy, hope, generosity, and trust in God's goodness. And when being thankful becomes the way we instinctively think, we will have provided ourselves with a valuable tool for the times of serious illness, the ravages of grief, and the occasions when we may not have full control of our thoughts.

Nevertheless, even if we want to be consistently thankful, there may be days when we need to hunt hard to find something *new* for which to be thankful. There may even be days when it is hard work to come up with something *old* to be thankful for. We all have times when it is seems more natural *not* to give thanks. God recognizes that reality. God, in fact, recognizes that being thankful when life is pressing relentlessly upon us is a sacrifice that shows our trust in Him, for He says, "Giving thanks is a sacrifice that truly honors me" (Ps. 50:23).

And that is the essence of thankfulness. Thankfulness has little to do with our circumstances. It is possible to be thankful with little. It is possible to be thankless with much. May we be people who are not only *genuinely* thankful but *consistently* thankful.

WEEK 109

I Need to Know Now!

Proverbs 24–27; Psalms 92–93; 1 Thessalonians 4

"It is God's privilege to conceal things" (Prov. 25:2). And don't we dislike it when He does—especially in times that are hard to bear or confusing to us. The more difficult our situation, the more intense our longing for knowing the concealed things. We want to know why this is happening to us and what the days ahead will look like. We want to know what the outcome will be.

Because we are in the dark about many things that matter tremendously to us, we sometimes begin to question God's love and wisdom in withholding information from us. We think that we would cope better if we knew even a little bit more.

And so we worry about the things hidden from us. We believe that with additional knowledge or understanding, we could have some control over our circumstances. Makes sense, doesn't it?

It makes sense to us, but Scripture tells us that our thought process is flawed. Knowing the hidden things about our circumstances will not impact the outcome or our peace of mind to the extent that trust in God will. God wants us to believe as the psalmist who declared, "The Lord is just! He is my rock! There is nothing but goodness in Him!" (Ps. 92:15). And if there is "nothing but goodness in Him," there can be nothing but eventual goodness for us with whatever comes into our lives—concealed or not.

Waiting for that eventual goodness doesn't come easily to us and neither does the belief in the constancy of God's goodness. For that matter, trusting God does not come easily either, since He too is partly concealed from us.

Learning to trust God is a journey often built on the hardships of our lives. With each jarring experience, each unexpected setback, and each concealed answer, we can learn to hang on and consistently trust in God and in His constant goodness until our journey ends. God knows why these things have come into our lives, even if we do not.

What we will eventually know are the results of trusting God when we have limited information. Our faith in God will grow. Our reliance on Him will deepen. We will have greater emotional strength, more compassion, and increased love for others. These outcomes are easier to see as we look back over our lives. It is not unusual to meet people who, though wearied from facing great hardships in life, are thankful for what they have gained from them. They know they have been molded both by the hardship and by trusting God with the things concealed from them. They know they would not have gained as much from their times of trouble if they understood all that was happening, while it was happening. You may be one of those people.

It is not the "not knowing" that is the issue; it is the "not trusting" God that brings us the most despair. It is a lifetime process, but with prayer and learning from the concealed times, we can become people who know in the depths of our being that "there is nothing but goodness" in God.

Arlina Yates

The Prayer of Agur

Proverbs 28–31; Psalm 94; 1 Thessalonians 5; 2 Thessalonians 1

"O God, I beg two favors from you before I die. First, help me never to tell a lie. Second, give me neither poverty nor riches! Give me just enough to satisfy my needs" (Prov. 30:7-8).

Because of the best-selling book *The Prayer of Jabez*, many of us are familiar with the now-famous prayer found in First Chronicles 4, but we may not be familiar with this lesser known prayer of Agur in Proverbs 30. Agur's prayer concerns two important topics: truthfulness and provision for our needs. We'll look at the first part of the prayer—the request for help "never to tell a lie."

What a pleasing prayer this must be to God, for Jesus considered truthfulness to be of supreme importance. In fact, Jesus describes Himself in John 14:6 as "the way, *the truth*, and the life." Jesus wasn't only saying He approves of truthfulness but that He *is* "the truth." Truth originates with Jesus and radiates from Him. It is one of God's loving gifts to us that He does not hide truth from us but has given us the Bible so that we, too, can know "the truth."

If Jesus is the essence of truth, is it any wonder that He condemns Satan by saying, "…there is no truth in him. When he lies, it is consistent with his character; for he is a liar and the father of lies" (John 8:44). What a complete contrast to Jesus! Just as truth originates from Jesus, lies originate from Satan.

Lying is so prevalent in our society that even Christians may take it lightly, but God does not. When we begin to understand that lying aligns us with Satan and his goals, it is frightening. Think about the kinds of lies that are part of our day-to-day existence.

There are the little white lies and bending of the truth that, in the strange twist of human reasoning, are often not considered actual lies. There are the outright lies told to protect ourselves or to gain something we think we cannot gain by being truthful. We purposely mislead someone. We make promises with little concern for keeping them. We lie to ourselves regarding the intent of our actions. We participate in lying by keeping silent rather than countering the lies we hear. On and on it goes.

Each and every lie originates from Satan—in whose ballpark I do not want to be playing, but where I have spent too much time as part of the lying team. Satan wants each of us on that team because it destroys our integrity as witnesses of Jesus Christ.

How do we get off the lying team? Agur's prayer is an excellent starting place, for it is surely a prayer of wisdom. It is also a prayer that recognizes the danger and ease of lying, for Agur begs God for help in always telling the truth. How often do we beg anyone for anything? Agur was not ashamed to beg for help, and his prayer shows how serious he was in his quest to be truthful.

When we become committed to telling the truth, the Holy Spirit will make us aware of approaching danger when we are headed toward the lying zone. We will be given adequate warning to avoid lying. And when we ignore the warning and lie, we need to confess it quickly—both to God and to the person to whom we lied. For sure, correcting mistruths is an uncomfortable and humbling experience, but it protects our Christian witness, honors God, and is an effective deterrent against future lying.

Agur's prayer leads to control of our mouth, our thoughts, and our actions. As these are brought under "the truth" of Christ's control, we will be known as people of integrity. Honesty, coupled with love for others, will allow people to rely on us, trust us, and be refreshed by our presence, for we will reflect our Father's nature and values.

"O God, I beg…help me never to tell a lie."

Well-Placed Confidence

Ecclesiastes 1–5; 2 Thessalonians 2–3

"For you know that you ought to follow our example" (2 Thess. 3:7). Paul's words to the Thessalonian church make one pause and think. How often would we urge others, much less an entire *group* of people, to look to us as examples of the way they should conduct themselves?

In this passage, as well as in other passages such as First Corinthians 4:16, Paul was confident that his life as a Christian would hold up under scrutiny. What are some of the areas in which Paul needed to be confident before he could make such a bold statement?

Paul was confident of *his beliefs.* Paul was a follower who believed passionately in Jesus Christ, but during the first part of his life he believed just as passionately that Jesus was not the Savior promised by the prophets in Scripture. He hung on to that belief until his life was completely transformed by his extraordinary encounter with Jesus. From the moment Paul saw the bright light and heard the voice of Jesus, he became a follower, more fervent in his belief than he had been in his disbelief (Acts 9).

Paul was confident of *his knowledge of God.* From his earliest days, he had been taught by some of the most knowledgeable and respected scholars of Hebrew Scripture. He was well-grounded in what the Old Testament texts said about God. And Paul knew the Jesus of our New Testament in a most intimate way, for he said his knowledge of Jesus "came by a direct revelation from Jesus Christ himself. No one else taught me" (Gal. 1:12). How could you get a better teacher than Jesus Christ Himself?

Paul was confident that *his life was aligned with godly principles.* Regardless of the circumstance, regardless of the time or the season, regardless of the place, Paul was confident others would see that his behavior, words, plans for the future, love for them, and love for God honored his Lord (Phil. 1:20).

Paul was confident that *he was not perfect.* As he so aptly put it, "I don't understand myself at all, for I really want to do what is right, but I don't do it. Instead, I do the very thing I hate" (Rom. 7:15). Paul knew that although he sometimes did the things he hated, he served as a good example of a repentant heart receiving God's forgiveness when he confessed those sins, resolutely turned away from them, and moved forward to serve God (Rom. 6:12-13).

Paul was confident of the *consistency of his life*. Although Paul's obedience to God may not have been perfect, his desire to please God was unwavering; and he was willing to commit his time, effort, and life to that end (1 Cor. 9:24-27).

Paul was confident of the *source of power in his life*. We know living an obedient, consistent, unselfish life takes a level of perseverance and discipline that does not come naturally to us. Paul knew it, too, and said his life could only be an example to others because "I can do everything with the help of Christ who gives me the strength I need" (Phil. 4:13).

Paul was confident of *his purpose in life*. Paul's life was forever changed by his encounter with Jesus Christ, and he wanted others to experience the same belief in and love for Christ. We know Paul experienced times of inconceivable suffering as well as times of incredible joy, but nothing deterred him from his purpose in life. What an example Paul has provided for each of us!

How would we rate our own confidence level regarding someone following our Christian example? It is a question worthy of our honest assessment.

WEEK 112

The Day Death Came

Ecclesiastes 6–9; Psalms 95–96; 1 Timothy 1

"None of us can hold back our spirit from departing. None of us has the power to prevent the day of our death. There is no escaping that obligation, that dark battle. And in the face of death, wickedness will certainly not rescue those who practice it" (Eccl. 8:8).

We know these words of Solomon to be true. There is no escaping the day of our death. But there is a way to assure that on that day we will indeed be rescued. Unlike those who practice wickedness with no hope of rescue, First Timothy 1:15 emphatically says, "This is a true saying, and everyone should believe it: Christ Jesus came into the world to save sinners."

Two true stories follow. These are the stories of two people who, though they had sinned, believed that Jesus Christ came into the world to save them. That belief profoundly affected the day of their deaths.

Brenda was a close friend during my teen years. Brenda's father and mother had been missionaries in Africa. When their family returned to the United States, Brenda's father became the pastor of the church I attended. About the same time that Brenda left for college, her father became director of mission work for the denomination. Brenda's father traveled often to the various mission ministries and while on a trip in Africa was killed in a car accident. He was buried in Sierra Leone, where he and his wife had ministered together.

After college, Brenda married, and soon after the birth of her second child, she was diagnosed with a cancerous brain tumor. Her last days were spent in a coma-like state. Brenda's husband and mother stayed by her bedside during those last days of her life—except to care for Brenda's young children. They were there when the unexpected happened. Brenda became conscious, looked into the distance, smiled, and said, "Daddy!" In the next instant her spirit departed this world. In the face of death, Brenda was rescued.

Sonia was a dear friend during my adult years. We met when I read a newspaper article about Sonia's twenty-year battle with cancer and her ministry to others with cancer. Sonia was a gifted speaker who spoke often to groups about her Lord, she was a popular Bible teacher with the female inmates at our county prison, and she went to the streets ministering to prostitutes. Sonia reached out to every hurting soul who crossed her path, and she never wavered from believing that Jesus Christ was the answer for all the wounded people she met. During the years I knew Sonia, her life was marked by pain and loss from the cancer that was relentlessly destroying her body, but she never lost hope in her Savior. In her weakness and pain, Jesus made her an effective witness to His love and mercy.

During Sonia's last few months on earth, her body became weaker, and her pain became almost unbearable. On the night of her death, tears streamed down Sonia's face as she tried to rest and cope with the pain. Finally she fell asleep for a few hours. Her family was there when the unexpected happened. Sonia awoke singing—yes, singing—a hymn of praise to her beloved Savior, took another breath, and in the next instant her spirit departed this world. In the face of death, Sonia was rescued.

Both of my friends experienced great suffering during their lifetimes, for they were, as we all are, bound by the forces of the "dark battle" of this life. But both of my friends accepted the salvation given to them by Jesus Christ, served Him wholeheartedly, and died gloriously rescued by Jesus. When they faced the final enemy of death, they knew the reality of Paul's words to Timothy that God is "our Savior" and "Jesus Christ our hope" (1 Tim. 1:1).

Solomon came to this conclusion regarding the day of our death: "Even though a person sins a hundred times…I know that those who fear God will be better off" (Eccl. 8:12). And to that we say, "Thank You, Lord Jesus, and amen!"

WEEK 113

Pleading on Behalf of Another

Ecclesiastes 10–12; Song of Songs 1–2; 1 Timothy 2–3

"I urge you, first of all, to pray for all people. As you make your requests, plead for God's mercy upon them, and give thanks" (1 Tim. 2:1). This verse calls us to a worthy undertaking—praying for others. With only a few words, Paul outlined four building blocks for this type of prayer: "pray for all people," "make your requests," "plead for God's mercy," and "give thanks." Let's take a closer look.

Paul began by *urging* us to make our requests for all people. Paul wasn't making a casual suggestion; he felt an urgent importance for this type of prayer. Our awareness of the many problems faced by family, friends, acquaintances, and even those we do not know personally points to this truth. There is no shortage of people needing a touch from God.

Knowing this, Paul said to pray "for all people." To follow this command is to give a great gift to others. But the truth is that this gift is not without cost, for as we earnestly pray for others, there is a physical, emotional, and spiritual commitment. Knowing Paul's passion and prayers for the new believers of his time, it is not hard to imagine that he intimately understood the strength that is used up in intense prayer.

As needs stack up, making our requests for others on a regular basis almost guarantees we will be vulnerable to times of feeling overwhelmed. We may stagger under the burden of others' pain, suffering, or poor decisions. We may feel that we cannot bear hearing about one more terrible situation for which prayer is needed. We may feel disappointed with the answers to our prayers or disillusioned when we feel God is not responding to our requests. We may wonder why so much suffering is allowed. If we are honest with ourselves and with God, we may have experienced all of these feelings—and more—during our times of prayer for others.

But honesty is the perfect place to begin our prayers. God already knows how we feel, so why try to hide the truth from ourselves? As we pray, let us do so with the same honesty we find in prayers throughout Scripture, sharing our real emotions with God. But acknowledging our raw emotions regarding our prayer requests does not mean we need to wallow in them.

Paul explained how we can move forward when praying for someone who faces extreme difficulties. He said to "plead for God's mercy upon them." We don't have to come to God with the perfect words. In these deeply personal prayers, it is God's mercy for which we plead on behalf of another person who is weighed down by life.

God's mercy may not look like or take the form we think it should. We may not even recognize it when it appears. But we can be sure that God's mercy flows from His love for each of us. And when that truth is firmly settled in our minds, we will be able to follow Paul's last guideline and "give thanks," for we will know—truly know—that no matter how our prayer is answered, it will be answered with God's mercy and His love.

Pleading with God for others is hard work, but we are not without hope or triumph. Paul has also said, "I can do everything with the help of Christ who gives me the strength I need" (Phil. 4:13). Our ability to intercede in prayer, to cope, to have hope for situations that seem hopeless, comes from Christ's strength, not ours. And if we come to the place where we are having trouble hanging on to that strength, we have the promise that "the Holy Spirit prays for us" (Rom. 8:26).

When our requests seem insurmountable, God is there extending mercy, love, and hope.

WEEK 114

Wait...No, Come...No, Wait...

Song of Songs 3–6; Psalms 97–98; 1 Timothy 4

"For the Lord is coming to judge the earth. He will judge the world with justice, and the nations with fairness" (Ps. 98:9).

The psalmists, the prophets, the apostles, and other believers of the Old and New Testament looked with optimism and hope for the coming of the Lord.

More than ever, I can relate to their longing. I long for our world to be ruled by Christ's justice rather than by the sin that currently affects so much of what we know. As hatred among different groups escalates, as violence and crime ooze into all segments of society, as pain and suffering increase, as worldwide financial and political systems crack and crumble, and as the consequences of sin pile up, my heart cries out, "How long, Jesus, how long until Your perfect justice and love rule over us?" I want to be rescued from the mess sin has caused. I want to go back to the joy of God's original plan for us and have hope, peace, and love govern our world and our lives.

And yet, I am conflicted; for as much as I want sin's power to be broken in this world and its effects to be removed, I know there are people who are rejecting Jesus. And with that thought my heart cries out, "Not yet, Lord! First, help them to believe in You as their Savior." And not only believe, but to follow.

How well I remember my own reaction years ago to discussions of Jesus' return to earth. Those discussions used to scare me rather than bring me peace because I knew my life and loyalty were more aligned to what I wanted than to what God wanted. I was a believer but a halfhearted follower.

Those halfhearted days are over, and now I long for Christ to come just as I long for Christ to wait because of those not ready for His return. Maybe you share those feelings, too. If so, together we can trust that God in His mercy and love will choose the perfect time to set this earth and its people free.

Until then, we can pray that those who reject Jesus will come into His family, that those who are lax about their walk with God will grow in their commitment, and that all of us will grow in our love for Him and others until it is time for all the earth to join together in the great celebration of the Lord's return. On that day, "the sea and everything in it [will] shout his praise, the earth and all living things [will] join in, the rivers [will] clap their hands in glee! The hills [will] sing out their songs of joy before the Lord" (Ps. 98:7-8).

It is going to be a loud, melodious song of joy. The King is coming!

WEEK 115

"At Home" Behavior

Song of Songs 7–8; Isaiah 1; Psalms 99–101; 1 Timothy 5

"For the Lord is good. His unfailing love continues forever, and his faithfulness continues to each generation" (Ps. 100:5). The words "each generation" may make us think of the *next* generation…and beyond: our children, our grandchildren, possibly even our great-grandchildren, as well as other people's children. Many times the thought of these lives brings us joy. But as troubling news continues to roll in, we may find ourselves wondering, *What is this world going to be like for the next generation?*

It is a reasonable question and probably has been asked by many generations before us. The frequent reminders of the numerous problems confronting our nation and our world is enough to make us feel despair. The far-reaching changes we have seen in our generation may lead us to fear for the future of the next generation. And going back more than one generation can make the changes more distinct and disturbing. Even though we may push our concerns aside, nagging questions can return quickly when we look at those who are precious to us and depend upon us for protection from harm.

Followers of Jesus recognize that no amount of wealth or power can insulate those we love from the ills of this world. It is God who is our help and deliverer. So how do we help ensure that those for whom we have responsibility go forward in their lives with the trust in God needed to overcome the issues of their own generation? David suggested one important action to take in accomplishing this goal. He stated, "I will be careful to live a blameless life…I will lead a life of integrity in my own home" (Ps. 101:2).

It makes perfect sense. If there is ever a place where the next generation can receive the training and examples needed to survive and to stand out as people of God in a world entangled in chaos, it is in our own homes. Living a life of integrity in our own homes is a worthy goal but not an easy one, for it is at home where our real values, truest actions and reactions, and most authentic beliefs are on display. How are our lives being evaluated by those who have shared our home?

Maybe we have already decided that, with God's help, we will "live a blameless life, a life of integrity," and those who know us best would attest to our desire and example. Maybe we have made that choice but failed, as David did. David's failure to carry out his goal to live such a life led to serious consequences for his family. But like David, we can return to a life of integrity as we pray for God's help. Maybe we haven't given much thought to the extent of our influence in our own home and haven't made living a life of integrity a priority. If so, may the Holy Spirit help us to realize our influence, give us the desire to lead blameless lives of integrity, and guide us in how to reclaim the times when we have not.

The impact of our "at home" behavior and attitudes on the next generation is enormous. But there is an influence far greater and more powerful than our own, and that is God's. There is hope for future generations because "the Lord is good. His unfailing love continues forever, and his faithfulness continues to each generation" (Ps. 100:5). We may fail; God will not.

God's goodness, His never-ending love, and His faithfulness continue to each generation and make all the difference in the world for those who trust in and obey Him.

By our influence we can give the next generation the tools of faith in the Lord Jesus Christ. By God's word, He will do the rest.

WEEK 116

Out of Focus

Isaiah 2–6; 1 Timothy 6; 2 Timothy 1

"But you never think about the Lord or notice what he is doing" (Isa. 5:12). This verse brings to mind an elderly friend whose strength has deteriorated to the point where she is incapable of doing many things for herself. Blessed with good health for most of her eighty-four years, this change has shaken her faith.

Losing the ability to be independent would be a difficult transition for almost anyone, but my friend firmly believes God has abandoned her. She is so focused on her losses that she no longer notices what God is doing for her.

God is far from uncaring about my friend's situation. Even though she was an only child and never married, she is not alone, for God has sent loyal friends who work many hours to ensure her safety, dignity, and comfort.

When I hear my friend say that God has abandoned her, one part of me grieves because no amount of discussion helps her notice what God is doing. But another part smiles, because in spite of her not noticing, God continues in His loving way to provide for her needs.

And I smile because I realize how I am sometimes like my friend, failing to notice the things in the background that God is quietly taking care of for me. It is a fault most of us share. Whether it is times of ease lulling us into complacency or the many demands of life pressing hard upon us, we stop noticing what God is doing on our behalf.

It may be that we are prone to this obliviousness because we are not thinking about God. Isaiah 5:12 gives as much importance to our thoughts of God as it does to our awareness of what He is doing. This makes sense, for we become attuned to a person when we allow our thoughts to dwell on him or her. Our thoughts may be positive or negative ones, but either way, focusing on someone allows that person to have influence over us.

It is the same when we focus our thoughts on God. Without that focus, we miss what God is doing in our lives, and that can easily lead to fear, anger, self-absorption, ungratefulness, or indifference. Eventually, we become accustomed to not seeing what God is doing for us, and our thoughts of Him may become negative as we associate God with all we see wrong in our lives...while missing what is good.

But God's influence over us *is* a good thing. If we do not dwell on what we perceive as God's injustice to us but think instead of all His attributes, it is likely that we will become open to His goodness and glory. The seraphim know God's goodness firsthand, and their words ring out this truth as they stand in the Lord's presence exclaiming, "Holy, holy, holy is the Lord Almighty! The whole earth is filled with his glory!" (Isa. 6:3).

God's glory flows over the entire earth. Don't miss what He is doing.

Week 117

Exceptional Service

Isaiah 7–11; Psalm 102; 2 Timothy 2

There are many well-known people in the Bible who called themselves, or were called, "servant of the Lord." Even a short list is impressive. There is the patriarch Abraham, the great leaders Moses and Joshua, the prophet Samuel, King David, the prophet Isaiah, Mary the mother of Jesus, and the apostle Paul (Gen. 26:24; Deut. 34:5; Josh. 24:29; 1 Sam. 3:10; Luke 1:69; Isa. 20:3; Luke 1:38; Rom. 1:1).

We hear the word "servant" and think of a number of traits: obedience, attentiveness to the master's priorities rather than to the servant's, and a passive demeanor. As each of these people's stories unfolded in Scripture, we see how they were indeed focused on their Master's priorities rather than on their own. But there certainly wasn't anything passive about any of their personalities.

With such distinct personalities, how did each of these individuals grow into his or her role of "servant of the Lord"? Paul, noted for his strong personality, gave a few guidelines. He wrote, "The Lord's servants must not quarrel but must be kind to everyone. They must be able to teach effectively and be patient with difficult people" (2 Tim. 2:24). These are practical guidelines—but not easy ones.

First guideline: Don't "quarrel but be kind to everyone." Oh my... does that mean be kind to the person who was rude or the person spoiling for a fight as we happen to come into their line of fire? Should we be kind to the person who makes us feel as though we can't do anything right? What about when we are the person feeling rude, critical, quarrelsome, or out of patience? Yes, hard as it may be, it means all that. As Solomon said in his wisdom, "A gentle answer turns away wrath, but harsh words stir up anger" (Prov. 15:1).

Carrying out this guideline will require quite a bit of practice. Along with practicing, we will need to shore up our ability to be kind to everyone with prayer. And we'll undoubtedly need to be humble enough to apologize for the times when we have been the troublemaker or when we have met quarrelsome words with our own unkind reactions. There is no doubt that working toward this first guideline is difficult and certainly the opposite of our natural reactions. But there's still more to accomplish if we desire to be servants of the Lord.

Second guideline: "Teach effectively." To teach effectively, instructors must know their subject matter. The knowledge the servant of the Lord needs is found in the Bible. We need to read *and* study our Textbook. Of course, the most effective teaching comes about when our knowledge, words, and actions mesh. Time restraints and difficult circumstances make this another guideline not easily accomplished. More practice, more prayer, more humility needed.

Final guideline in this verse: "Be patient with difficult people." By this point, we may find ourselves looking for exceptions or loopholes to these guidelines. Are we actually supposed to be patient with the person whose opinions or habits drive us to distraction? Be patient with the person who continues to seek our advice but never follows it? Be patient with those quarrelsome people we have to be kind to in the first guideline? You bet. More practice, more prayer, more humility needed.

Paul's list in Second Timothy 2:24 of the characteristics of a servant of God is not exhaustive—perhaps just exhausting! That is, until enough prayer makes it our desire and paves the way forward, enough humility makes us cautious of our words and actions, and enough practice makes it natural.

Being a true servant of the Lord is an exceptional thing in this world and takes exceptional dedication. How exceptional are you willing to be?

WEEK 118

The Power, The Plan, The Promise

Isaiah 12–16; 2 Timothy 3–4

"I have a plan for the whole earth, for my mighty power reaches throughout the world" (Isa. 14:26). When God gave this message to Isaiah, large areas of the world were embroiled in war against the powerful and exceptionally cruel Assyrian army. Wherever they marched, intense suffering was inflicted upon the people.

This time of despair was not unique in history. Financial, moral, and social breakdowns; horrific natural calamities; despotic governments; deadly epidemics; and devastating warfare continue. So it has been for the days that have come before our time and so it is for the times in which we live. It would be easy to despair and be overcome by fear.

Except we have one immensely important thing to cling to during periods of upheaval—the steadiness of God. God has "a plan for the whole earth," and He has the mighty power to realize His plan. Nothing—

no matter how evil, widespread, or insidious—has the power of God. Despite ongoing calamity, God has a plan with a magnificent ending.

It is surely comforting to know there is such a plan because these in-between times would be unsettling if we did not have God's promises to give us hope. Isaiah 14:26 is one of those promises. There is hope for us because there is a time coming when God's plan to extinguish evil and its consequences will be fully implemented. At that time a new earth, free of the evil that causes so much anguish and calamity, will be called into existence (Rev. 21).

Since God has a plan to destroy evil, we may wonder why He doesn't implement it. The times of Isaiah help us address this question, for they show us God's plan to destroy evil is delayed by His mercy, patience, and love.

We see this delay played out in different ways in the northern and southern kingdoms of Israel. God withholds His judgment of sin in both nations, waiting patiently for those who had rejected Him to turn from evil. The northern kingdom wasted this valuable time to pursue everything but God. In spite of God's love for the people, the time finally came for judgment, and the Assyrians moved in to destroy the northern nation. This painful plan to restore goodness was not implemented without ample warning to those who were sinning.

In contrast to the northern kingdom, the people of the southern kingdom took this time of mercy from God to listen to His warning, turn from their sin, and receive His forgiveness. God in turn rescued them from annihilation when a deadly epidemic destroyed the Assyrian army as they prepared to attack.

That, of course, is ancient history. But although times change, the basic story of the world does not, nor does God's plan for the world. God has not made a secret of the things to come for those who follow Him and for those who do not. Followers of Jesus Christ need not fear what is happening today or what is to come in our world—for we have the hope of Heaven. But knowledge of our own eternal rescue should do more than merely comfort us, for we have family, friends, and acquaintances who need to understand God's plan for them and for the world. Paul summed it up when he told Timothy we must "work at bringing others to Christ," for God "does not want anyone to perish"—and neither should we (2 Tim. 4:5; 2 Pet. 3:9).

God has the power. God has the plan. God has given us His promise. And therein lies our hope. In a deeply troubled world, share the hope of Christ.

WEEK 119

A to Z

Isaiah 17–21; Psalm 103; Titus 1

"Praise the Lord, I tell myself; with my whole heart, I will praise his holy name. Praise the Lord, I tell myself, and never forget the good things he does for me" (Ps. 103:1-2).

Psalm 103 is a magnificent psalm of praise, but that is not the only thing that struck me as I read it. What stood out to me is that David "tells" himself to "praise the Lord." We do not know the specific circumstances of David's life at the time this psalm was written, but based on the words he chose, we can probably conclude that thoughts of praise were not hovering near the surface ready to be expressed.

Sometimes our praise to the Lord is spontaneous, and sometimes it is not. In this case, it seems as if David had to make a conscious decision to praise God. He pulled his thoughts from the situations he was dealing with and told himself to praise God with his "whole heart," remembering "the good things" God was doing for him. And by directing and disciplining his thoughts, David came up with an impressive list of things for which to be thankful.

In the next twenty verses of this psalm, David recounted twenty-three different reasons to praise God. His list included specific points of who God is, what God does, and what God does not do. You can almost feel David's gusto building as, one by one, he recalled these blessings and characteristics of God. Before long, his enthusiasm caused him to repeat a few points that were too remarkable to be adequately expressed by his first attempt.

David begins Psalm 103 with the need to jump-start his praise to God by telling himself to just do it, but he ends the psalm with a triumphant call to everything that God has created in Heaven and earth to join him in praise to the Lord. His final words of the psalm indicate that he no longer needed to be persuaded to praise God with his whole heart. David's emotions followed his thoughts, and he remembered twenty-three reasons to celebrate!

Perhaps we are like David at the beginning of this psalm, and our truest feeling at the moment is not praise for God. Perhaps we are feeling overwrought, overwhelmed, or overcome. But David had the smart answer to the burdens we carry when he told himself to praise the Lord with his whole heart and then immediately followed through on his own advice by listing the good things God had done for him. God has done the same things for us, so David's reasons to rejoice can be ours, too. And like David, as we thoughtfully and deliberately go through his list, we may soon be feeling much better and more thankful.

David listed twenty-three profound points, and sometimes we may share those thoughts. On other days, our list of things for which to be thankful may contain items that seem ordinary in comparison to David's, but that doesn't mean they are unimportant.

Here is a simple way to recall some good things. Starting with A, name something good God has done for you or given you. One day it could be God's acceptance and the next day it could be apples. Keep on going until you get to Z.

Twenty-six reasons to be thankful. It is an easy way to tell ourselves to praise the Lord.

WEEK 120

A Productive Life

Isaiah 22–26; Titus 2–3

The Bible is packed with practical advice about how to live life successfully. Paul's letter to his close friend, Titus, contained one of these valuable guidelines. "For our people should not have unproductive lives. They must learn to do good by helping others who have urgent needs" (Titus 3:14).

In today's world, the productivity of a person's life is often measured by the amount of wealth and possessions accumulated. Paul's definition and measurement of a successful, productive life were completely different. He believed lives were productive when people spent their time and resources "learning to do good" for others.

Notice that Paul believed this was a learned response, not a natural one, for he undoubtedly recognized our tendency toward focusing on our own desires. While we may know people who naturally seem to do good to others, it is likely their behavior is not the result of a core personality trait but from much practice in giving up their own plans so that they can help others.

While the shift from being self-absorbed starts with learning to do good, it deepens as we begin "helping others who have urgent needs." This makes sense. To help people with "urgent needs" is to do so with no expectation of repayment. And when no repayment is expected, compassion and kindness guide our behavior.

This world certainly does not lack those with urgent needs. We often think urgent needs—such as physical needs for food, clean water, adequate shelter, warm clothing, and medical care—are met through monetary help. While this is true, there are many urgent needs that are met in other ways. Emotional needs for friendship, acceptance, encouragement, respect, and comfort are met as we give our time and companionship. And it is often time and companionship that help to meet spiritual needs, such as guidance on how to begin and grow in a relationship with Jesus, reminders of God's greatness, and prayer for others.

Urgent needs often trigger powerful emotions for both the giver and the receiver. As we become people who practice doing good to help others, it is easy to become overwhelmed by the enormity of the needs and discouraged as we wonder if what we are able to do makes much difference. As these thoughts arise, we need to remind ourselves that we are not in this alone. We can ask God for wisdom to know what we are to do and what should be left to others, for strength, and for more people to be willing to live productive lives by helping others.

Being on the receiving end of help can bring a different set of emotions. While it would be rare for any person to travel through life without experiencing urgent physical, emotional, or spiritual needs, we may feel embarrassed when these situations occur in our lives. May God help us to remember that it may be our need that allows another to "learn to do good."

And isn't it true that having an urgent need in one area of our life does not preclude us from helping others in another area? You may have heard stories of people who, while helping someone in need, were also renewed by what they had received in return.

This is not surprising, for aren't we often amazed by how God works in our lives? We think we are giving to another and we are also receiving. We think we are receiving and we are also giving. Yes, there may be times of discouragement associated with urgent needs, but there are also times of joy and thankfulness from seeing God at work through us and for us.

Once again, the Bible's values stand in contrast to the values of our society, for it is not what we accumulate but what we give that makes us productive. By God's standards, are we living productive lives?

WEEK 121

What a Voice!

Isaiah 27–30; Psalm 104; Philemon; Hebrews 1

Words. We are surrounded by words and the voices behind those words; some of those voices hold our attention while many merely fade into the background.

Think about the voices that make up our lives. Hearing the voice of someone we love can instantly bring joy, a sense of belonging and comfort...or it may bring pain and despair. Hearing the voice of authority can pull us up short, get us busy, keep us steady, and bring order out of chaos...or anger us and cause us to rebel. Hearing the voice of someone we respect can cause us to reconsider a viewpoint or course of action and challenge us to better things...or bring a sense of guilt or shame.

Have you thought much about the actual voice of God and what this voice means to us? If our own voices reflect our thoughts, desires, intentions, and emotions, then does the voice of God not reflect these same things and so much more? But to truly understand the voice of God, we need to understand all that God is—yet what human has that capacity? Even our best attempts at understanding fall short, but Scripture provides many opportunities to learn about the voice of God.

Psalm 104:7-9 speaks of the absolute power of God's voice. "At the sound of your rebuke, the water fled.... Mountains rose and valleys sank to the levels you decreed. Then you set a firm boundary for the seas, so they would never again cover the earth." Think about the sound of a voice that carries enough power to be the creating force of the earth, as "mountains rose and valleys sank." Think about the authority behind a voice that can cause the elements of nature to obey as "the water fled" and a "firm boundary" was "set for the seas." If we aren't astounded and amazed and humbled, we ought to be.

Hebrews tells of the total domination of Jesus' voice: "He sustains the universe by the mighty power of his command" (Heb. 1:3). By only the sound of "his command," our world and the entire universe were not only created but are continually controlled and sustained. Think about a

God of such supreme power and control that His voice alone maintains order and harmony throughout the vast universe. If we aren't astounded and amazed and humbled, we ought to be.

But Isaiah tells us of the enormous difference in God's voice when He communicates with us rather than the universe. When the universe hears God's voice of command, it does not have the option of deciding if it will listen and obey. It is commanded to do so and does. But when God speaks to us, He gives us the choice to listen to His voice or to ignore it. And too often we choose to ignore God's voice of love, treating it as one of those background voices that never fully capture our attention.

But we have fully captured God's attention. In a voice of infinite patience, God tells us repeatedly what He wants us to understand: "So the Lord will spell out his message for them again, repeating it over and over, a line at a time, in very simple words" (Isa. 28:13).

Do you hear God's voice as He spells out His simple messages "a line at a time"? Through Bible reading and through prayer, we hear God saying again and again, "Come and talk with Me. I love you. Believe in Me and be saved. I am merciful and will forgive you if you ask. Love Me enough to obey. I am worthy of your trust. I go to prepare a place for you so that you can be with Me always." Think hard about these simple messages from God. If we aren't listening to God's voice, we are cheating ourselves out of the most fulfilling life conceivable.

And yet too often that is the case. Isaiah 28:13 continues, saying of the ancient Israelites: "yet they will stumble over this simple, straight-forward message." The Israelites stumbled over the "straight-forward message" and suffered because of it, and so do we, time and time again. There are plenty of reasons why this occurs, and each individual must honestly assess the things that keep us from living by the simple, straight-forward message of God.

Regardless of our response to His messages, we are assured that God desires—more than anyone else—to keep us from the suffering that comes with ignoring His voice. "But the Lord still waits for you to come to him so he can show you his love and compassion. For the Lord is a faithful God…He will be gracious if you ask for help. …He will respond instantly to the sound of your cries" (Isa. 30:18-19). What a message of love, forgiveness, and mercy.

There are many things to *learn* about God by listening to His voice. There are many things to *gain* by listening to God's voice. It is the voice above all others. Has it captured your attention?

WEEK 122

Important to God

Isaiah 31–35; Psalm 105; Hebrews 2

How do you picture God? Do you see His magnificence, power, and knowledge as the Creator who designed the far-flung universes and their countless planets and features? Do you think of God as the dynamic force who holds together all that has been, now is, and will be? No description can completely capture the greatness of God, but we can glimpse it in His handiwork at the uppermost levels of all that exists.

And yet this is only one side of God, for He is also God of the smallest details that make up the day-to-day concerns and activities of His creation. This may sound like foolishness to people who view God as being uninvolved and aloof from His creation, but that is not how God describes Himself.

God said of Himself, "Search the book of the Lord, and see what he will do. He will not miss a single detail" (Isa. 34:16). This is not the first time in the Bible that God has declared He is involved in the smallest details of all that exists. And now God promises that "He will not miss a single detail"—not one. This is God at an intimate, personal level.

Isaiah 34 is a chapter concerning God's fury against sin. In it, we see the power of God as His patience finally comes to an end, and the consequences are catastrophic. But in the midst of this sweeping condemnation, we see God's attention to detail as He promises to repopulate the destroyed land with specific birds and animals.

In its complete contrast to the destruction described in the first half of the chapter, God's care and concern for repopulating the land with a handful of animals is all the more striking. Can we doubt that God is involved with and cares about *us* down to the smallest detail of our lives, if He makes promises to the wild creatures and their mates? If they have God's attention and promises, how much more so will we?

There are times in each of our lives when, if we are attuned to God's presence, we will be aware of His attention to the details of our lives. Sometimes this detailed care is easy to recognize as it occurs, but it often takes time for us to put all the pieces together. But when we finally do recognize God's involvement in the details of our lives, it helps us understand how tenderly we are loved by God. These times deepen our awareness of God's presence and reenergize our faith.

But there are many times when we aren't able to sense God's involvement at a detailed level in our lives. Just as the birds and animals did not completely understand or know the full scope of God's detailed interaction on their behalf, so it is with us. And our not knowing may cause us sometimes to feel as if God has forgotten us. But He has not. God is so confident that He will keep His specific promises that He urges us to "Search the book of the Lord, and see what he will do" (Isa. 34:16). Go ahead and take up the challenge!

God is never disinterested in or uncaring about our family, our loved ones, or us. He is God with us, and He will do what He has promised. Count on it...and Him.

WEEK 123

Changing Circumstances

Isaiah 36–40; Hebrews 3–4

You have probably heard the saying, "Prayer changes things." Many times when people quote this, they believe that the "things" being changed are not the circumstances being prayed about but the attitudes and the behavior of the person who is doing the praying. And that is undoubtedly true.

But sometimes the "things" being changed include the circumstances. Sometimes our prayers actually do change the course of events. We read of such a case in Isaiah 38.

The king of Judah, Hezekiah, was going to die. Although he was a young man, he "became deathly ill, and the prophet Isaiah went to visit him. He gave the king this message: 'This is what the Lord says: "Set your affairs in order, for you are going to die. You will not recover from this illness"'" (Isa. 38:1). God had spoken.

"When Hezekiah heard this, he turned his face to the wall... broke down and wept bitterly" (Isa. 38:2-3). This announcement was devastating to him, as it would be to most of us. Of all the hard times Hezekiah had faced in his life, this was the hardest. As in the past when he faced hard times, Hezekiah spoke honestly to God, pleading for his life. "Remember, O Lord, how I have always tried to be faithful to you and do what is pleasing in your sight" (Isa. 38:2-3).

Hezekiah had a history of talking with God, and God had a history of listening. God saw Hezekiah's despair, and He heard Hezekiah's plea. In many instances like the one Hezekiah faced that day, God does not change our circumstances but answers our pleas by fulfilling His promise in Psalm 34:18 to be close to us in our despair.

But on that day, God offered Hezekiah something more than His comfort and help in accepting the difficult situation. On that day, God not only changed what was going to happen, but He responded so swiftly that Isaiah barely had time to depart from Hezekiah's rooms in the palace before God called him back. "Before Isaiah had left the middle courtyard, this message came to him from the Lord: 'Go back to Hezekiah. Tell him, "This is what the Lord, the God of your ancestor David, says: I have heard your prayer and seen your tears. I will heal you, and three days from now you will get out of bed and go to the Temple of the Lord. I will add fifteen years to your life, and I will rescue you and this city from the king of Assyria"'" (2 Kings 20:4-6; Isa. 38:5-6). God had changed His mind.

In three days, Hezekiah would move from a terminal illness to renewed health. Not only was he going to live, but for good measure, God was going to give him an additional gift—a gift for which Hezekiah, in his despair over his own predicted death, had not even asked. Like Hezekiah, Jerusalem was also going to be given another chance at life. God was going to rescue this besieged city from the mighty Assyrian army. God was going to do far more than Hezekiah had hoped or asked.

As is often the case, though, Hezekiah had a part to play in God's plan. His recovery and answer to his prayer were dependent on his obedience to God's direction. In this instance, an ointment of figs was to be made and spread over Hezekiah's boil before he would recover. Now we may wonder, why figs? And why wait three days? But why not? God is not limited by time or by the method He chooses to use in touching our lives. Rather, it is we who may limit God by our lack of trust and obedience. But even then, God understands our weaknesses.

Hezekiah is the perfect example of some of these weaknesses. He was lightning-quick to believe Isaiah's message that he was going to die; no other proof was needed. But when he was told that God had heard his prayer, would heal him within three days if he applied the fig ointment, and was giving him fifteen more years of life—plus victory over his enemies, Hezekiah asked for proof. "What sign will prove that I will go to the Temple of the Lord three days from now?" (Isa. 38:22).

Do you find it strange that Hezekiah needed a sign that God would keep His promise? After all, in three days he would know. But those three days of continuing suffering may have been more than Hezekiah's faith could handle at that moment. It is easy to imagine that many people would have been getting irritated with Hezekiah by this time, but God was not. Instead of irritation, God responds to Hezekiah with spectacular proof. "'And this is the sign that the Lord will give you to prove he will do as he promised: I will cause the sun's shadow to move ten steps backward on the sundial of Ahaz!' So the shadow on the sundial moved backward ten steps" (Isa. 38:7-8). Hezekiah had his proof.

God knows us so well. When circumstances have wearied us and broken our spirit and health, "He gives power to those who are tired and worn out; he offers strength to the weak" (Isa. 40:29). When our faith is weak, God understands our frailties, for "…no one can measure the depths of his understanding" (Isa. 40:28). When we wonder if we can be honest with God about our crushing disappointments and sorrows, we are reminded of His tenderness toward us: "Comfort, comfort my people" (Isa. 40:1).

Let us lay to rest any belief that prayer only changes the way we think, act, or feel but can never change our circumstances. *Prayer* is too powerful to be limited to one type of response from God. *God* is too powerful to be limited to one type of response to prayer.

WEEK 124

Our Choice

Isaiah 41–44; Psalm 106; Hebrews 5–6

"The people refused to enter the pleasant land, for they wouldn't believe his promise to care for them. Instead, they grumbled in their tents and refused to obey the Lord" (Ps. 106:24-25).

Oh, those Israelites! They were stubborn to the point of their own harm. God wanted to bring them into their own country, a wonderful place. All they needed to do was obey Him, so they could be prepared to govern their new homeland, but "they refused to enter the pleasant land," and they "refused to obey the Lord." It was not that they were confused about how to enter or obey—they simply refused to do so.

They were also shortsighted, apparently having learned little from such experiences as God's amazing rescue of them from the powerful Egyptians and His care for them as they wandered in the desert. In spite of what God had done for them, they looked ahead and "wouldn't believe his promise to care for them." It was not that they couldn't believe, but that they wouldn't believe.

They were ungrateful as well and spent their time grumbling in their tents. They were not thankful for what they had. They were oblivious to harm they had avoided and forgetful of the awful conditions from which they had been rescued. They were fretful over their circumstances and their future. They were whining because things did not go the way they thought they should. It was not that God had actually failed them; they grumbled about what they supposed were God's failings.

What a mess! The Israelites couldn't see their own failings, mistrust, and disobedience. They couldn't see that it was their actions and beliefs that kept them from the good God wanted for them.

Hundreds of years later, these same peoples' descendants were embroiled in warfare that would come close to annihilating them. God asked, "Will not even one of you apply these lessons from the past and see the ruin that awaits you?" (Isa. 42:23). This wasn't a question asked in anger but a question of loving despair, as God longed for "even one" of them to trust that what He wanted for them was good. But God knew the people would not "apply these lessons" from the past. Even so, He clearly restated to the people how their actions were leading to their destruction. And the people's response? "The people would not go where he sent them, nor would they obey his law" (Isa. 42:24).

However, let's not feel any superiority in this matter, for we, too, struggle with obedience to God. That struggle begins with our inability to believe that God only commands us to do what is in our best interest. But belief in this basic truth is the foundation upon which obedience to God is built. Without this belief, we pull the rug out from under ourselves when it comes to obedience. If we rely on our own understanding of what serves our best interests, we often go with our misleading thought processes rather than obey God's perfect plan.

More consistent obedience is possible, though. Jesus Christ was the greatest example of obedience of all time. We are told "even though Jesus was God's Son, he learned obedience" (Heb. 5:8). Jesus was God, but Jesus was also human and had to learn to be obedient as all humans do. How did Jesus learn to be obedient to God? He learned it "from the things he suffered" (Heb. 5:8). Jesus was willing to obey in spite of suffering because He did believe and trust that God's plan was in the best interests of all people.

Although it is normal to want to avoid suffering, it is often only the pain of suffering that gets and keeps our attention while we learn valuable lessons. One of those lessons is that our sins truly do harm us. Just as children learn that fire hurts and to keep their distance, so we learn that sin hurts; and once we have suffered from a sin, we, too, may learn to keep our distance.

We can learn because the consequences of sin are eventually always painful. Our suffering may be physical, our bodies broken by sin. Our suffering may be emotional, leaving us without hope. But our suffering will always be spiritual, separating us from close companionship with God.

How much better it is to be counted among those "who have trained themselves to recognize the difference between right and wrong and then do what is right" (Heb. 5:14). How much better it is to be counted among those who have come truly to believe that whatever God has commanded us to do will lead us to the "pleasant land."

But even if it is our deep desire to be obedient, we often fail, for there always seems to be new sins to ensnare us. It would become downright discouraging, were it not for one amazing phenomenon—the joy of learning to obey.

When we first become determined to obey and resist sin, it is far from easy. We don't have much experience under our belts, and we haven't known the sweetness of a close and intimate relationship with Jesus—one unmarred by purposeful sin. It is hard work at first, but then amazing things begin to happen.

We begin to see the positive outcomes of our obedience. We start to believe God's plan for our lives is good, and our trust increases. Our way of thinking changes and we find we want to obey. Obeying is no longer a duty but a joy.

And as we learn the joy of obedience, we become the opposite of who we were. We become people who enter the pleasant land, believing in God's promise to care for us, and rejoicing as we obey the Lord.

Believing, obeying, rejoicing. Disbelieving, disobeying, grumbling. Choices...always choices.

WEEK 125

What's Your Name?

Isaiah 45–49; Psalm 107; Hebrews 7

Have you ever thought about the significance of a person's name? A name, first and foremost, is an identifier. Now that may seem simplistic, but identification by name often goes beyond mere superficial acknowledgment of a person. A name can be a happy or unhappy reminder of another person and create many emotions.

There is also something intimate about being known by name. To be known by your name is to be no longer one of many or a stranger. As in the case of the person who speaks our name, *hearing* our name may create emotions for us. We may not even be aware of these fleeting feelings since our attention is quickly captured by the reason we are being called by name.

Someone God called by name was the mighty ruler, Cyrus. "I am the Lord, the God of Israel, the one who calls you by name. ...I called you by name when you did not know me..." (Isa. 45:3-4). What makes this an intriguing statement is that Cyrus could not possibly have known God at the time God called him by name, for Cyrus had not been born. Cyrus was not an empire builder when God first spoke his name; he was not an adult, he was not a child, he would not even "be" for more than one hundred years. But God knew him by name.

And although his birth was more than a century away, God stated the powerful emotions that would arise when the name of Cyrus was spoken. "Mighty kings will be paralyzed with fear. ...They will follow you as prisoners in chains" (Isa. 45:1,14).

God had an explanation as to why He called Cyrus by name long before his existence became a reality. "And why have I called you for this work? I have prepared you, even though you do not know me. ...I will raise up Cyrus to fulfill my righteous purpose, and I will guide all his actions. He will restore my city and free my captive people...!" (Isa. 45:4-5,13).

Cyrus would enable Jerusalem to be rebuilt from the rubble that remained after the Israelites were captured by the Babylonians. He would be the person to free the Israelites from yet another exile. He had a specific purpose, and to God, Cyrus' name spoke of that purpose.

Cyrus would not free the Israelites of his generation in the same way Pharaoh had freed their ancestors. What Pharaoh did involuntarily, Cyrus would do willingly. This would not be without cost to Cyrus, for he would need to make sacrifices in order to send the Israelites home to Jerusalem—sacrifices he was willing to make. For the Israelites to be able to return to Jerusalem, Cyrus had to be willing to give up the skills of a people who were important to his empire. He had to be willing to give up some of his wealth so the Israelites would have what they needed to make the trip and to rebuild Jerusalem. He had to make sure the way was safe for the Israelites to return to Jerusalem, for there were dangerous lands and situations to pass through. Cyrus had been created for a purpose, and history verifies that he followed God's plan and fulfilled that purpose.

Cyrus' story is not unique. God knows each of us by name and has created us for a purpose to fulfill in this life. Are we fulfilling our purpose as Cyrus did? Do we even know our purpose?

If not, we can ask God's help in making it clear to us. Then as we go forward, we will have started the journey of our life's purpose. God guided Cyrus in "all his actions." God will guide us, too, if we are willing to do what He asks.

There will also be sacrifices for us to make to fulfill our purpose, but I know we will think those sacrifices were worth it when we hear Jesus greet us by name as we enter Heaven.

WEEK 126

Scorn and Slander

Isaiah 50–54; Hebrews 8–9

"Listen to me, you who know right from wrong and cherish my law in your hearts" (Isa. 51:7). God, through Isaiah, has an important message. We can hear the urgency in the words and almost see an exclamation point. "Listen to me…" Those words say it all. Stop, be still, pay attention, there is a message you need to hear.

To whom does God want to give this message? The message is to those who believe and follow Him. It is to those who turn to God's laws for help in determining the differences between "right from wrong." The message is to believers who not only "cherish" God's law but are determined to obey it. The message is to us.

Now that God has the believers' attention, He gives this message: "Do not be afraid of people's scorn or their slanderous talk" (Isa. 51:7). Wait a minute! If God is addressing believers who cherish His law, He is talking to people whose lives will be characterized by their love for Him and for others. Yet God is saying to expect "scorn or slanderous talk." Why would we expect love to be met with such negative reactions?

Why indeed? It seems reasonable to believe that goodwill would be the normal response to receiving love. That belief may be reasonable, but it is not always reality. No matter how much love we extend, there will be times in our lives when those who receive our love will be disdainful toward us. Their reactions may hurt our feelings or puzzle us, but most times they will not cause us to be afraid.

Why then did God choose the words "Do not be afraid" when warning about scorn being directed toward a believer? It is likely that God is speaking of the type of scorn that occurs when someone takes exception to our faith in Him.

God's warning is fitting. A believer who chooses to live by the rules of God rather than join in activities that go against godly principles may seem bizarre and become an object of ridicule.

At a deeper level, true hostility may spring forth from those whose values and actions are in direct opposition to God's laws. Even if a believer makes no judgment of another, a life lived by God's principles will contrast with, and possibly condemn, a life that is not lived this way. And feelings of condemnation, even self-condemnation, may result in bitter opposition toward a believer.

It is difficult not to defend ourselves at the injustice of it all. Sometimes it feels so right to give back the same as we get. You know… an eye for an eye, unkindness for unkindness, anger for anger.

But is that not the reason for this verse of warning? During those times when our own anger rises in response to how we are being treated, when our feelings are hurt, when we want to belong but do not, or when our reputations are being destroyed, we may not feel up to cherishing and obeying the greatest of God's laws—to love Him and love others.

But hold steady! There is a purpose in all of this. God is telling us to be ready for hostility, to seek His help in our reactions, and to practice being different by showing kindness to those who are not easy to love. It is exactly this type of consistent kindness in the face of scorn and slander that may eventually cause a hostile person to take another look at what our faith means. It is also this type of behavior that helps us to be an example for believers who have not yet had a chance to learn these lessons.

We have been given the perfect example of how to react during these times, for Jesus showed us the way as He prepared to die for our sins. "He was oppressed and treated harshly, yet he never said a word" (Isa. 53:7). Not to say "a word" in defense of ourselves may take more God-control and humility than any of us possesses, but we can pray that the words and actions we do use are pleasing to God.

And it will take a combination of prayer and determination. When the scorn and slanderous talk leave us heartsick, ready to give up, or angry, we have Jesus' example of how to react. And with that in mind, we can once again gather ourselves to try to love others as God wants us to—even in the face of scorn or slander.

Week 127

Need Rescued?

Isaiah 55–58; Psalms 108–109; Hebrews 10

David said, "For I am poor and needy, and my heart is full of pain" (Ps. 109:22). How true this rings. We know this intimately through our own situations, and we know it as we listen to others and look around us. We are indeed a poor and needy people.

We may be poor and in need financially—burdened day after day in a struggle to provide the basic necessities for ourselves and those we love. We may be poor and in need physically—engulfed by pain, illness, addictions, or looming death. We may be poor and in need emotionally—

overwhelmed by disappointment, fear, worry, depression, guilt, rejection, or grief. We may be poor and in need spiritually—rebellious, doubtful, ungrateful, or struggling with feelings of being separated from God.

There are so many problems, but few solutions to those problems come solely through our own efforts. We stagger under the sheer magnitude of our needs and the needs of those around us. And then there are the times when we no longer stagger but lie broken and weary—barely able to lift our eyes toward God.

But David lifted his eyes and his voice to cry out to God, saying, "Help me, O Lord my God! Use your strong right arm to save me" (Ps. 109:26; 108:6). In the midst of cruel life circumstances, our cries echo with David's as we plead for relief, for help in our distress. Our cries are those of a wounded heart. Our cries are the cries of a soul that has lost hope. Our cries are the cries of desperation.

God heard David's cries and rescued him, for "He stands beside the needy, ready to save them…" (Ps. 109:31). And God hears our cries and vows, "I am ready to make an everlasting covenant with you. I will give you all the mercies and unfailing love that I promised David" (Isa. 55:3).

But we cry out, "When, Lord?" For we need relief and healing and solutions now. We do not have, or know, the answers to our problems, but God does. What seems so confusing, so insurmountable to us, is not to God. God reminds us, "My thoughts are completely different from yours, and my ways are far beyond anything you could imagine" (Isa. 55:8).

During our most difficult times, solutions are beyond our imagination, but not beyond God's. With the full voice of authority and power, God declares, "My thoughts are different." With the gentle whisper of love, God says, "My ways are far beyond anything you could imagine." With the compelling voice of assurance, God says, "Seek the Lord while you can find him. Call on him now while he is near" (Isa. 55:6). And when we find Him, we can also find healing and comfort for our physical needs, rest and encouragement for our emotional needs, reassurance and guidance for our spiritual needs, and patience and trust as we wait for better days.

Poor or needy? Need rescued? Tried all that you know to do? Well then, "let us go right into the presence of God, with true hearts fully trusting him. …without wavering, let us hold tightly to the hope we say we have, for God can be trusted to keep his promise" (Heb. 10:22-23).

And so, "without wavering," we can "go right into the presence of God"—a presence so mighty that it is beyond our imagination. And with hope, we can believe that "God can be trusted to keep his promise." Our hope is built on nothing less than God. Our hope could not be built on anything greater.

Week 128

Let's Get Together

Isaiah 59–62; Psalms 110–111; Hebrews 11

"Praise the Lord! I will thank the Lord with all my heart as I meet with his godly people" (Ps. 111:1). This psalmist knew of what he wrote. Here was a person who understood the immense benefits of meeting together with godly people. Now many readers of this verse will think that the writer was referring to meeting together in a churchlike setting, and they might be correct, for there is great joy in gathering in groups to worship God.

But if you have family members or cherished friends with whom you can discuss the things of God, then you can also picture the psalmist's words referring to meeting with only a few people. There is something especially pleasing and inspiring about gathering informally with people to talk about the amazing things God has done and is doing. The psalmist knew this as well, for he continued with, "How amazing are the deeds of the Lord! All who delight in him should ponder them" (Ps. 111:2).

Ah, yes, the joy that can come to us when we ponder what God has done! And if we have experienced the joy of being aware of God's presence in our lives, we most likely know how that joy multiplies each time we talk about these things with others who also love Him. Even during times when our hearts are heavy, talking about godly things while being with a godly person can uplift us.

Our conversations with other Christians can become one of the building blocks of our faith as we recognize through our shared experiences and insights that "everything he does reveals his glory and majesty" (Ps. 111:3). These times together do not need to focus on theological points, for God's "glory and majesty" are clearly evident as we recall our day-to-day experiences with the Lord as our Leader, Savior, and Counselor. As we share our feelings about God and His amazing deeds, He will not be a distant deity but will become real to us. This is no flight of imagination, for God is pleased when we reflect on Him as we make our way through our days.

As we recall times of God's faithfulness, we will begin to see more readily just how much God is involved in our lives. Answers to prayers and stories of sins forgiven and lives changed, will increase our trust. Recollections of the blessings that have come from obedience, and the negative consequences that have come from disobedience, will help us understand more clearly why God has given us the guidelines He has. We will rejoice in the evidence of God's power and be strengthened in our spirits as we look back on the difficulties we have faced and how God has used these times to benefit us in ways we could not have anticipated. Thankfulness, even awe, will be a natural by-product of these conversations as we focus on God and His work on our behalf, His kindness, and His goodness to us.

The psalmist asks, "Who can forget the wonders he performs?" (Ps. 111:4). Indeed, who could possibly forget? Not us, as we remember these wonders among ourselves. It is so simple, so ordinary, and so natural to have family or friends with whom we can comfortably talk about anything. It is so powerful, so life-changing, and so uplifting when part of that time together is about the wonders God performs in our lives.

Week 129

Answers Before We Ask

Isaiah 63–66; Hebrews 12–13; John 1

"I will answer them before they even call to me. While they are still talking to me about their needs, I will go ahead and answer their prayers!"

(Isa. 65:24). This has to be one of the most hope-giving verses in all of Scripture. It is a significant verse when life is humming along, and it is even more so when life is not. It is a direct promise from God to His followers, who can believe in and count on what He promises to do. There are three reassuring parts to this special promise. Let's look at each.

God knows our needs. He knew before we prayed about them. He knew even before they occurred. As we face difficult life situations and circumstances that bring us to despair, God's promise to us is that He knows all about them and that He is with us. It is a promise for the times when our needs, struggles, heartbreaks, and confusion pile up, corner us, and leave us dazed.

God has an answer for us. He states it clearly, "I will answer them." Just as God knows the adversities we face, He knows what answers best fit our specific and unique needs.

God will not withhold this perfect answer from us. "Before" we pray, God promises to have the answer on the way. This suggests that God understands us so intimately that even before we talk to Him, He knows about the things we will request, and He is ready with an answer. While we "are still talking to" God about our needs, He has taken the initiative and sent the answer.

Now some may read this statement by God and think they have plenty of examples of answers that did not come to their prayers. All of us can think this way if we believe that prayer is only answered when our request has been met in the exact manner and time frame in which we asked—in other words, by a resounding "Yes!" from God. God's answer may be "Yes," but it may also be "No, I have something better for you." Or it may be "Wait, trust Me, and learn." How clearly I remember a time, however, when there was no doubt that God had sent the answer to my prayer, quite literally, while I was still talking to Him.

We live in the woods. It had been a year with little rain, and it was a calm autumn day without even a hint of wind—a perfect day to begin raking our many leaves. In those days we burned our leaves, and my plan was to do exactly that. It was no problem deciding where to start, since everywhere I turned was covered with dry leaves. Before long I had a large pile raked, and I lit the fire. As I continued raking leaves onto the pile, the fire leaped up and blazed away. It was a lovely, sunny day—the sky so blue I wanted to stare at it. And then, without warning, a wind whipped in, picking up burning leaves and scattering them throughout the woods. Smaller fires started to flare up everywhere as burning ash singed my hair and burned a hole in my coat. I knew in that instant—with a sickening certainty and dread—that our home, our neighbors' homes, and the trees and land surrounding us were in danger, and there was nothing I could do to stop the fires.

Instinctively I cried out, "God, help me!" Those were my only words, but before I completed the sentence, I felt something hit me. At first I thought it was more ash from the many fires, but it was God's answer sent to me before I even finished calling out to Him. It was rain. The sky was still blue, and the sun still shone; but there was a gentle rain falling. In a few minutes all of the fires were out, and only smoke remained from the main fire. Everything was safe. I was weak with relief, gratitude, and wonderment, for long before I knew the words of Isaiah 65:24, I knew that God had answered my cry for help while I was still praying.

Regardless of His timing and His methods, I am convinced that God does answer our prayers, each and every time. Even while we are still talking to Him.

WEEK 130

Yes, We Will Come

Jeremiah 1–4; Psalms 112–113; John 2

"Your own wickedness will punish you. You will see what an evil, bitter thing it is to forsake the Lord your God, having no fear of him. I, the Lord, the Lord Almighty, have spoken!" (Jer. 2:19). What a sobering verse of warning. And yet a warning is a blessing, for it can keep us from the harm it warns against. Let us look at this lesson, this warning, this blessing.

There is, first and foremost, the serious matter of forsaking the Lord. There are two levels on which people can forsake God: as an individual or acting together as a society or nation. Jeremiah's warning was addressed both to the nation of Judah (the *southern* kingdom of the once united Israel) and to the individuals who made up that nation.

His warning was already a reality for the destroyed *northern* kingdom of Israel, for her people knew what an "evil, bitter thing" it was to forsake the Lord. They had forsaken the Lord when they lost their fear of His superiority, and their nation had crumbled—the land destroyed, and the people killed, maimed, tortured, and enslaved. Don't skim over these things as a dry rehash of history. Consider the dread, panic, fear, sorrow, pain, and the end of hope that the northern kingdom had experienced when their "own wickedness" punished them. Put yourself into these people's lives, and see it as Jeremiah saw it. His words show his anguish that the same type of destruction was coming quickly to Judah: "My heart, my heart—I writhe in pain! My heart pounds within me!" (Jer. 4:19).

Judah had two possible responses to God's warning. They could continue to go their own way as the northern kingdom of Israel had, rejecting God and claiming they had not sinned (Jer. 2:35). Or they could accept God's invitation to return to Him: "I am still calling you to come back to me. Only acknowledge your guilt" (Jer. 3:1,13). Their response carried consequences for this life and for eternity.

Judah tried to have it both ways. They answered with words of devotion while continuing to reject God. God, of course, knew their words were exactly that—only words. "Judah has never sincerely returned to me. She has only pretended to be sorry" (Jer. 3:10). Their forgiveness and healing were just one humble, honest step away, but Judah would not take it. They would not ask for God's forgiveness or His help to turn from, and keep away from, sin.

If we have ever rejected and abandoned God, we are undoubtedly aware what "an evil, bitter thing" it is to be separated from Him. We understand the bleakness of life without the Holy Spirit to guide and comfort us. We understand the sense of fear and doom when we stand on our own without the towering strength of God to overshadow us. We understand the darkness of spirit, soul, and mind without God's light to warm and brighten our world.

Obedience is not a onetime decision but a continuous choice. Sometimes we choose wisely and sometimes we do not. May we remember the warning given to us in Jeremiah 2:19 of continually choosing poorly.

But may we also remember the blessing of this warning, for it points us to God's mercy and forgiveness.

We see this amazing mercy and forgiveness at a later time in Judah's history, after they suffered the same fate as the northern kingdom. God's prior offer still stood: "'My wayward children,' says the Lord, 'come back to me, and I will heal your wayward hearts.'" This time the people's response was sincere, "Yes, we will come, for you are the Lord our God" (Jer. 3:22).

It is the choice that each of us must make. It is the choice we made yesterday, the one we must make today, and the one we will need to make again tomorrow. Whom will we serve?

Week 131

After Dark Encounter

Jeremiah 5–8; Psalms 114–115; John 3

Night time was coming on quickly. Nicodemus—a man well-known, well-respected, well-versed in biblical texts—wrestled with a decision. Word on the streets of Jerusalem had told him where Jesus would be that evening, and Nicodemus wished to talk with Him. He was drawn to Jesus, and yet he sensed he was alone in this feeling among the religious leaders. Since Jesus had burst into the Temple a few days earlier, sweeping it clear of the money-changers and merchants, as well as challenging Nicodemus' fellow Pharisees on how they conducted Temple worship and business, he had heard nothing but fury, grumbling, and talk of payback for the lack of respect Jesus had shown them.

But something deep inside Nicodemus believed Jesus was right in what He had done and said that day, and he wanted to learn more about this Man. Still, he was enough of a realist to know that openly seeking out Jesus would be detrimental to his position in the religious hierarchy and in the community. He could become a laughingstock or, even worse, labeled a traitor. There was much to lose and maybe nothing to gain by approaching Jesus. However, this was possibly his only chance to talk to Him, for Nicodemus also had heard that Jesus and His handful of disciples were leaving Jerusalem tomorrow. He would go.

Walking the streets, with little light to show the way, Nicodemus wrestled with what he knew of prophecies concerning the Messiah, what he had seen of Jesus, and what question he would ask first. Soon he came upon Jesus, and there was no turning back, for Jesus was looking right at him. Nicodemus did not know *how* he knew it, but he was aware that Jesus *wanted* him to come and talk with Him. And so he did just that.

There were so many things he wanted to talk about with this Man of obvious wisdom and knowledge. He began, "Teacher, we all know that God has sent you to teach us. Your miraculous signs are proof enough that God is with you" (John 3:2). These words had no more than died away in the night air when "Jesus replied, 'I assure you, unless you are born again, you can never see the Kingdom of God'" (John 3:3).

Nicodemus struggled with confusion. He had not even asked one of his carefully thought-out questions, and Jesus had responded to his first words with this strange statement. The things Nicodemus did *not* know were the things Jesus *did* know. Jesus knew how quickly their time together would pass and how critical it was to come right to the heart of all Nicodemus needed to understand but did not know how to ask.

Nicodemus' mind raced, for he wasn't sure if Jesus was using everyday images to explain a spiritual concept he already understood or if Jesus was talking about something entirely new. He believed, as all Pharisees did, that there was resurrection after death based on a person's righteousness and adherence to Jewish law. Jesus' words sounded like there was something else other than Nicodemus' own righteousness that would allow him to see the Kingdom of God. His confusion came to a head, and he exclaimed, "What do you mean? How can an old man go back into his mother's womb and be born again?" (John 3:4). "What" and "How"—questions to God that were as old as humanity.

Focused intently on Jesus so he would not miss a word, Nicodemus listened to this new and confusing twist on rebirth that had not been heard, taught, or known by God's people. "Jesus replied, 'The truth is, no one can enter the Kingdom of God without being born of water and the Spirit. Humans can reproduce only human life, but the Holy Spirit gives new life from heaven. So don't be surprised at my statement that you must be born again'" (John 3:5-7). Again Nicodemus asked, "What do you mean?" (v. 9). Jesus' words were not making sense to him.

Jesus, acknowledging how difficult this was to understand in human terms, went back a step to the root of the issue. "I am telling you what we know and have seen, and yet you won't believe us. But if you don't even believe me when I tell you about things that happen here on earth, how can you possibly believe if I tell you what is going on in heaven?" (John 3:11-12).

Jesus was doing it again. Nicodemus had not spoken of his disbelief, but Jesus once again went directly to what Nicodemus truly felt rather than what he was expressing. Jesus had intentionally spoken of Himself in the plural—"what we know…what we have seen…you won't believe us…"—for a reason. Jesus was saying: I am the Son of God; in fact, I am God, in human form; I am more than a teacher. Nicodemus fervently believed in God, and now he had to decide if he would believe that Jesus was actually God in person. Until Nicodemus could understand and believe this, he could not believe all the other things Jesus was telling him.

If Nicodemus could believe that Jesus was God, then he had taken the first step in being assured of eternal life. The next step was becoming a new person through that belief. Jesus said there was only one way for this to happen. A new person could not be created through good intentions, desires, resolutions, or rituals. A new person required change that occurred from the inside out; it was almost like becoming a new species of human. To become a new person required a powerful, supernatural Master Change Agent—the Holy Spirit. And believing in Jesus activated the Change Agent of the Holy Spirit who could make Nicodemus into a person ready for God's Kingdom.

Before they parted that night, Jesus talked with Nicodemus about life after this earthly one. Those words from Jesus were comforting, frightening, or maddening—depending on what or in whom you believe and trust. "There is no judgment awaiting those who trust him [Jesus]. But those who do not trust him have already been judged for not believing in the only Son of God" (John 3:18).

The words were true for Nicodemus, for each person who *has* lived, who *is* living, or who *will* live. "Those who believe him [Jesus] discover that God is true" (John 3:33). And that is the most life-giving, life-changing, and life-enhancing discovery of all time!

The Most Important Message

Jeremiah 9–13; John 4–5

God had a message for Israel's neighbors. "And if these nations quickly learn the ways of my people, and if they learn to swear by my name, saying, 'As surely as the Lord lives' (just as they taught my people to swear by the name of Baal), then they will be given a place among my people" (Jer. 12:16).

Let's take a look at how these two calls to action leading to a gift from God were important not only to the people of Jeremiah's time but to our own times as well.

The first call to action for the neighboring nations was to "quickly learn the ways of my people." God's people, the Israelites, were to be characterized by their love for God, obedience to His guidelines, humility, kindness, and justice to others. But during the time of this message, the majority of God's own people were not living by the ways in which they had been instructed. Their neighbors would have had a hard time finding Israelites who could guide them in quickly learning God's way.

God's second call to action was for the neighboring nations to "learn to swear by my name saying, 'As surely as the Lord lives.'" In other words, these nations were to be so convinced of the Lord's existence that they could confirm the absolute truth about any situation by declaring it to be as real as the Lord. And with this oath, they would also be acknowledging that all of what God declared about Himself was true, including that He alone is God.

It follows that, if the other nations agreed the Lord is the only God, *His* name would replace the name of Baal, and they would willingly give up worshiping other gods. And when they did, the Lord promised "they will be given a place among my people." The Lord loved these nations and wanted them to be His people.

But they did not want Him. In fact, the stipulations and the promised outcome had to sound like sheer lunacy to the neighboring nations. The Israelites' persistent disobedience had led them to the brink of disaster, and their sorry state was clearly evident to their neighbors. Sadly, the results of the Israelites' continual disobedience contributed greatly to the unwillingness of others to listen to God.

And then there was the matter of making the Lord their *only* god. This wasn't the first time the people had heard the message about discarding their gods in favor of worshiping only the Lord. The harping on the same subject was starting to grow old. Baal worship was widespread at this time, and most people weren't willing to take the chance of possibly losing the blessing of Baal.

But Jeremiah understood the special gift God was offering when He promised to give the nations a place among my people. His obedience to God and concern for others caused him to faithfully share that message. But Jeremiah paid a price for being this messenger. He became an object of scorn and was ignored by most people (Jer. 6:10). Those who did listen were more often angered by his message than accepting of it, and even Jeremiah's own brothers plotted to kill him. The Israelite religious and political leaders, who should have been his allies, countered his message (Jer. 5:5). And yet to those few who listened to Jeremiah and followed his lead, his message became the most important one they would ever receive.

The principles given to Jeremiah from God still apply today. We are to live our lives by God's standards so that others can learn of His ways. We are to swear by the truth that "the Lord is the only true God, the living God" (Jer. 10:10). And we are to be the message that shows that all other so-called gods are as worthless as Baal.

The message that God is who He says He is—the one and only God—may still be ignored, met with scorn, or endanger our lives if we proclaim it. We may be labeled arrogant or close-minded if it matters to us what or who other people worship...or if they worship at all. But regardless of others' reactions, the message is still valid. As we bring the most important message ever to those willing to hear, we can trust that God will use that message to rescue those who are open to His truth.

Jeremiah faithfully gave the Lord's message. Will we?

Take, Eat, Give

Jeremiah 14–18; Psalm 116; John 6

Matthew, Mark, Luke, and John all wrote of the time Jesus fed more than five thousand people with two fish and five loaves of bread. The story is so familiar to us that eventually we stop thinking about how incredible it was.

At the same time, the sheer magnitude of the miracle of five loaves and two fish stretching to feed a crowd of that size can cause us to miss other important points of this story. Let's take a look at two of those points.

Jesus knew, before anyone else did, that He was only a few minutes away from performing a miracle that would not only capture the attention of the crowd but also the attention of people like us centuries later. His ministry was made up of many great moments and this one would once again reinforce who He was. As Jesus began the miraculous process of providing food for this crowd of people, He stopped for something critically important. "Then Jesus took the loaves, gave thanks to God, and passed them out to the people. Afterward he did the same with the fish…" (John 6:11).

Jesus was grateful for the food God was going to provide, and He gave His prayerful thanks for it. This prayer was not merely a ritual or force of habit. These were not routine, quickly mumbled words but a meaningful response to a great gift. Are we as thankful for *our* food?

We are people who, for the most part, have ample food to meet our needs. But perhaps because of its abundance, easy availability, and variety, we may take our food supply for granted. We have a hunger pang and, with little thought, reach for a snack. We sit down to full meals. We may even complain if we aren't in the mood for what we have to eat. But look again at the words of the verse: "Jesus took the loaves, gave thanks... and afterward he did the same with the fish." Jesus was mindful of and thankful for the loaves, and he was equally mindful of and thankful for the fish.

Have we also stopped to consider that the gift of being able to eat goes beyond having adequate food? Each time we bite, chew, swallow, and digest our food properly we have reason to be thankful. If you are skeptical, talk to anyone who is physically unable to do so.

Sometimes it is a worshipful thing to ask God, "Why us?" When we have a snack, when we sit down to a meal, when we are strong enough to prepare our own food, and when we are healthy enough to eat and enjoy it, we need to pause to think, "Why us?" and then thank God.

But let's not stop with a prayer of thanks, for Jesus did not stop there. After Jesus thanked God for His food, He shared it with the crowd, "and they all ate until they were full" (John 6:11). No one went away hungry. No one. The conditions in which Jesus lived while on earth are much like the conditions in which many people live today. Food is precious to them. We are not so isolated as to be unaware of the wars, financial upheavals, natural disasters, and corrupt governments that cause food to be in short supply for many people. Millions labor hard all day, every day, for only enough food to take the edge off their hunger. Millions more cannot feed themselves or those they love because food is not available to them, no matter how hard they work. People will die today, and every day, from lack of food. We need to be responsive to their plight.

Jesus gave us a perfect model to follow. As we thank God for what we have been given, let us engage in helping those who need the blessing of something to eat. We can pray for those who are too ill to eat or who do not have food. We can get involved in a local food ministry. We can support Christian organizations that work throughout the world to help feed both the physical and spiritual hunger of those who live where food is not easily available. If we ask, God will guide us in what He wants us to do.

On that day so long ago, Jesus fed thousands of people. We may never have the same opportunity for such great service to God, but we can become keenly aware of and thankful for the gift we have been given. And we can make a life-long commitment to help others have that same blessing every day of their lives and ours.

WEEK 134

Two Paths

Jeremiah 19–22; Psalm 117; John 7–8

This is the story of the interaction between two men. Each of their vocations involved direct service to God. Knowing God's direction and following it were critical to their success.

Pashhur was the priest in charge of the Temple of the Lord. He had the sacred responsibility to maintain the accuracy and holiness of worship within the Temple. This included deciding who, of the many speakers who came to the Temple, spoke the truth and who did not. Those who claimed to speak for God but did not were to be punished severely because their false words would dilute or contradict God's true words.

Jeremiah was a prophet. He had the sacred responsibility to speak God's words of truth to others. Jeremiah and Pashhur's paths crossed at the Temple when Jeremiah brought God's message of judgment and doom to the political and spiritual leaders assembled there. Standing before them, he cried out, "This is what the Lord Almighty, the God of Israel, says: 'I will bring disaster upon this city and its surrounding towns just as I promised, because you have stubbornly refused to listen to me'" (Jer. 19:15).

It was Pashhur's duty to decide if this was a message of a deranged person or one that was numbingly frightening in its truth. Jeremiah's message was in exact opposition to the messages from numerous other prophets who were saying all was well. Pashhur's decision would publicly align the religious leaders with one or the other of these messages.

If Pashhur ever needed God's direction, it was at that moment. And God's guidance was available to him through Scripture and through prayer. By humbly asking God for wisdom, Pashhur would have had help judging the truth of Jeremiah's message.

Pashhur reacted. "So he arrested Jeremiah the prophet and had him whipped and put in stocks at the Benjamin Gate of the Lord's Temple" (Jer. 20:2). Pashhur did *not* humbly seek God, did *not* go to Scripture for guidance, and did *not* want to know the truth. Pashhur failed in the responsibility he had been given by God.

In contrast, Jeremiah succeeded in the responsibility he had been given by God. But that success did not have much physical appeal. Jeremiah, whipped and put in stocks for a day, would have had plenty of time to nurse any grudges against God or others. As he watched those for whom he had predicted punishment walking by him—mocking him and appearing unconcerned—he may have wondered about God's protection. During those hours he may have questioned how much more pain and humiliation he could endure…and if he would continue to speak for God.

He made his decision. "The next day, when Pashhur finally released him, Jeremiah said, 'Pashhur, the Lord has changed your name. From now on you are to be called "The Man Who Lives in Terror." For this is what the Lord says: …you and all your household will go as captives to Babylon. There you will die and be buried, you and all your friends to whom you promised that everything would be all right'" (Jer. 20:3-4,6).

Destiny hung in the balance for many people at this moment. Jeremiah had been giving the same message for many years. Would God's hard-to-accept message finally break through to Pashhur? Would this influential spiritual leader help to spread Jeremiah's message, turning people toward God and away from destruction? Sadly, he would not. And so he spent his final days in a foreign land with the memories of how he allowed his pride and power to bring devastation to many by assuring them "that everything would be all right" when God had clearly said it would not. Pashhur chose the easier, self-centered path that ended in pain and destruction.

For many years, until disaster struck Jerusalem, Jeremiah's was the harder path compared to Pashhur's. Throughout this lengthy time, he lamented—in real pain, justified fear, and true rejection—that "my entire life has been filled with trouble, sorrow, and shame" (Jer. 20:18). Jeremiah often had his fill of the consequences of following God and being the deliverer of His message. But he continued to choose the harder, selfless path.

He did this because there was something so compelling about his relationship with God and His message that he was drawn to proclaim it in spite of the pain. Jeremiah himself marveled at the fact that "I can't stop! If I say I'll never mention the Lord or speak in his name, his word burns in my heart like a fire. It's like a fire in my bones! I am weary of holding it in" (Jer. 20:9).

The lives of Jeremiah and other devoted followers of God demonstrate that suffering and discouragement often are part of being faithful to God and His message. The clash between evil and God—and the fallout from this clash—is as old as humanity. But just as ancient and sure is God's eventual deliverance of His followers from this fallout. Holding on to faith may be difficult during these times, but the process of spiritual maturing brought about by it also brings a thankfulness that eases the pain. In time, even Jeremiah said, "Now I will sing out my thanks to the Lord! Praise the Lord! For though I was poor and needy, he delivered me from my oppressors" (Jer. 20:13).

Knowing there are always consequences along the way, would it be better to be left standing in Jeremiah's place or Pashhur's? With God's help and strength, let it be Jeremiah's way we choose—faithful to the end.

WEEK 135

When?

Jeremiah 23–26; Psalm 118; John 9–10

Typically, people are not good at waiting. If there is anything associated with waiting, it is the question of "when" the wait will be over. Jeremiah 25 tells us about a wait that had already lasted twenty-three years and had not yet reached its conclusion.

"Jeremiah the prophet said to the people in Judah and Jerusalem, 'For the past twenty-three years the Lord has been giving me his messages. I have faithfully passed them on to you, but you have not listened'" (Jer. 25:2-3).

The messages were clear. If the people continued to disobey God, they would be punished. If they began to obey, they would be forgiven. For twenty-three years, Jeremiah waited for the Lord to fulfill these words of warning and promise. And for twenty-three years, the people in Judah and Jerusalem had waited for Jeremiah to stop talking.

It does not take much imagination to picture the people wondering "when" Jeremiah would give up. Nor is it difficult to understand why most people had dismissed his message after hearing the same thing again and again without seeing anything that proved the truth of it. They never understood that the long wait was due to God's mercy and desire to give them multiple chances to change, obey, and escape punishment. To the people of Judah, the prolonged wait only made them doubt the validity and probability of Jeremiah's message.

It also does not take much imagination to have a sense of the misery Jeremiah must have experienced during those long years. Twenty-three years is a long time to stick with something that has not produced the results you expected. Jeremiah must have wondered "when" there would be action that would cause the people to stop thinking of him as an irrational annoyance and start thinking of him as a prophet who faithfully passed on God's messages.

There are at least three parallels from this story to our lives today. First, we continue to be limited and ruled by time, while God is not (2 Pet. 3:8).

Second, God continues to give us warnings to help us avoid things that would harm us. And He continues to give us promises that apply to things occurring today as well as to significant future events. These messages to us are found throughout the Bible.

The third parallel relates to our reactions to God's warnings and promises when our wait for them to become reality does not match our sense of timing. We, too, may become confused, doubtful, or dismissive until finally, much to our detriment, we no longer think of the messages at all.

These parallels serve as important lessons to us even now. We need to guard against dismissing God's warnings and promises because we are not able to recognize them as they happen or because we no longer anticipate them as future events. If we trust the Message Giver, we must trust His messages and His timing.

Week 136

Deceived by Liars

Jeremiah 27–31; Psalm 119; John 11

Four people claimed they brought messages from the Lord to the people of Judah, but the Lord said they did not speak for Him. In fact, God said their messages were lies that were causing the people of Judah to turn away from the real message God was trying to give them through Jeremiah. There is no mistaking how serious God considered this matter when we read these four men's stories.

There was Hananiah. "Then Jeremiah the prophet said to Hananiah, 'Listen Hananiah! The Lord has not sent you, but the people believe your lies. Therefore, the Lord says you must die. Your life will end this very year because you have rebelled against the Lord.' Two months later, Hananiah died" (Jer. 28:15-17).

There were Ahab and Zedekiah. "This is what the Lord Almighty, the God of Israel, says about your prophets—Ahab and Zedekiah—who are telling you lies in my name: 'I will turn them over to Nebuchadnezzar for a public execution. Their terrible fate will become proverbial, so that whenever the Judean exiles want to curse someone they will say, "May the Lord make you like Zedekiah and Ahab, whom the king of Babylon burned alive!"'" (Jer. 29:21-22).

And there was Shemaiah. "…This is what the Lord says concerning Shemaiah: Since he has prophesied to you when I did not send him and has tricked you into believing his lies, I will punish him and his family. None of his descendants will see the good things I will do for my people" (Jer. 29:31-32).

Now in addition to these four men, the Israelites played an important role in these stories. They had been given contradictory messages, each supposedly from God. As God's people, it was crucial for them to choose, believe, and follow the true message from the Lord. But they chose to believe the liars' messages and suffered for it.

What caused the Israelites to be deceived? Several factors stand out. First, they preferred to believe the four men who said all would be well and they would be rescued from their enemies because they were God's people, rather than believe Jeremiah who spoke of punishment for disobedience and the need for change.

Second, the lies contained just enough truth to make them believable; after all, the Israelites were God's people, and He had rescued them from their enemies in the past. Why should this time be any different?

Third, the false message-givers were popular with well-known Israelites whose support lent credibility to their lies. But none of these factors made the four men's messages true.

What should the Israelites have done? If they actually recognized the truth but ignored it, they needed to begin obeying the Lord straightaway. If they were genuinely confused about what was true, they needed to ask the Lord for help, for He never hides the truth from those who seek to know it. They also needed to evaluate what they heard against Scripture, for God reveals Himself through it. And then, if they were still confused, they needed to seek godly counsel from those who were true in their devotion to the Lord. How different it would have been for the Israelites in the days that were to come if they had taken these steps.

Why is this relevant to us? Because damaging mistruths about God, the Bible, and the legitimacy of other gods continue today. These deceptions can be as harmful to us as they were to the Israelites if we fail to recognize that they are not true.

So the question becomes: what should we do to keep from being deceived? And the answer is that we need to do exactly what the Israelites should have done. We need to study Scripture, for we will always need the knowledge found there to help us judge the truth of what others say about God.

We need to pray that God will show us the truth. God will answer our sincere prayer for good judgment to know the truth.

If we are still unsure about what is true, we should discuss our questions with others—not someone like the four men who had little concern about accurately representing God, but people who desire to please God first and foremost.

The Israelites eventually found out who was telling the truth when God allowed them to be conquered by their enemies. After a harsh time of war and defeat, the Israelites finally chose God over the deception they had embraced for so long. God said because of that choice, "tears of joy will stream down their faces, and I will lead them home with great care" (Jer. 31:9). What a day that was for the Israelites, and what a day it is for all who choose to follow God's truth. Because of that day, it is worth every effort to know The Way, choose The Truth, and follow The Life (John 14:6).

Week 137

Winners and Losers

Jeremiah 32–36; John 12–13

"A dinner was prepared in Jesus' honor. Martha served, and Lazarus sat at the table with him. When all the people heard of Jesus' arrival, they flocked to see him and also to see Lazarus, the man Jesus had raised from the dead. Then the leading priests decided to kill Lazarus, too, for it was because of him that many of the people had deserted them and believed in Jesus" (John 12:2,9-11).

No matter how you look at it, Lazarus had a one-of-a-kind life. While the Bible documents a handful of adults and children who were raised from the dead, only Lazarus had been dead for four days—long enough to be laid in a dark, closed burial cave alongside others who had died. Lazarus' family, upon learning of Jesus' intention to call Lazarus back to life, felt obligated to mention that his body was decomposing due to the length of time since his death. It was a hopeless situation to all but Jesus (John 11:39-44).

And now here was Lazarus sitting, eating, and talking at the dinner table with Jesus. Sharing a meal seems almost too ordinary when compared to Lazarus' dramatic and amazing encounter with Jesus at the cemetery. But while one part of Lazarus' relationship with Jesus was unique, other aspects were common to all sincere followers.

The first of these was Lazarus' obedience to the Lord's voice even in a daunting situation. Think about it! With three words—"Lazarus, come out!"—Jesus set into motion an event for which Lazarus had no preparation or experience. As life and consciousness returned, was Lazarus joyful, confused, or dismayed? Whatever his thoughts, Lazarus obeyed and left the tomb because God enabled him to do so.

Leaving that tomb took courage and trust in Jesus, and living his life after leaving the tomb required more of the same. Lazarus had not been consulted about coming back to life, and he had no strategy ready to deal with the outcomes of that action. Here was a man who had led a quiet, simple life but who now lived with no privacy, for his name was on everyone's lips. Lazarus had not sought fame or its chaotic upheaval, but it came to him, and God enabled him to cope.

And that fame served an important purpose, for it pointed others toward Jesus and His ability to change a life. Lazarus became an easy-to-understand example of the power, wisdom, and love of Jesus. So many people sought after them to know more that the religious leaders became jealous and threatened by Lazarus—just as they were of Jesus. They decided both needed to die to stop this message that was spreading like a wildfire.

It is almost humorous, isn't it? Didn't the religious leaders see the irony of plotting Lazarus' death? Hadn't he just been through that, and wasn't it the root of what they considered their current problem? In spite of the Pharisees' faulty thinking, their threats—along with the major changes in how he had to live his life—were real to Lazarus.

With all the changes Lazarus faced, it is safe to say he would have been thankful for Jesus' friendship and guidance. As they sat at that dinner table, did Lazarus ask questions to help him understand what had happened to him? Did he need Jesus' help to see how this event and his fame were being used by God to spread the message of who Jesus was? Staying in close contact with Jesus enabled Lazarus to look toward his future with faith rather than fear.

We, too, have many situations thrown at us with which we must cope. Sometimes they may be enough almost to scare us to death. Sometimes they are new experiences, and we do not know how to respond. Sometimes they are detrimental to our health, livelihood, or security.

Although it may sound simplistic, obeying and trusting Jesus is the first and best course of action for these times. Jesus has the power, wisdom, and love that make obedience to Him and trust in Him reasonable actions. In Lazarus' story, we saw that Jesus even conquered our greatest enemy: death. Lazarus walked out of the tomb and faced both the crowds and his future because Jesus enabled him to do so. Jesus will do no less for us.

The story of Lazarus teaches us that we need to stay in close contact with Jesus. Lazarus did this face-to-face as he sat at the table with Jesus. We stay in close contact through prayer and studying God's words to us in the Bible. Talk to Jesus in prayer as you would your dearest confidant, one you can trust completely with your feelings. Seek to know Him better as your loving guide through the Bible.

As his story concludes, Lazarus' obedience, trust, and closeness with Jesus destroyed the Pharisees' plans. Lazarus' story of his relationship with Jesus was too powerful. The Pharisees begrudgingly admitted about Jesus, "We've lost. Look, the whole world has gone after him!" (John 12:19).

Those are sweet words to a Christian. When it comes to *our* life's story, may our enemies, Satan and his minions, echo the Pharisees' words, "We've lost...."

Week 138

Peace—the Source Makes the Difference

Jeremiah 37–41; John 14–15

"I am leaving you with a gift—peace of mind and heart. And the peace I give isn't like the peace the world gives. So don't be troubled or afraid" (John 14:27). These are Jesus' words.

Jesus had several points to make about peace. He noted there are two sources of peace. There is the peace that comes from Him and "the peace the world gives." The source of peace makes all the difference when it comes to its quality. A peace whose source is other than God is sometimes based on our relationships, our circumstances, what we can do, or on our own determination to have it. These types of peace are shallow and easily lost. As it is lost and regained and lost again, the pursuit of an inferior peace takes shape.

Jesus said true peace will come from Him as His gift through "the Holy Spirit, who leads into all truth" (John 14:17). But how do we go about getting this gift that is not from our world? Jesus bluntly and simply answered that question when He said, "Apart from me you can do nothing" (John 15:5). No matter how hard we try, we cannot force peace into existence. When we try to do so, we have substituted our activity for the Holy Spirit's, shoved Jesus to the side, and gained nothing.

But there are things we can do that will keep us connected to Jesus and His gifts. Peace can be found as we read the Bible and as we pray—actions which join us directly with God. Come to the Father asking for His peace. As humans bound by the constraints of this world, we may not fully understand how the Holy Spirit gives us peace through prayer and God's Word, but we can experience the comfort of it.

There is another activity that helps us keep connected to Jesus, and it is clearly evident throughout the verses of John, Jeremiah, and most other books of Scripture. It is the act of obedience. God's principles are not designed to bring us misery but to lead us toward genuine happiness and peace. When we are obeying, our lives may not be carefree or trouble-free, but they will be free of the excesses and consequences of our disobedience to the Lord's guidelines.

Jeremiah and Zedekiah are two individuals whose lives prove out Jesus' teaching about peace.

Jeremiah lived a life of hardship. He suffered one painful blow after another over a period of forty years—spanning the entire time he was God's spokesperson. During those years, he was a social outcast; mocked, ignored, and unwanted. He had powerful enemies who hated him enough to kill him. He was beaten. He was unfairly imprisoned numerous times. He was thrown into a muddy cistern to starve to death. Jeremiah summarized the uniformity of his life with the understatement, "Lord, you know I am suffering for your sake" (Jer. 15:15).

Jeremiah suffered, but he did so willingly and with surety of purpose. In his faithful service to the Lord, Jeremiah found peace. "Your words are what sustain me. They bring me great joy and are my heart's delight, for I bear your name, O Lord God Almighty" (Jer. 15:16). And that is Jeremiah's story.

Zedekiah was the last king of Judah. Although he was the king of a land under Babylonian siege, he still commanded great power within the city of Jerusalem and the land of Judah. His word was law, others lived or died at his command, and his attention was sought. He had the finest of what remained in the land: homes, furnishings, jewels, servants, livestock, and fields.

But Zedekiah was a man torn between what he wanted to do and what he knew was right. He wanted to outsmart the Babylonians and remain king. He wanted to live life by his rules and for his desires, ignoring Jeremiah and the Lord's call for repentance and a changed life. But Zedekiah could not ignore the fact that the Lord was real, powerful, and deserving of obedience. He was a man at war with himself, with God, and with other nations.

During his reign, Zedekiah made one smart move when he asked Jeremiah to "Please pray to the Lord our God for us" (Jer. 37:3). Jeremiah did so, and God answered, telling Zedekiah what he needed to do to save his life and obtain peace. What was Zedekiah's response? He said, "But I am afraid..."; afraid to obey, afraid to give up what he was used to trusting, and afraid to stop living life on his own terms (Jer. 38:19). Zedekiah's vacillation lasted until his final day as king, the day his land was conquered and Jerusalem burned to the ground. After the Babylonians captured Zedekiah, they forced him to watch his sons being murdered; then they blinded him, leaving that gruesome scene seared into his mind's eye before he was imprisoned for life. We are not told whether or not during his years of imprisonment Zedekiah finally accepted the peace that only God could give him.

Zedekiah, as king, had all that the world could offer, but real peace eluded him. Jeremiah, whose earthly possessions were meager and whose circumstances were constantly unsettling, had great peace through God. And so can we—even during times when it would seem impossible. It is a gift from Jesus, who has shown us the way.

WEEK 139

Doing It Our Way

Jeremiah 42–47; John 16

Judah, and Jerusalem with it, was now under Babylonian rule. Babylon wanted an Israelite to govern on their behalf, but there were few natives left, as most had died during the long siege or been forced to relocate outside of Judah. Yet the land needed a leader, so Gedaliah was appointed by Babylon as the head of its newest territory.

But now Gedaliah was dead, assassinated by Judean rebels. The few Israelites remaining in the land were justifiably afraid of Babylonian retribution. But they had a plan, and it involved the God they had rejected for so many years.

"And all the people, from the least to the greatest, approached Jeremiah the prophet. They said, 'Please pray to the Lord your God for us. As you know, we are only a tiny remnant compared to what we were before. Beg the Lord your God to show us what to do and where to go.

...Whether we like it or not, we will obey the Lord our God to whom we send you with our plea. For if we obey him, everything will turn out well for us" (Jer. 42:1-3,6).

The people started their plea to Jeremiah by speaking of the Lord as "your God" rather than "our God." They were stubborn, but they were not stupid. They knew they could not claim God and His power as their own if they were unwilling to obey Him as Jeremiah did. However, they had run out of options. By the time they finished speaking, they stood, seemingly contrite, before "the Lord *our* God" and Jeremiah wanting to know "what to do and where to go."

The realization that "if we obey him, everything will turn out well for us" was pressing along the edges of their consciousness, but old beliefs die hard. Even now, the people anticipated they would not want to do what the Lord told them to do. "Whether we like it or not" summed up their belief that whatever God wanted of them was going to be a bitter disappointment and hard to accept.

Jeremiah, more than most, knew how unlikely it was that they would do what they said, but he agreed to their request. "Ten days later, the Lord gave his reply to Jeremiah" (Jer. 42:7). Ten days must have seemed like an eternity to these people who were looking over their shoulders in anticipation of Babylonian vengeance at any moment. They had promised to obey in exchange for direction on how to get out of this mess, so what was taking God so long with the answer?

Jeremiah gathered the people together to hear God's answer. "'Stay here in this land. If you do, I will build you up and not tear you down; I will plant you and not uproot you. For I am sorry for all the punishment I have had to bring upon you. Do not fear the king of Babylon anymore,' says the Lord. 'For I am with you and will save you and rescue you from his power. I will be merciful to you by making him kind, so he will let you stay here in your land'" (Jer. 42:10-12).

God's words of hope, mercy, and protection should have brought authentic joy to these people, for they had known great suffering during the siege and expected worse to come. But the people only heard *part* of the message, and it was every bit as bad as they had imagined it would be. What was God thinking to tell them to "stay here in your land" when they had asked "where to go?" They were not going to stay. The land was destroyed, and they would be next. They were so fixed on their disappointment over God's plan not matching up to their own thoughts that they completely missed God's promise of rescue and care.

Since it looked like God couldn't figure it out, they needed to take control. They would go to Egypt. They didn't need to count on the kindness of the king of Babylon; they would outrun him. As usual, they thought they were one step ahead of God. And as usual, their thoughts and actions were no surprise to God, who had also sent along a warning for Jeremiah to deliver: "...If you insist on going to Egypt, the war and famine you fear will follow close behind you, and you will die there" (Jer. 42:15-16).

But the people did insist on going to Egypt. There was another message waiting for them when they arrived. "And now the Lord God Almighty, the God of Israel, asks you: Why are you destroying yourselves?" (Jer. 44:7). It does make one wonder, doesn't it? Why did they continue to think they knew better than God, and why did they ignore God's promise of goodness if they would only obey? Why did they cling to doing the exact thing that brought hardship and death?

The clues are found in their final response to Jeremiah's message. "We will not listen to your messages from the Lord! We will do whatever we want" (Jer. 44:16-17). Pride and stubbornness kept them from believing, obeying, and following a loving God.

God summed up their lives. "To this very hour you have shown no remorse or reverence. No one has chosen to follow my law and the decrees I gave to you and your ancestors before you" (Jer. 44:10). It was not what God wanted for them, but He allowed them to choose what and whom they would believe and follow.

There are many lessons to learn from the people of this story. We need to avoid being as these people were—too proud and stubborn to follow God, too willful to put aside a course of action that they had decided was best, and too suspicious of a loving God. We need to embrace their original words, "show us what to do and where to go." What better prayer is there for a follower of Jesus Christ?

There Are No Hopeless Cases

Jeremiah 48–52; John 17–18

"My people have been lost sheep. Their shepherds have led them astray and turned them loose in the mountains. They have lost their way and cannot remember how to get back to the fold" (Jer. 50:6).

The Lord wanted to be these people's Shepherd. He was the Shepherd who would provide everything they needed, give them rest in green meadows, offer them tranquility beside peaceful streams, renew their strength, and guide them along the correct paths (Ps. 23:1-3).

What a contrast to the leaders of Israel and Judah who had failed as shepherds. They did not protect or guide the people of their nations but "led them astray" to the things that brought them pain and harm. "Turned loose in the mountains," they faced danger by getting off the right paths and onto paths where they stumbled and fell until their strength and hope were gone.

It seemed as though they knew no other path. After making wrong choices for so long, the people had walled themselves off from God's help. They had stubbornly rejected their true leader and were now lost, vulnerable, and confused—with no memory of "how to get back to the fold." But though their memory of the Lord had become weak during the many years they had wandered away from Him, His memory of them had not weakened. He had never stopped loving them or reaching out to offer His protection and guidance.

When the only things left were despair over the past, ongoing misery, and hopelessness for the future, the people finally allowed themselves to hear the voice of the Lord calling to them. "'Then the people of Israel and Judah will join together,' says the Lord, 'weeping and seeking the Lord their God. They will ask the way to Jerusalem and will start back home again. They will bind themselves to the Lord with an eternal covenant that will never again be broken'" (Jer. 50:4-5).

They thought they could not "get back to the fold," but all they needed to do was to "ask the way," and then take that path home. Even though they did not "remember how to get back," there were those, like Jeremiah, who had remained faithful to God and could tell them the way back. And so, they started "back home again," this time binding "themselves to the Lord." They had seemed hopelessly lost, but they were not.

Do you know or love someone who has lost his or her way, making choices that have led to deepening pain and suffering? Do you know someone who has been "led astray" from God by choosing the wrong path for so long that it now seems completely ingrained? Do you know someone who seems like a hopeless case with no remembrance of "how to get back to the fold?" Are *you* that someone? Do you think of yourself as the hopeless case?

With God there is always hope. Sometimes our trust in God's ability to rescue those who have lost their way falters. Sometimes the anguish of these situations brings us to the end of our physical, emotional, and spiritual resources. Yet God's strength does not falter. His goodness and unfailing love will pursue us all the days of our lives (Ps. 23:6).

God, our true Shepherd, still calls to us and will rescue us. With one, just one, honest step seeking to come home, the Lord meets us "with an eternal covenant that will never again be broken."

Week 141

Opening a Locked Door

Lamentations 1–5; John 19–20

So much had happened in just a few days to the devoted friends and disciples of Jesus. Could it have been such a short time since they felt the jubilation of the Passover crowds cheering for Jesus as He entered Jerusalem? With each shout of approval, it had seemed like the cheers were also meant for them.

And now they didn't know what to think. The One they believed was from God had been arrested, tortured, publicly humiliated, and executed.

Only the strongest of believers could hold on to their hope and belief that Jesus was their rescuer after those gruesome, frightening, crushing hours. This was not the first time they had faced the fact that following Jesus was different from what they had first believed it would be. But this was without a doubt the most troubling and traumatic of those times.

Hours lengthened into days as they mulled over the hatred of the crowd, Jesus' death, and the fact that He was gone from them. Confused and scared, they wondered if they were next in this manhunt.

Scenes of their time together with Jesus played again and again in their thoughts as they tried to make sense of it all. Adding to their confusion was Mary, John, and Peter's insistence that Jesus was alive. It was a muddle to their exhausted minds and bodies.

For now, they "were meeting behind locked doors because they were afraid of the Jewish leaders" (John 20:19). They knew a locked door would not keep them safe from those intent on destroying them, but it made them feel a little bit more secure at a time when security was in short supply. That locked door represented their attempt to have some control over their destiny if those they feared pursued them, but it also represented the wall they had built between themselves and everyone else in Jerusalem.

They were indeed correct to think that someone was pursuing them, but to their real pursuer the locked door was of no importance. "Suddenly, Jesus was standing there among them! 'Peace be with you,' he said" (John 20:19). Jesus had broken through their feeble defenses, and their useless attempt at control. And He did it in an amazing, unexpected way. As He often had done, Jesus went right to the heart of their situation. With their previous beliefs now in question, their hopes shattered, and future unsure, Jesus spoke of the peace available through Him for their minds, souls, and bodies.

Jesus understood that all they had based their lives and futures on had been shaken by the events of the past few days, so "he held out his hands for them to see, and he showed them his side" (John 20:20). He was real; He was alive; His promises could be counted on! As that reality sank in, "They were filled with joy when they saw their Lord!" (John 20:20).

But so much had happened, so much remained confusing, and so much was still unknown that their doubts wrestled with their joy as they stood together in that room. Jesus understood and "spoke to them again and said, 'Peace be with you'" (John 20:21).

They needed not only peace but refocusing. Standing among them, Jesus gave them that refocus, saying, "As the Father has sent me, so I send you" (John 20:21). Images of Jesus' ministry—to them and to others— flashed across their minds, and they knew what they were being sent to do. It was time to come out from behind those locked doors. There was an entire world that needed to know what they knew and have what they had.

Jesus knew they could not do this without help. "Then he breathed on them and said to them, 'Receive the Holy Spirit'" (John 20:22). And with that breath there was renewed strength, courage, and wisdom. There was an assurance for that day and all future days. There was empowerment to carry out the great work they were being sent to do.

And so it can be with us. It starts with our belief in the reality of Jesus' resurrection. That belief moves us to trust Him for everything we need and gets us out from behind our locked doors.

Week 142

Always with Us

Ezekiel 1–5; John 21; James 1

Seven disciples were gathered at the Sea of Galilee. They were going fishing. These men did not fish for pleasure; fishing was their livelihood. They fished all night but caught nothing. No fish meant no income. They had a problem.

In the faint light of early dawn, "the disciples saw Jesus standing on the beach, but they couldn't see who he was." Jesus called out from the shore, "'Friends, have you caught any fish?' 'No,' they replied" (John 21:4-5). Surprisingly, they did not recognize His voice even though they had heard it for three years. Had the characteristics of Jesus' voice changed along with other features of His resurrected body? Were the disciples too tired from a long night of hard work or too disappointed by their lack of success to pay close attention? Or was it because they were not expecting to hear from Jesus at that moment?

They may not have recognized the voice as being that of Jesus, but there was still something persuasive about it. When He advised them to "throw out your net on the right-hand side of the boat, and you'll get plenty of fish," they began to prepare the nets once again (John 21:6). As they worked, they must have wondered how throwing their nets on the right side of the boat rather than the left would change the outcome. Although the instructions did not make much sense, and they did not recognize the Messenger, they had enough faith in the message to carry out what they had been told to do.

Their obedient actions led to an incredible outcome when "they couldn't draw in the net because there were so many fish in it" (John 21:6). In fact, the outcome was so amazing that there was only one conclusion to be made, and John made it. He immediately said "to Peter, 'It is the Lord!'" (John 21:7). There was no mistaking God's involvement in their situation.

Even though the disciples were slow in recognizing Jesus, He was not slow in meeting their needs. It started with all those fish and continued as they came ashore and "saw that a charcoal fire was burning and fish were frying over it, and there was bread" (John 21:9). After the excitement of catching so many fish and a night of hard work, the smell of those fish frying must have made the disciples' mouths water. But before they ate, Jesus wanted them to be part of what He was doing. "'Bring some of the fish you've just caught,' Jesus said" (John 21:10). He did not need their fish to provide breakfast, but they needed the joy of helping and of sharing part of what they had been given.

To no one's surprise, Simon Peter, the man of action, "went aboard and dragged the net to the shore" (John 21:11). Since the net had been too heavy to drag into the boat with all seven disciples helping, Peter would have had to exert great effort to bring it to shore by himself, for there were "153 large fish" in that net (John 21:11). It's easy to see Peter standing there after meeting this challenge—soaking wet, breathing heavily, tired, and dirty, but jubilant over the number of fish in the net and Jesus being with them once again.

"'Now come and have some breakfast!' Jesus said. ...Then Jesus served them the bread and the fish" (John 21:12-13). At that moment, they did not serve Jesus; He served them. But the fact that they would have had no success without His help could not have escaped their thoughts as Jesus handed them fish and bread. All that they had came from Him.

And once again they knew that Jesus was always with them. He was with them during this ordinary time of a shared breakfast, during the difficult time of having no source of income, and during the noteworthy time when fishing on the right-hand side of the boat had provided a firsthand glimpse of God's power, love, and provision for them.

What was true for the disciples is true for us as well. We can be assured that Jesus is *always* with us and for us—during the ordinary times of our lives, during the difficult times of our lives, and during the noteworthy times of our lives.

Week 143

Awesome Images

Ezekiel 6–11; James 2

What would someone think if they had never seen an animal, fish, or bird and suddenly saw a whale arc out of the ocean, a giraffe stretch its long neck, an armadillo shuffle by, or a brilliantly colored hummingbird in stationary flight? I think they would be amazed but not as amazed as Ezekiel was when he encountered some intriguing beings.

One of these beings seemed to be a man, but "from the waist down he looked like a burning flame," and "from the waist up he looked like gleaming amber." This figure sat on a throne made of material that looked like "blue sapphire," and "all around him was a glowing halo, like a rainbow shining through the clouds." The figure lifted Ezekiel into the sky and transported him in a vision from Babylon to Jerusalem. In Ezekiel's own words, this being was "the Sovereign Lord," who had taken on an appearance recognizable to man (Ezek. 1:26-28; 8:1-3).

During his vision of Jerusalem, Ezekiel saw not only the Sovereign Lord but the cherubim who were depicted on the Ark of the Covenant inside the Most Holy Place of the Temple. Ezekiel did not see the cherubim as artistic depictions but as living beings.

Each of these cherubim had four faces—human, lion, ox, and eagle. They looked as brilliant as fire, and lightning flashed back and forth among them. Their hands were hidden by four wings, and they were able to fly in any direction without turning around. "As they flew their wings roared like waves crashing against the shore" (Ezek. 1:5-25; 10:2-22).

But that wasn't all that was unusual about these living beings. Each had an "awesomely tall" wheel with "a second wheel turning crosswise within it. Both the cherubim and the wheels were covered with eyes" and somehow Ezekiel knew that "the spirit of the living beings was in the wheels" (Ezek. 1:18; 10:10,12,17).

Is it any wonder that after seeing these things Ezekiel was overwhelmed by God's undeniable majesty and power and "fell face down in the dust" (Ezek. 9:8)? Seeing these displays of God's creative ability for the first time would have to be a humbling experience.

For the reader of Scripture today, Ezekiel's descriptions of the Sovereign Lord and the cherubim/living beings may not evoke the sense of awe they did for Ezekiel because they are often considered to be symbolic rather than literal descriptions. But even that possibility does not contradict the fact that God, as the Creator of this world and of all worlds, is certainly capable of creating and sustaining cherubim or anything else He desires.

As we contemplate God's power, we should be in awe. But those thoughts should also bring great comfort to us. If God is capable of creating and sustaining such variety, He is certainly capable of caring for us. We can count on Him.

Mastering Wisdom

Ezekiel 12–15; James 3–5

James and Proverbs are both books that discuss the benefits of wisdom while giving many practical examples on how to obtain or measure it. This may be one of the reasons that these biblical books are often among people's favorites, for few of us would claim to have mastered wisdom.

But James declares that wisdom can be mastered and tells of the choices made by those who are wise. "If you are wise and understand God's ways, live a life of steady goodness so that only good deeds will pour forth. And if you don't brag about the good you do, then you will be truly wise!" (James 3:13).

James says if we are wise, one of our choices will be to live a life of steady goodness. Steady goodness is consistent and without noteworthy changes in pace or goals. In contrast, an unsteady goodness would be weak, wavering, and causing others to be unsure of what to expect.

Goodness has many traits, and James gives some examples of goodness in relationship to wisdom. He says it is "first of all pure. It is also peace-loving, gentle at all times, and willing to yield to others. It is full of mercy and good deeds. It shows no partiality and is always sincere" (James 3:17). James' explanation of steady goodness echoes many aspects of the description of love found in First Corinthians 13. Those echoes are fitting, for a life of steady goodness will be characterized by loving action to others.

As we take a hard look at the list in verse 17, we will more than likely see areas where God has brought us into maturity *and* areas where we need to focus if we are to become more like Jesus. Are we "pure," seeking to please God at all times, or only when it conveniently lines up with what we want? Are we globally "peace-loving," trying to make a difference in the midst of the turbulence faced by many around the world, or are we indifferent to those needs? Are we locally "peace-loving," or do we participate in petty quarrels, backbiting, and gossip? Are we "gentle at all times" with others, or is it hard to keep our frustration in check with those who differ from us or with us? Do we "yield to others," or do we insist on our rights and expect others to yield to us? Do we show "mercy" to others, or do we judge them? Do we see the value in each person, even those who are not valued by this world, or do we show "partiality"? Are we "always sincere" when we deal with others, or do we have hidden motives? Where is God showing us we need to change, if we are to become truly wise?

James ends verse 13 by reminding us that, to be truly wise, we should not "brag about the good" we do. James is not saying we should not talk about the ways we are living a life of steady goodness, for our examples can be an encouragement to others to do the same. But he is saying that we need to credit God, not ourselves, since it is God who enables us to be steady in doing good.

Pursuing a life of steady goodness becomes both possible and desirable as we depend on God for help in aligning our actions and thoughts with His. There can be no better goal and no better life.

WEEK 145

Misused Gifts

Ezekiel 16–21; 1 Peter 1

We give gifts throughout our lifetime. Sometimes we give gifts with little thought, but much thought may go into gifts for those we love.

These special gifts are given with the hope they will be valued and bring happiness to our loved ones. We desire to make their lives more enjoyable or easier by our gift. We want it to serve as a reminder of what is shared between us.

How satisfying it is to give of ourselves and our resources and to have our gift appreciated and used in the way it was intended. But what a disappointment it is if our special gifts are taken for granted. It would be an even greater letdown if we were ignored and others were credited with spending their time, thought, and resources on the gift. That is the situation God faced with the Israelites.

Ezekiel 16 tells the story of God giving many gifts to His beloved people, carefully considered gifts to enhance their lives and delight their senses. It is the story of the people taking these gifts for granted and using them in ways God never intended.

God gave them riches of "jewels and gold and silver ornaments," and the people, rejecting God, "made statues of men and worshiped them" (Ezek. 16:17). God gave them children, and the people sacrificed these children to their man-made gods. God gave them the best foods, and the people used the "fine flour and oil and honey" as "a lovely sacrifice" to these "gods" (v. 19). They did not reject the gifts, but they completely and thoroughly misused them while rejecting God as their Gift-giver.

God asks, almost in disbelief and indignation, if we can "Imagine it!" (Ezek. 16:19). And the truth is, we may not have given it much thought...until we consider the gifts *we* have given and our hopes for those gifts. It is then we begin to understand how deeply it must have hurt God to have His loving gifts, planned for the Israelites' highest good and greatest happiness, taken for granted. We can begin to sense what it meant to God to have His gifts so completely misused and to grasp what it cost God to be totally ignored as the Gift-giver. The gratitude that should have flowed to God was diverted to a powerless, metal object that could never give back.

Today God continues to be the Giver of our most needed and important gifts. Do we recognize, appreciate, and properly use all the gifts God has given us? Or do we credit the wrong person or thing, chalking up God's gifts to luck or believing it is only our own hard work and efforts that provide for us? Do we use our gifts the way God intended, or do we squander them on the wrong things?

When God says "Imagine it!" about our use of His gifts, may it be with the voice of approval rather than the voice of dismay.

WEEK 146

Silent Grief

Ezekiel 22–24; Psalms 120–122; 1 Peter 2

"Then this message came to me from the Lord: 'Son of man, I am going to take away your dearest treasure. Suddenly she will die'" (Ezek. 24:15-16).

God didn't need to name names for Ezekiel. Ezekiel knew who his dearest treasure was. It was his wife. And with these devastating words, Ezekiel learned she was going to die. It doesn't take much imagination to visualize the shock Ezekiel felt as he went to his wife to share this message...or their sorrow and grief at the thought of their coming separation. What we may find difficult to imagine is their continuing trust in and obedience to God.

That obedience would have been called upon immediately, for God also had a task for Ezekiel. He was to tell his Israelite neighbors what God had said. Ezekiel obeyed and "proclaimed this to the people the next morning, and in the evening my wife died" (Ezek. 24:18).

By Jewish custom, the entire community would have come together for seven emotional days to mourn for Ezekiel's wife—weeping loudly, tearing their clothing, and visiting Ezekiel with gifts of food. But God wanted this time of mourning to be completely different. "You must not show any sorrow. Do not weep; let there be no tears. Let there be no wailing at her grave. ...Do not perform the rituals of mourning or accept any food brought to you by consoling friends" (Ezek. 24:16-17).

God was not forbidding Ezekiel to feel this great loss. Ezekiel mourned. But he did not do so in public. No public mourning was so dramatically different from the norm that the people asked Ezekiel, "What does all this mean? What are you trying to tell us?" (Ezek. 24:19).

There were few situations that could have made the people as curious and concerned as Ezekiel's lack of public mourning. Ezekiel had a captive audience as he explained that the death of his wife paralleled the widespread death that was coming to Jerusalem. The destruction to that beloved city—at the hands of the Babylonians—was going to be so far-reaching that there would be no time and no resources to mourn the many who died. And the grief of those who survived would be too deep and all-encompassing to express, just as Ezekiel's was for his wife. This grief would be caused not only by the many deaths but by the horrors preceding those deaths and by the people's recognition that their sin had led to this destruction.

Ezekiel's loss was truly staggering. First God took his wife, and then He took away his public mourning. Through it all, Ezekiel obeyed God, even though it was probably the hardest thing he ever did. But let us not conclude God was cruel or uncaring. Ezekiel had a more in-depth relationship with God than most people, and through Ezekiel's experiences, his wife shared this intimate knowledge. Compared to most people, they had a much clearer picture of God's holiness, power, and sovereignty and a more concrete comprehension of heaven to console them.

There was a purpose for God's action, and Ezekiel understood this purpose. His understanding could not, in itself, take away the sting of such great loss, but the trust in God that Ezekiel and his wife had already established could bring comfort.

Someday, if it has not already happened, we too will also lose our dearest treasure. The grief and pain will overwhelm us. But as the loneliness and sorrow threaten to overcome us, we will have the Holy Spirit to comfort us and God's promises to which to cling. If there is any question of the power of the Holy Spirit and God's promises in our lives, that question will be answered as we look to God for help in the hardest of all times. And Heaven will take on a new meaning when our "dearest treasure" has preceded us there.

There is little doubt that, if given a choice, Ezekiel would have chosen to keep his dearest treasure, but he was not given this choice. As is often the case for us during difficult times, Ezekiel's only choice was whether or not he would obey and trust. Ezekiel did. May we allow God to help us to do the same when we come to this devastating time in our lives—remembering Him, His promises, and the home He has prepared for us.

A New View on Suffering

Ezekiel 25–29; 1 Peter 3–4

"Christ also suffered when he died for our sins once for all time. He never sinned, but he died for sinners that he might bring us safely home to God..." (1 Pet. 3:18).

It is important to remember who wrote these words regarding the suffering of Jesus Christ. It was Peter. And Peter had not chosen the word "suffered" lightly. He had observed how this single word played out in Jesus' earthly life.

Long before Peter wrote about suffering, he had formed the opinion that it should be avoided when possible. That opinion influenced his thinking as he heard Jesus speak about why He was willing to die and the suffering He would experience as He was put on trial and killed. Peter caught a glimpse of how gruesome that suffering would be and loathed the thought of it. Convinced that horrific suffering should not be part of the plan, Peter tried to persuade Jesus to find a different way to "bring us safely home to God," but his words of counsel were swiftly rejected by Jesus (Matt. 16:21-23).

When those words of predicted suffering began to come true in the Garden of Gethsemane, it was Peter who drew his sword and readied for battle as the mob approached. In his attempt to defend Jesus, he cut off the ear of the high priest's servant, creating a gaping wound that Jesus immediately healed (John 18:1-11).

Hours later the friends of Jesus stood at a distance watching Christ's final agonizing hours on the cross (Luke 23:49). Peter saw exactly how real, raw, and relentless Jesus' suffering was during His final earthly hours so sinners could be brought "safely home to God."

Worse yet, Peter knew he had added to Jesus' suffering. While Peter's love for Jesus had drawn him to the fringes of the crowd gathered to watch Jesus' trial, beating, and crucifixion, his fear caused him to declare publicly that he did not know or associate with Jesus. When his love was most needed, he chose personal safety over Jesus. It was a choice not easily forgotten. How many times did Peter recall the moment when Jesus turned to look at him after hearing him angrily cursing at a servant girl who insisted that he was a disciple of Jesus? How many times did Peter remember the bitter tears he wept when he realized what he had done? (Matt. 26:72; Luke 22:54-62). Those three denials became a low point in Peter's life, and because of it, he began to understand suffering in a new way.

Peter experienced the agony of turning away from Christ for a time, but this, more than anything else, may have helped him to understand his own need for the redemption made possible by Christ's suffering on the cross. Christ's resurrection was the dividing point between the weak and unpredictable Peter of old and the bold and courageous Peter who had experienced God's forgiveness and the life-changing power of the Holy Spirit. Peter's guilt and regret regarding his role in Christ's suffering were transformed by the resurrection, and his life was never the same.

The man who cut off a servant's ear was the same man who later wrote, "Don't repay evil for evil. Don't retaliate. Work hard at living in peace with others" (1 Pet. 3:9,11). The man who, out of fear, cursed at a servant girl for questioning if he was aligned with Jesus was the same man who later wrote, "Be happy if you are insulted for being a Christian, for then the glorious Spirit of God will come upon you. It is no shame to suffer for being a Christian. Praise God for the privilege of being called by his wonderful name!" (1 Pet. 4:14,16). The man who recoiled at the thought of suffering became a person who was willing to—and who did—suffer horribly because of his unbendable devotion to Jesus Christ. He had a new opinion about suffering because God had made him a new person.

Are we like the old Peter, afraid of suffering and trying to avoid the unavoidable? If so, God can strengthen us. Are we like Peter, weighed down with deep regret for past failures? If so, God can forgive us because Jesus died on the cross with open arms. As we move into those arms, God can renew us and use our experiences to help others, just as He did with Peter.

Week 148

Watchfulness Goes Both Ways

Ezekiel 30–32; Psalms 123–125; 1 Peter 5

This week our reading included two verses that share the themes of being focused and watchful. But the object of focus in each verse is nothing like the other.

In the first verse, an unidentified psalmist urges us to keep our focus on God: "We look to the Lord our God for his mercy, just as servants keep their eyes on their master, as a slave girl watches her mistress for the slightest signal" (Ps. 123:2). Focusing on God is not unusual advice to find in the Bible, but the level of concentration suggested in this verse elevates that activity to the highest level.

There are different reasons why a slave, or servant, would watch his or her master intently. If the master was cruel, the slave would mistrust the master and watch carefully as a matter of self-preservation. If employment by the master made the difference between the servant having basic needs met or being destitute, the servant would keep a careful watch so as to maintain the master's goodwill. If a master was consistently kind, a servant may eventually become devoted to the master.

The true Master of this psalm is God. And the psalmist is aware of God's mercy. How comforting it is to serve a master who is merciful, for mercy is comprised of compassion, kindness, understanding, and forgiveness. So the psalmist is urging us to be alert to God's never-ending stream of compassion for our plights, kindness for our needs, understanding for our weaknesses, and forgiveness for our failures. It is good to be focused on such a loving Master.

Life would be so much simpler if that was the only focus that required constant vigilance. But it is not. Peter warned of another: "Be careful! Watch out for attacks from the devil, your great enemy. He prowls around like a roaring lion, looking for some victim to devour" (1 Pet. 5:8). Once again, we see the advice to watch and keep focused.

But there is a different reason behind this directive to keep watch. The devil has opposite motives and goals to those of the Lord. Cruelty, not mercy, characterizes this master. Harshness, hatred, ruthlessness, pain, and sorrow are his gifts to those who serve him. And yes, just like a lion, this would-be master will hunt, stalk, and ambush his prey. We need not fear this evil being who is vastly inferior to God, but we do need to respect his power and cunning and keep a close watch for the traps in which he specializes.

Peter and the psalmist knew that focus and watchfulness go both ways. Even if our ability to focus is often weak, we ourselves are the focus of strong spiritual forces. Our loving Master, Jesus Christ, watches over us in mercy and love. Our enemy, the devil, watches us to try to bring about our destruction.

Where is our focus? The psalmist and Peter had wise words of advice for us. In turn, we need to be wise and heed what they say by staying attuned to our true Master and keeping a cautious eye on the evil one who wants to rule over us.

Bargaining with God

Ezekiel 33–37; 2 Peter 1–2

"Then this message came to me from the Lord: 'Son of man, the scattered remnants of Judah living among the ruined cities keep saying, "Abraham was only one man, and yet he gained possession of the entire land! We are many; surely the land should be given to us as a possession"'" (Ezek. 33:23-24).

This verse contains a fitting description of Israel after many years of warfare. The land lay in ruins, and the Israelites were few though they still saw themselves as many. Most of the people who had survived the war, the famine, and the diseases had been moved to other countries by the conquering Assyrians and Babylonians. A small group of survivors had escaped both death and deportation, but these scattered remnants were exactly that—the bits and pieces of a once great nation scattered around the land.

They had hit bottom. To go on, they needed hope, and they needed comfort. Looking out over their destroyed land, these remaining few clung to their history, thinking that if Abraham, as one man, had "gained possession of the entire land," surely they, being more than one, could do the same.

And so the bargaining with God began. "Surely the land should be given" to them. The stories from long ago told of the great promise made between God and Abraham, the promise that the land now known as Israel would be the home of the descendants of Abraham. They were descendants of Abraham, and they were ready to claim what was rightfully theirs. It was so clear, so logical. Yes, "surely the land should be given" to them.

There was one flaw in their reasoning and therefore with their bargaining power. They were remembering what they wanted to remember and forgetting what was not to their liking about God's promise to Abraham. There was that sticky part about obedience that they preferred to forget.

Stubborn and deluded as they were, God still loved them enough to try once again to set them straight. God had heard their reasoning, and now He would respond through Ezekiel. "Now give these people this message from the Sovereign Lord: 'You eat meat with blood in it, you worship idols, and you murder the innocent. Do you really think the land should be yours?'" (Ezek. 33:25).

After pointing out only a few of the ongoing issues with the people's obedience, God stops and asks the most logical question. "Do you *really* think the land should be yours?" God was challenging them to remember the entire story of His promise to Abraham, not their watered-down version.

God was keeping His promise, as He always does, for He had promised the people punishment if they did not obey and His blessing if they did. They had not obeyed, and God had punished them. They continued in their disobedience, and God continued withholding His blessing. But it wasn't what God wanted for them any more than it was what the people wanted. "'As surely as I live,' says the Sovereign Lord, 'I take no pleasure in the death of wicked people. I only want them to turn from their wicked ways so they can live'" (Ezek. 33:11).

The ancient Israelites are not the only ones who have tried to bargain with God or bend God's will to their own. If we are honest with ourselves we can probably remember doing the same thing at some point in our lives. Maybe we are at that point right now.

Are we bargaining with God about an issue in our lives, saying or thinking, "God, if You do this, then I promise I'll...."? God wants us to come to Him wholeheartedly and without conditions on our part, trusting Him to know what is best for us on our journey through life.

Do we read God's promises in Scripture and expect God to uphold His part while we renege on ours? God's promises often have actions that we need to take for the promises to be fulfilled in our lives. Are we taking them?

Do we subconsciously feel we deserve a specific response or gift from God based on our relationship with Him, thereby making God almost like a divine Santa Claus? God wants us to have a relationship with Him based on love, gratitude, and trust for what He has *already* given us—His creation and His salvation.

And finally, have we attempted to rewrite part of our history to justify ourselves? God wants us to be honest about our lives so He can heal the broken parts.

God, who knows us better than we know ourselves, wants us to be obedient because being obedient leads to life the way God designed it to be. It is not a life to be lived among the ruins but a life guided by the God who loves us.

Week 150

Headed Home

Ezekiel 38–40; Psalms 126–128; 2 Peter 3

"When the Lord restored his exiles to Jerusalem, it was like a dream! We were filled with laughter, and we sang for joy. And the other nations said, 'What amazing things the Lord has done for them.' Yes the Lord has done amazing things for us! What joy!" (Ps. 126:1-3).

To the Israelites, Jerusalem represented not only their homeland but their special relationship with God. Year after year, going back to Jerusalem had been the dream of many who had been forcibly moved far from their home. And now their dream was a reality. Their sense of elation seemed to bubble up from the core of their being, and it filled these returning people with laughter, songs, and joy.

But before the Israelites experienced the full joy of returning to Jerusalem, they had to make the long, arduous journey to get there. Although they did not know what this journey held for them, their knowledge about their homeland gave them a clear understanding of where they were headed, and that knowledge alone brought much happiness and anticipation.

It was a good thing that they knew about and longed for their ending destination, for as we have seen in prior passages, their journey to Jerusalem was dangerous and filled with many hardships. The prayer of the people became, "restore our fortunes, Lord, as streams renew the desert" (Ps. 126:4). This prayer was not merely a figure of speech, for their long journey taught them much about the grueling demands of traveling through a hostile desert inhabited by equally hostile people. Every step they took toward Jerusalem would have been made only through gritty determination and faith.

But the people were not left to bear these hardships alone. Having their loved ones and friends on the journey would have brought some comfort. And knowing that God was with them and guiding them had to bring reassurance, even if it did not eliminate the pain of their circumstances.

What must it have been like for these weary, beat-up travelers when they first glimpsed their homeland? The joy of anticipation at the beginning of the journey could not compare to the joy of finally being home. The joy of this homecoming was beyond their imaginations; it had to be experienced.

The Israelites were traveling to Jerusalem. Our life's journey is toward Heaven. But the two journeys share many similarities. There will be difficulties on our journey, many of which we will never foresee. Our relationship with God can give us assurance and hope as we struggle through these difficulties. Our relationship with loved ones can give us support and encouragement. Our anticipation of Heaven can help us to keep moving forward, even when it is hard to do so.

And when the journey is over, the joy of coming home to Heaven will far surpass anything we can imagine now. The difficulties of the journey will dissolve into the joy of reaching the destination. And part of that joy will be sharing a home with God, for He has promised that "I will make my home among them. I will be their God, and they will be my people" (Ezek. 37:27).

It is a home where our laughter and joy will lead to the same conclusion as the Israelites' about their homecoming: "Yes, the Lord has done amazing things for us!"

Week 151

The Sound of Silence

Ezekiel 41–45; 1 John 1–2

The sound of water can be so soothing—the gurgle of a brook, the rhythmic lap of waves on a shore, or the splashing of children playing in a swimming pool. The sound of water can be exhilarating—just ask a dedicated white-water rafter or champion swimmer. But the sound of water can also be alarming—especially when it is the roar of rushing water.

Rushing, roaring water makes us wary because it is always a potent force and is often evidence of a natural disaster such as a hurricane, a tsunami, or a flood. Obstacles to flowing water such as immense rocks or the narrowing of a channel can also create the roar of rushing water, as can its plummet from one level to another. And, as Ezekiel experienced, so can God's presence.

It was God's presence returning to the Temple in Jerusalem that gave Ezekiel firsthand knowledge of the sound of God's overwhelming power. "Suddenly, the glory of the God of Israel appeared from the east. The sound of his coming was like the roar of rushing waters, and the whole landscape shone with his glory" (Ezek. 43:2). God's presence was such a powerful, holy force that it caused the air being displaced by it to sound like the roar of rushing water. Ezekiel said he was so overcome by the sound and the glory of God's presence that he "fell down before him with my face in the dust" (Ezek. 43:3).

Ezekiel not only *heard* the presence of God, he *felt* the presence of God, and he *saw* its grandeur. It is unlikely that he could ever doubt God's power or presence after that experience.

But we are not Ezekiel. Most of us will never experience God's presence in such a dramatic way in this life. Our experiences with God will more than likely be quieter times. Often, these times are so quiet that they cause us to begin to doubt God's presence. This may happen when the obstacles in our lives are so loud that they drown out our ability to sense God's presence with us. Or it may be when our lives are serene and we wait to hear the quiet whisper of the Holy Spirit but do not. It can even be when we are seeking God with all of our heart, mind, and soul but we only sense His silence.

These are the times when we may long to hear, feel, or see God's presence as Ezekiel did. But we must practice walking with God by faith alone and not by sight or by sound (2 Cor. 5:7). Most importantly, we must remember that even though God's presence sounded like the roar of rushing water as He entered the Temple, once His presence filled the Temple, there was silence. But He was still there.

As He is with us.

WEEK 152

All Our Actions

Ezekiel 46–48; Psalms 129–131; 1 John 3

"Dear children, let us stop just saying we love each other, let us really show it by our actions" (1 John 3:18). Sometimes this is hard to do. Our hearts may be willing, but we may feel too tired, stressed, or busy when an opportunity comes to show love by our actions. We may be in the middle of doing something and not want to stop. Or we may think that our day cannot accommodate one more thing when an unexpected need interrupts our plans.

That is what happened to me not long ago. It was a Monday morning at 7:10 when the doorbell rang. Wondering who would be at the door that early, I guessed that someone needed help. Opening the door, I saw my neighbor walking away. I called to John to see if everything was okay, since his wife had recently undergone major surgery. As he turned back toward me, I saw he was holding two miniature golf clubs. You see, John has been a lifelong golfer, but the passage of time has made playing no longer possible. He loves the game so much, though, that he has converted to miniature golf, which he plays faithfully each day, sometimes even when it is snowing.

As it turned out, all was fine at home, but John was feeling the need to get out on the course. So he had set out to walk the six miles of hilly, curvy roads, since he no longer drives. As he started his walk, he had stopped by for a little visit.

Even at that time in the morning it was a hot, humid, sticky day. Thoughts of the weather and of the danger of walking on our country roads prompted me to offer to drive John. So off we went. Two hours later we were back home. John had a fun time, and I was glad I had taken the time to help. As far as First John 3:18 goes, I had shown love by my actions. End of story. Or so I thought.

As I moved into my day's work, I suddenly began feeling overwhelmed by what I thought I needed to accomplish that day. Before long, my happiness at helping John began to turn into resentment. The more things stacked up that morning, the more aggravated I became. And then it hit me. There is more to our actions than what we do. There are also the actions of our mind—what we think. It didn't take long to recognize that, while my deeds had shown love to John, my thoughts were now anything but loving.

In reality, wasn't I rebelling against God, who had provided this chance for me to practice loving others? With the Holy Spirit's help, I began to understand that "it is by our actions that we know we are living in the truth" (1 John 3:19). Living in God's truth involves all of our actions. Confessing my resentful and rebellious thoughts as the sins they were, I asked once again for God's help to be consistent and pleasing to Him in what I did and what I thought.

And because God loves me so much, on that same day He provided three other unexpected opportunities to put aside my plans so I could live "in the truth" by showing love to others through all of my actions. No doubt about it—in my case, God knows that practice makes perfect and so my lessons continue.

Week 153

Is It Hot in Here?

Daniel 1–3; Psalms 132–134; 1 John 4

Shadrach, Meshach, and Abednego were caught between a rock and a hot place. They had deliberately disobeyed King Nebuchadnezzar's decree that all people under his rule were to worship a gold statue he had created or be thrown into a blazing furnace. Of course, troublemakers had hurried to the king as fast as they could to tell of the Israelites' disobedience. And now Nebuchadnezzar was furious enough to kill.

Standing before the king, there was only one question to be answered. Almost in disbelief that anyone would dare to disobey him, Nebuchadnezzar asked, "Is it true, Shadrach, Meshach, and Abednego, that you refuse to serve my gods or to worship the gold statue I have set up?" (Dan. 3:14).

These three men, who had refused to sin by worshiping a false god, were not going to sin by lying. So they answered truthfully, causing the king to become almost as hot as the furnace. In spite of his fury, he gave these valued members of his government one last chance to live. "If you bow down and worship the statute I have made when you hear the sound of the musical instruments, all will be well. But if you refuse, you will be thrown immediately into the blazing furnace. What god will be able to rescue you from my power then?" (Dan. 3:15).

Well, Shadrach, Meshach, and Abednego had the answer to that question and willingly shared it, "If we are thrown into the blazing furnace, the God whom we serve is able to save us" (Dan. 3:17). To Nebuchadnezzar, who thought of himself as being as powerful as any god, this was a challenge that could not be ignored.

Commanding "that the furnace be heated seven times hotter than usual," Nebuchadnezzar "ordered some of the strongest men of his army to bind Shadrach, Meshach, and Abednego and throw them into the blazing furnace" (Dan. 3:19-20).

But before they were sent to certain death, Shadrach, Meshach, and Abednego had one other thing to share with Nebuchadnezzar. They knew the power of the Lord and boldly proclaimed to the king, "…He will rescue us from your power, Your Majesty" (Dan. 3:17). They were not cringing and trembling in fear at their coming fate but standing firmly confident in the God they served.

Yes, they were definitely confident that God *could* rescue them. However, it was their final words to the king before being thrown into that raging fire that showed how much they trusted God. "*But even if he doesn't*, Your Majesty can be sure that we will never serve your gods or worship the gold statue you have set up" (Dan. 3:18).

"But even if he doesn't…." Even if they burned to death in that furnace, they would obey God's commands. Even if they were not rescued, their trust in God would not change. They were prepared to be rescued or prepared to die. Whatever God had for them, they would accept it—not begrudgingly or with resentment, but with a faith that was vibrant and flourishing.

You know the end of this story. God rescued Shadrach, Meshach, and Abednego—spectacularly so. Because they survived, many of us would conclude that their faith had been rewarded. But because they were confident of God's wisdom and care in all aspects of their lives, Shadrach, Meshach, and Abednego would have believed that their faith had been rewarded whether they lived or died.

There are many valuable lessons for us to take away from this story. Certainly Shadrach, Meshach, and Abednego's obedience to God in spite of the possibility of tremendous suffering or death is a worthy example to follow. Their understanding of God's characteristics and His promises help us understand God better.

But possibly their most notable trait was their unshakable faith in God. The words "but even if He doesn't" reflected their willingness to trust God even when the course of their lives might have diverged sharply from what they hoped it would be. That type of trust replaces fear with peace, weakness with strength, chaos with purpose, and vacillation with steadfastness.

Shadrach, Meshach, and Abednego knew God was worthy of that kind of trust and lived accordingly. Do we?

Courage Put to the Test

Daniel 4–8; 1 John 5; 2 John 1

No one could accuse Daniel of being cowardly or fearful. Strengthened by his faith in God, examples of his bravery are plentiful.

Possibly Daniel's best-known moment of bravery took place when he refused to obey King Darius' command to worship a god other than the Lord God. This refusal earned Daniel a night in the lion's den. It would take an extraordinary person to not be terrified of the prospect of being tossed into the midst of killer lions. And yet the Bible records no evidence of Daniel showing any fear.

Even as a young man, Daniel possessed unusual courage. Until the time Judah became subject to the Babylonians, Daniel would have lived the privileged life of Israelite nobility. But in a complete reversal of fortune, Daniel was taken from all that he knew and forcibly marched five hundred miles to Babylon as a prisoner of war. The march was arduous and made by people without hope. Many did not have the courage to keep going, but Daniel did (Dan. 1:1-3).

Arriving in Babylon, Daniel was singled out as a person with leadership potential and ordered into a three-year training program by King Nebuchadnezzar, the most powerful human being on earth at that time. But Daniel had a problem with the training program because the food being served was in conflict with the dietary laws given to Israel by God. Although Daniel was nothing more than a lowly captive in a new and strange land, he sought and gained permission to eat food that followed God's guidelines. Not many would have the strength to stand against a powerful ruler like King Nebuchadnezzar in order to stand for their allegiance to God. The Bible tells us that Daniel had that kind of courage (Dan. 1:4-20).

Between these noteworthy times, Daniel lived a life similarly marked by his bravery. Throughout his adult life he was an advisor to the four most powerful rulers of the day: Nebuchadnezzar, Belshazzar, Darius, and Cyrus. In the face of such absolute power, it would have been logical for Daniel to speak to these kings in ways that would keep them calm and happy. But Daniel was God's messenger to these rulers, and he often found it necessary to tell them the most unpleasant news. Certainly not a job for the faint of heart.

He told Nebuchadnezzar that because of his pride he would become insane "until you learn that the Most High rules over the kingdoms of the world and gives them to anyone he chooses" (Dan. 4:25). He told Belshazzar that "you have defied the Lord of heaven. God has numbered the days of your reign and has brought it to an end. You have been weighed on the balances and have failed the test" (Dan. 5:23,26-27). Daniel did not relish giving these shocking messages, but he did not fear being God's messenger.

There was something that did shake Daniel, however, and it shook him badly. It was a vision of things to come, including the rise and fall of four world powers: the Babylonian, Medo-Persian, Greek, and Roman empires. Daniel's vision of one empire overcoming the one before it was disturbing, since world powers do not quietly ebb away and new ones arise without great conflict and devastation. But there was something even more terrifying to Daniel in the vision. Daniel saw the coming deception and devastation of the holy people in the final battles between God and evil.

As this vision unfolded, the angel Gabriel was sent to Daniel to help him understand what would transpire. Daniel tells of his reaction to this vision: "I fainted and lay there with my face to the ground. Then I, Daniel, was overcome and lay sick for several days. I was greatly troubled by the vision and could not understand it" (Dan. 8:18,27).

We know that Daniel was not ruled by fear, so his extreme reaction to this vision was truly out of character for him. It is disconcerting to think of Daniel being in such distress, and it is even more troubling when we remember that the direst part of Daniel's vision has not yet been completely fulfilled.

Each generation has had holy people who have experienced the destruction Daniel saw in his vision. There have been countless believers who have had to face mistreatment, much of it severe. Many others have been killed because of their faithfulness to Jesus Christ. But the time has not yet come when widespread deception, devastation, and destruction threaten every believer.

For Christians who have not faced these types of hardships, these thoughts can be frightening and make us wonder if our faith would be strong enough to carry us through. The prospects of persecution can make us fearful about the future. But we can make choices that help prepare us for whatever sort of spiritual battle we may face.

Studying Daniel's life gives us not only the clues of his courage but also the sources of it. Like Daniel, we can make our relationship with God the cornerstone of everything we do. Daniel prayed three times a day; we can make prayer a priority. Daniel was a student of Scripture and gained wisdom; we can make Bible study a priority to keep us close to God and protect us from being deceived. Daniel determined ahead of time that he would be loyal to God no matter what; we can make the same decision.

And we can realize and understand that God will give His children strength and courage when it is needed. Daniel did not practice being willing to be thrown in the lion's den before it happened. He did not practice being a captive in a foreign country before he was one. He did not practice giving bad news to powerful people before he had to do it. But he did honor and obey God by living a consistent life, choosing God's way in each small, daily detail so it became second nature for him to do so in the more difficult circumstances.

And we can do the same.

WEEK 155

The Exact Moment

Daniel 9–12; Psalms 135–136; 3 John 1

After a long life marked by many years of turning to God in prayer, it was natural for Daniel to call out to God in honesty and openness when his world was out of balance. And once again, Daniel was wrestling with a situation that brought both joy and pain.

As Daniel studied the writings of the prophets, he realized that the time was quickly coming for the Israelites' punishment of exile to end. For an Israelite, fewer joys could surpass the end of their exile and the return to their homeland. Daniel felt this joy.

And yet, Daniel knew that before their exile could end, God still required the Israelites to confess and turn away from their sin of worshiping other gods. Daniel also knew that the people were not prepared to do so. Can you imagine his grief at this realization? But no matter how deep his grief or how frightening the consequences, Daniel could not make the disobedient people see the harm they were doing to themselves.

So Daniel did what he always did in times of deep distress and trouble. "I turned to the Lord God and pleaded with him in prayer and fasting…and confessed: 'O Lord, you are a great and awesome God! You always fulfill your promises of unfailing love to those who love you and keep your commands. But we have sinned and done wrong. But the Lord our God is merciful and forgiving, even though we have rebelled against him. The Lord has brought against us the disaster he prepared, for we did not obey him, and the Lord our God is just in everything he does'" (Dan. 9:3-5,9,14).

There is much to learn from Daniel's prayer. We learn that Daniel was spiritually humble in spite of his earthly prominence. Although Scripture is silent about Daniel's sins, he recognized that his sins—even if unknown by others—needed to be confessed to God as much as any other person's. Daniel prayed for himself as well as for others.

We learn that Daniel understood the justice of God's actions. God had warned His people about the consequences of turning away from

Him, so Daniel did not blame God for the choices that others made or for the consequences of those choices.

We learn that Daniel knew the characteristics of God that make Him God. He rejoiced in God's greatness, that God's justice is offset by His mercy, and that God's forgiveness is driven by His "unfailing love." Daniel's prayer captured his understanding of God's nature and the trust he felt in God.

Daniel's final cry to God captures the intensity of his emotion. "O Lord, hear. O Lord, forgive. O Lord, listen and act! For your own sake, O my God, do not delay..." (Dan. 9:19).

God did not delay but sent Gabriel, the mighty angel, with His response to Daniel's prayer. "Daniel, I have come here to give you insight and understanding. The moment you began praying, a command was given. I am here to tell you what it was, for God loves you very much. Now listen, so you can understand" (Dan. 9:23).

With only a few words, Gabriel told Daniel three important things. Daniel was assured that "God loves you very much." Daniel was promised that God wanted to give him "insight and understanding." Daniel was told that "the moment you began praying, a command was given."

No matter what the circumstances in our lives, God's responses to Daniel's prayer are the same for us as we pray. God loves us. God hears us. God responds to us. God will give us insight and understanding if we seek it.

WEEK 156

Difficult Relationships

Hosea 1–6; Jude

Is there a relationship that causes you so much pain that it would be easier for you to walk away from it? Is there a relationship that you wish with all your heart was different from what it is?

Then you may have a great deal in common with the prophet Hosea, for this was the kind of relationship he had with a woman named Gomer. At the beginning of his life's work as a prophet of God, Hosea was told to "Go and marry a prostitute, so some of her children will be born to you from other men" (Hos. 1:2).

We read those verses, and we know that, if he obeys God's directive, there is much heartache ahead for Hosea. Hosea had to know that too, but as hard as it must have been, he was obedient to God and married Gomer.

God had several reasons for asking such a hard thing of Hosea. One of those reasons was that God wanted to use Hosea's relationship with his wife as a vivid, living example to "illustrate the way my people have been untrue to me, openly committing adultery against the Lord by worshiping other gods" (Hos. 1:2). Hosea was going to pay a high price due to the sins of others.

Before long we read one of the more pain-filled verses in Scripture. "Then the Lord said to me, 'Go and get your wife again. Bring her back to you and love her, even though she loves adultery'" (Hos. 3:1).

"Go and get your wife again." The word "again" sums up a lifetime of hurt and pain. It is obvious that this was not the first time Hosea had to deal with his wife's sin. What is not as obvious is what Hosea must have felt as he once again started out on a journey to get his wife.

Hosea wasn't starting out blind as to the reason God asked him to go get Gomer again. God was using this as one more living illustration to show that "the Lord still loves Israel even though the people have turned to other gods, offering them choice gifts" (Hos. 3:1). But after Gomer's repeated abandonments of their marriage and their home did Hosea wonder about God's ways?

Did Hosea resent the harsh reality that once again his life would be disrupted as he obeyed God's command? Did he feel hurt? Hopeless? Angry? Used? Discouraged? Just plain weary? Was he wondering how he could force Gomer, who loved adultery, to make the right choices? Did his sense of honor and dignity make him question why he had to keep on being the object of gossip, derision, and even pity?

Regardless of his feelings, Hosea did bring Gomer home. But knowing Gomer's inclination for making wrong choices, Hosea set boundaries for her: "You must live in my house for many days and stop your prostitution. During this time, you will not have sexual intercourse with anyone, not even with me" (Hos. 3:3). Hosea did not allow Gomer the freedom to keep doing what could destroy them both.

As difficult as it would have been for Hosea to bring Gomer back, it was not the hardest part of what God asked of Hosea that day. The hardest part would have been to love Gomer. How could Hosea love Gomer considering her past betrayals and the real probability of future hurt? How could he love her in spite of no apparent remorse or desire to change on her part? How could he love her when she took advantage of his kindness and loyalty?

By most people's standards, Gomer did not deserve to be loved. Although Hosea had a long history of obedience to God, even he could not turn *emotional* love for his wife on and off at will. But he could practice *deliberate* love and seek what was best for her. He could feel compassion for the pain that her own actions caused her. He could show her respect even when she did not respect herself or him. He could offer godly guidance even if she did not want to hear it. He could be kind and patient. He could humbly examine his past actions and attitudes toward Gomer to determine if there was anything for which he needed to seek her forgiveness. And, most of all, he could have faith and hope that, through God, Gomer could change.

God tells us love should characterize all of our relationships, even those made difficult by sin. God does not ask us to condone the things that are wrong, nor does He ask us to ignore them. But He does ask us to love...even when it is the hardest thing to do, even when that love can only happen with His help.

Use with Care

Hosea 7–10; Psalms 137–138; Revelation 1

"I bow before your holy Temple as I worship. I will give thanks to your name for your unfailing love and faithfulness, because your promises are backed by all the honor of your name" (Ps. 138:2).

The promises of God are important to believers because they are one way in which God expresses His "unfailing love and faithfulness" to His followers. God's promises can give us strength when we are fearful, confused, or weak. They can give us hope when our problems feel overwhelming. They can help us follow the right path when we are tempted to take one that would harm us. They can help us understand God and who He is.

But we may feel somewhat jaded about promises because throughout our lives we have received many that were not kept by family, friends, businesses, and others. Regardless of the sincerity of a person making a promise, circumstances may come along that make it impossible to fulfill that promise. Not so with God's promises. They will always be kept. We can build our lives on that certainty.

Psalm 138 tells us why that is so. David praises God because he recognizes God's "promises are backed by all the honor of your name." Look again at what David is saying. God's promises are dependable because they are backed by all, not some, of the honor of God's name. These promises are supported by nothing less than the reputation that God's name carries.

And what a reputation! God's name stands for His superior position as the Creator and Provider of all life. That alone would ensure His authority to keep promises—but there is more. God's name also stands for His nature—His power, justice, kindness, faithfulness, and love. Everything that there is to God, what we know and understand and what we do not, is captured in His name. God's name is of unmatched value and is to be respected.

But far too often that is not the case in this world, is it? God's various names are not respected or given the honor they deserve. How often do we hear or see "God," "Jesus," "Christ," "Lord," "omg," or another of God's names scattered mindlessly throughout conversations or writings? How often are God's names used flippantly, arrogantly, or as an angry curse? It is even easy to stop thinking about the true meaning of God's names when continually surrounded by their disrespectful or careless use.

It is important to stop and focus on what His name means to us. How has your life been changed by God? How is each day different because of God? What does God mean to your future? As these thoughts settle into our consciousness, our use of any of God's names will stand out as the name that means everything to us because of who He is and what He has done for us. And our words will convey the reverence, honor, love, and enthusiasm God deserves.

"'I am the Alpha and the Omega—the beginning and the end,' says the Lord God. 'I am the one who is, who always was, and who is still to come, the Almighty One!'" (Rev. 1:8). Blessed be the glorious names of the Lord!

WEEK 158

Can't Wait for Sunday!

Hosea 11–14; Revelation 2–4

The book of Revelation can cause us to experience many conflicting emotions: joy and fear, comfort and distress, assurance and confusion, longing to know more and wondering how to best respond to what we do know.

It may have produced the same emotions among the members of the seven churches of Asia Minor for which Revelation was originally written. God knew these church communities intimately. They were important to Him, and He desired to guide them into the relationship with Him that they were meant to have.

And these churches *needed* God's attention and guidance. The churches each faced issues that could destroy them. Some were experiencing faith-testing hardships such as poverty, suffering, and persecution for being Christians. Others were blessed with riches that made it easy to become complacent, proud, and seemingly self-sufficient. Still others were allowing teaching that was contrary to God's Word, leading not only to confusion but eventually to the acceptance of sin.

But the stories of these churches included triumphs as well as problems. There were examples of love, faith, obedience, hard work, service to others, resistance to evil influences, opposition to false teaching, growth in relationship with the Lord, and unwavering devotion to Him.

It is no small matter to be complimented by God. His words of praise to the churches that remained faithful and active in spite of their troubles and hardships must have lifted their spirits. Knowing that God recognized their deepening relationship of love and obedience to Him must have encouraged and thrilled each person to whom these messages were given.

It is also no small matter to be reprimanded by God. God clearly warned of the serious consequences for the churches that had become halfhearted in their devotion to Him, who did not practice loving service to others, and who tolerated sin and false teachings about Him. Was there sorrow and fear among the people of these churches when they heard Jesus' command to repent of these sins? Or had some moved so far away in their relationship with Him that they no longer cared?

Whether its members were following God's guidelines and doing much good or falling short of His desires and causing much damage, each of these churches and its future was God's focus in Revelation. This final, great book of Scripture is directed to local churches, not only to individuals. Yet these days many Christians are not part of any church or are only marginally so. Others have been so wounded by their experiences within a church that they actively avoid participation. But God wants to bless us through the church.

Perhaps the greatest benefit of being an active part of a church is that it helps us obey God's command to love the Lord our God with all our heart, soul, strength, and mind (Luke 10:27). There is something spiritually powerful, exciting, and life-changing when we gather with a group of people who are focused on God and joined together in praise, learning, singing hymns, and prayer.

Another blessing of being part of a church is that it can help us put into practice God's command that we love others (Luke 10:27). The most loving thing we can do for others is share with them what Jesus Christ means to us and how He is the answer to our heart's deepest longings. Being part of a church whose main purpose is to tell others about the wonderful message of Jesus Christ gives us encouragement and tools to do exactly that.

Being part of a church can provide opportunities for service to others that may not be possible for us as individuals. Our interaction with people who have different talents and abilities from our own can lead to ideas we would not have and provide new ways to put action to our faith.

Another powerful aspect of a church family is its encouragement, help, and friendship during life's hardest times. As we become part of a church, there is a support system available that would not otherwise be part of our lives.

If you are part of a church that pleases God, you already experience these things. If you are part of a church that would be in line for a warning from Jesus, then determine to be an example to the people of your church. The church at Sardis was "dead" and their deeds were "far from right in the sight of God" (Rev. 3:1-2). But even in this church, there were a few individuals who had "not soiled their garments with evil deeds" (Rev. 3:4). These were the people God could use to bring the Sardis church back to Him. Like these few, it may be your role to be a communicator of God's truth and an example of Christ's love to your church community.

And if you are not currently attending a church, become part of one that is built on the characteristics for which God praised the Revelation churches. If you have been hurt by someone or something in the church, seek God's healing and His help. It is true that we can do many of the things as individuals that are done by a church congregation; but if our relationship with God is built only on our personal times with Him without the give-and-take of worshiping, learning, and serving together with others, something vital will be missing in our Christian life. Then again, this is also true if our worship and seeking of God occurs only during our times in church. Group and personal worship balance each other, if our desire is to become more like Jesus.

God has great things to accomplish through us, His church.

The Prayers of God's People

Joel 1–3; Amos 1–2; Psalm 139; Revelation 5

Revelation 5 opens on a pivotal moment, as the apostle John finds himself observing not only the activities of Heaven but the activities occurring at the actual throne of God. With God are the "twenty-four elders," "millions of angels," and the "four living beings" (Rev. 4:4,6; 5:11). What an astounding sight it must have been.

As riveting as this was, there was something that drew John's attention away. It was a scroll, a scroll of utmost importance, and it had to be opened. The scroll had seized all of Heaven's attention, for "no one in heaven or on earth or under the earth was able to open the scroll and read it" (Rev. 5:3). John did not know what was on the scroll, but understanding instinctively that it needed to be opened for the sake of all of us, he wept (Rev. 5:4). How intense John's sorrow and disappointment must have been. In the midst of that place of unimaginable power, how could it be that "no one could be found who was worthy to open the scroll and read it" (Rev. 5:4)?

But the angels, living beings, and elders were not weeping or mourning. They knew there was someone worthy to open the scroll! It was "the Lion of the tribe of Judah" (Rev. 5:5).

And as John's vision—cloudy from weeping—clears, he finally saw what the others were seeing. But it is not a lion he sees. It is a "Lamb that had been killed but was now standing between the throne and the four living beings and among the twenty-four elders" (Rev. 5:6). Then John knew he was looking at his Savior and his friend, Jesus Christ.

John was an elderly man by this time, and he had experienced many amazing things, but it is hard to imagine his joy as he recognized Jesus. He was not alone in this emotion, for at the sight of the Lamb, joy broke out in Heaven, the kind of unrestrained joy that makes you want to laugh and cry and sing out. And so they did.

As Jesus the Lamb "took the scroll, the four living beings and the twenty-four elders fell down before the Lamb. Each one had a harp, and they held gold bowls filled with incense—the prayers of God's people" (Rev. 5:7-8). At this central moment in human history, when an important promise of God begins to unfold, we, too, are represented. Not by John, but by our prayers.

What could show more clearly the immense value of our prayers to God than the revelation that they are kept near His throne? The next time you wonder whether God hears, cares about, or answers your prayers, remember that of all the things throughout the universes that God could choose to have near Him, He has chosen "the prayers of God's people."

God hears. God cares. God answers our prayers.

Week 160

Balancing Act

Amos 3–6; Psalms 140–141; Revelation 6

From Genesis to Revelation, the message has been the same. And while the stories behind the message have varied, the emphasis has remained unchanged. This week's reading again touched on these important points:

People sin: "For I know the vast number of your sins and the depth of your rebellions" (Amos 5:12).

God warns about the consequences of sin: "But always, first of all, I warn you through my servants the prophets. I, the Sovereign Lord, have now done this. Come back to me and live!" (Amos 3:7; 5:4).

People reject this warning and God's love: "But still you would not return to me,' says the Lord" (Amos 4:6).

Sin causes much heartache: "There will be crying in all the public squares and in every street" (Amos 5:16).

God judges and punishes sin: "You push away every thought of coming disaster, but your actions only bring the day of judgment closer. Prepare to meet your God as he comes in judgment" (Amos 6:3; 4:12).

God judges but forgives the sins of those who seek Him: "Come back to the Lord and live! ...Surely the godly are praising your name, for they will live in your presence" (Amos 5:6; Ps. 140:13).

These verses show us, once again, that God's actions are guided by two of His major attributes working in harmony—His holiness operating hand in hand with His love.

We know that God is holy, without sin. We know that sin cannot exist in His presence. We know that sin must be judged and judgment leads to punishment. That is bad news since sin is a factor in each of our lives.

At the same time, we know that God is love. We know that, because of this love, a way to escape the immense punishment that results from sin was provided by Jesus, through His horrific crucifixion and temporary separation from God. We also know that, because of God's love, the Holy Spirit has been sent to "convince the world of its sin, and of God's righteousness, and of the coming judgment" (John 16:8). Judgment will lead to eternal life in God's loving presence for those who are convinced by the Spirit of their need for forgiveness of sin and that Jesus Christ is their pathway to a holy God.

And so we see that God is completely holy *and* completely loving. But that is a hard concept for humans to understand. We tend to end up emphasizing one over the other, and as a result, we misrepresent what God is truly like, causing confusion for ourselves and others.

On the one hand, there are believers who tend to emphasize God's holiness and His judgment of sin. When God's love does not balance His holiness in our thinking, there are several false beliefs we may slip into. Our faith can easily become one of rules, where we begin to think it is our actions that either save or condemn us. Judging others whose behavior does not rise to *our* standard of conduct can quickly follow. And when our relationship with God is based mainly on following rules, we may never feel truly safe with Him, since we are incapable of being sinless, no matter how much we want to be. When we have made God's holiness His primary characteristic and failed to balance it with His love, we have created a god who is inconsistent with whom God says He is in Scripture.

But just as dangerous is an overemphasis on God's love and mercy coupled with little thought to His holiness. When God's love, mercy, and forgiveness are not balanced by His requirement for holiness, we may begin to take Jesus' great sacrifice on our behalf for granted. By minimizing God's holiness, we may no longer see the danger of sin and fall into the trap of an "anything goes" Christianity. We can make God's love into something so cheaply given to us that we become indifferent about our need for His forgiveness. Yet sin—and its judgment—should be taken seriously, since the Bible spends a lot of time warning us about it. Christ's love should not lead us to a careless relationship with Him or a disregard for His commandments.

It is only when we keep both of these major attributes of God in perspective that we begin to have a better understanding of God. As we develop respect for God's holiness and His warning that He must judge sin, we also begin to understand the amazing gift of God's merciful love as He extends it to us through Jesus Christ. Jesus' sacrifice for us is our only hope of rescue from the demands of God's holiness. And God's love, Jesus' sacrifice, and the Holy Spirit's guidance will help us to be living examples of His grace and our need for it. We can accept it in awestruck gratitude or ignore it with eternal regret.

WEEK 161

One Half Hour

Amos 7–9; Obadiah; Revelation 7–9

"When the Lamb broke the seventh seal, there was silence throughout heaven for about half an hour" (Rev. 8:1).

How extraordinary. Millions of angels, twenty-four elders, four living beings, and "a vast crowd, too great to count, from every nation and tribe and people and language, standing in front of the throne and before the Lamb" joined together in complete silence (Rev. 5:11; 7:9).

What was it about Jesus breaking the seventh seal that caused this astonishing reaction? At the breaking of this seal "the seven angels who stand before God were given seven trumpets" (Rev. 8:2). And with these trumpets the second phase of the long-promised judgment of sin commences.

Is it any wonder that Heaven grew still and silent? What was about to unfold was worthy of total silence.

The land, plant life, and water take the initial blows of this judgment of sin. As the first trumpet sounds, one-third of the earth is set on fire, causing one-third of the trees to burn and all of the grass. As the second trumpet sounds, one-third of the water in the oceans turns to blood, destroying one-third of the ships on the sea and causing one-third of all sea life to die. The third trumpet sounds, and one-third of the water in all of the rivers and springs becomes so bitter that drinking it leads to death. The fourth trumpet sounds, and one-third of the sun, moon, and stars turn dark, causing the light of day and night to diminish significantly. God's gifts making up the natural world, one dependent upon the other, become drastically altered. The stability, which people have counted on since creation, is gone—wreaking havoc on food, water, and climate.

Human devastation commingles with this ecological disaster. The fifth trumpet sounds, and people are tortured so severely by evil forces that they long to die. And with the sounding of the sixth trumpet, plagues are released, killing one-third of all remaining people. The results of God loosening His restraint on evil in this world are too terrible to fully grasp.

As the image brought about by the sixth trumpet fades away, complete and total silence seems an appropriate response. There comes a time when depth of emotion allows for nothing else. Whether or not we believe that every word of Revelation regarding God's judgment of sin is to be taken literally, there are enough other Scriptures, including Jesus' own words, which tell of a time of final judgment of sin and the eternal consequences of not choosing to repent. As we contemplate the words of judgment in Revelation, we, too, may feel emotion so great that it leaves us silent.

We may feel horrified by the destruction and suffering. Our hearts may shrink back from so much pain and sorrow. We may long for it to be avoided, for those being judged to have another chance. These longings would seem to match God's. Before the seventh, and last, trumpet is blown, there is a time lapse that gives those who have survived this period of judgment and punishment an opportunity to turn to God and away from what is causing their destruction. Will they?

In this case, the answer is "no." "The people who did not die in these plagues still refused to turn from their evil deeds. And they did not repent…" (Rev. 9:20-21). Those few words sum up the greatest tragedy ever to face humanity. And yet their refusal should not destroy the hope that those who come *before* these people will answer "yes" to God's offer of salvation.

It may seem strange to talk about a sense of hope after devastation of this kind, but we discover even in these scenes of judgment that God will show mercy to those who turn to Him. Just as there are many passages of Scripture telling of God's judgment of sin, there are many passages telling of His mercy to any who call out to Him. The horrors of God's promised judgment of sin and the beauty of His promised mercy should move us to share our reason for hope with those who need to hear it.

There is even reason to feel gratitude as we contemplate these scenes of judgment, for we know that with the final judgment of sin comes the destruction of its power. Until that time, we live in a world reeling from the effects of sin that are not yet judged and punished. But we also live with God's promise that the Holy Spirit will be with us, giving us the strength and comfort we need to cope. We need not fear what life has for us today or in the future, not even a future as described in these passages, for "Salvation comes from our God on the throne and from the Lamb!" (Rev. 7:10).

As children of God, we have reason to rejoice that when sin's destruction is brought to a close by God, there will be a new earth, and we will be a new people, where "He who sits on the throne will live among them and shelter them…. For the Lamb who stands in front of the throne will be their Shepherd. He will lead them to the springs of life-giving water. And God will wipe away all their tears" (Rev. 7:15,17).

The days leading up to *that* day will indeed be difficult ones, marked by many tears. But there is a new day coming, and what a day it will be!

Lessons from a Fish

Jonah 1–4; Psalms 142–143; Revelation 10

"'Get up and go to the great city of Nineveh! Announce my judgment against it because I have seen how wicked its people are.' But Jonah got up and went in the opposite direction in order to get away from the Lord" (Jonah 1:2-3).

"Then the Lord ordered the fish to spit up Jonah on the beach, and it did" (Jonah 2:10).

God told Jonah to do something, and he did not do it. God told the fish to do something, and it did it. That raises questions about levels of intelligence and wisdom, doesn't it? Supposedly, Jonah, the man, had the greater of these two attributes, but in this instance he seemed to have less than a fish.

What Jonah did have that the fish did not was a freedom given to all people by God—the freedom to choose our path and make our own decisions, even if they conflict with what God desires for us. Using this freedom, Jonah decided the best way to get out of doing what God wanted was to find "a ship leaving for Tarshish, hoping that by going away to the west he could escape from the Lord" (Jonah 1:3).

Freedom of choice does not mean that God turns away from us when we choose poorly. God is the God of second chances, and He will try to get our attention in an attempt to guide us back to doing what is best for us. If we are attuned to the Holy Spirit, this guidance may be as simple as our sensing that we need to rethink an action or an attitude. But sometimes it takes much more to get our attention. In Jonah's case, God used an extraordinary creature to capture his attention.

Our poor choices, including the times we deliberately disobey God, often have a way of leading to rough circumstances for others as well as ourselves. Just ask the people on board the ship with Jonah. Jonah involved every person on that ship in the troubles that resulted from doing things his way rather than God's. And they were significant troubles, for the Lord unleashed "a powerful wind over the sea, causing a violent storm that threatened to send them to the bottom" (Jonah 1:4). There is no doubt about it, when you are Master of all creation, you can whip up an attention-grabbing storm.

Now at that moment Jonah deserved at least a little credit. Unlike many of us, he did not question or blame God for allowing this difficult situation. He admitted that it was his actions and disobedience to God's directive that started the disaster he and his shipmates were facing. As he looked into the wet, windswept, terrified faces of the sailors, Jonah "told them that he was running away from the Lord" (Jonah 1:10).

The sailors, who were not followers of the Lord God, showed much greater wisdom concerning obedience to God than Jonah had, for they "were terrified when they heard this. 'Oh, why did you do it?' they groaned" (Jonah 1:10). Well, as we know, there was only one solution Jonah could think of to end the chaos they were in; and so he was tossed overboard, "and the storm stopped at once! The sailors were awestruck by the Lord's great power, and they offered him a sacrifice and vowed to serve him" (Jonah 1:15-16). What a great reminder that God can use even the most trying, even terrifying, circumstances for good.

Meanwhile, the most interesting part of Jonah's experience of running away from God was about to begin, for "the Lord had arranged for a great fish to swallow Jonah. And Jonah was inside the fish for three days and three nights" (Jonah 1:17). Three days and three nights is a long time to be alone in a strange place. In fact, it is plenty of time to rethink how to do things differently if given another chance. Jonah was given that additional chance when the fish obeyed God's command.

What would the world be like if all creatures, human and otherwise, wanted to do God's will and were quick to obey His direction? Now that would be one terrific place to live, wouldn't it? A place *ruled* by love, *guided* by love, *created* through love. It would be a place like…Heaven!

Be wise, and start practicing now for life in your final home. Obey like the fish, not like Jonah.

Before, Behind, Beside

Micah 1–5; Psalm 144; Revelation 11

A major hurricane had hit, and a fairly strong spin-off storm was headed our way. My husband was in Siberia, and I was home alone.

It was evident the remnants of the storm would soon hit our area. By mid-afternoon the rain began, and it was much heavier than most storms. As night approached, so did the wind.

Our house sits in a forest, surrounded by trees that are sixty to eighty feet tall. Now wind gusts up to seventy miles per hour were pounding them. The sound of branches breaking off and hitting the side of the house and the steadily mounting roar of the wind became frightening. And then the electrical power went off.

After praying for safety and peace of mind, there was little else to do but to go to bed. As I lay awake praying, a loud thud sounded above the wind and rain, shaking the ground and the house. Because it was pitch-black inside and out, I could only guess that a tree had fallen nearby. My prayers became more urgent as another thud sounded, followed by another and another.

Suddenly there was a booming crash, and the house shook violently. There was no doubt that a tree had hit it. Leaping up, I expected to collide with branches or plummet into holes that had been created by the fallen tree. Instead I only hit walls and furniture as I tried to make my way by the dim light of my nearly dead flashlight. Puzzled, but realizing there was nothing I could do at that moment, I lay down again, fearfully continuing to pray for safety. I fell into a surprisingly peaceful sleep as the storm continued to rage and trees continued to fall.

By dawn the rain and wind had moved on. As I looked outside, God's protection was unmistakable. Twelve trees surrounding our house had fallen. Two had hit the house but had fallen on the end farthest from where I had spent the night. Amazingly, those trees had not crushed the roof, and their trunks and limbs had sealed the holes that had been created so that no water had come into the house. Two other trees had landed within inches of either side of the room where I had slept. I marveled at God's hand on my life, for I surely would have been hurt if those trees had fallen at a slightly different angle.

That morning, I clearly understood David's words that God "is my loving ally and my fortress, my tower of safety, my deliverer. He stands before me as a shield, and I take refuge in him…" (Ps. 144:2).

God "stands before" us "as a shield." When life presses down on us harshly, it may be hard to believe this statement, for it is not often that God's protection on our lives is clearly seen and obvious to us. And yet, we who are God's followers do not know what it is like to live without Him going before us as a shield, deflecting multiple instances of harm and danger. We only know what we have experienced, not what we have been sheltered from and never experienced.

But we are promised that God is even more than the God who goes before us. He is also our "loving ally" standing alongside us. He is fighting for us, not against us. In a world that can be frightening, He is our "deliverer" and our "tower of safety."

Even knowing this and believing it, we can still have lingering wounds from the difficulties of our lives. In spite of recognizing God's protection, the night of the storm had been a long and terrifying one, and high-wind storms can now make me uneasy if my focus is on the storm rather than on God. David understood the issue of the scars that remain from our life experiences, for he acknowledged needing to "take refuge" in God. God is our place of safety and healing. And God will always be that for His children.

As we remember past difficulties, live with today's issues, or look out at the future with possible fear and apprehension, we need Someone greater than our problems and ourselves. We need God. Who better to have going before us, standing beside us, and sheltering us on life's journey?

Powerful Enemies

Micah 6–7; Nahum 1–3; Revelation 12–13

There are several subjects in the Bible that many people tend to skim over. But because they are contained in Scripture, it is vitally important that we pay attention to these topics. Let's focus on one such topic.

"This great dragon—the ancient serpent called the devil, or Satan, the one deceiving the whole world—was thrown down to the earth with all his angels…. Terror will come on the earth and the sea. For the devil has come down to you in great anger, and he knows that he has little time…. He declared war against…all who keep God's commandments and confess that they belong to Jesus" (Rev. 12:9,12,17).

These verses ring out with an unmistakable warning for all people, believers and unbelievers alike, about the existence of powerful enemies. If we take these verses seriously, as we should, they are disturbing and provide a good reason for us to understand all we can about these adversaries.

The first thing we are told is the identity of our enemies. The leader is given many titles: "this great dragon, the ancient serpent, the devil, or Satan." But Satan is not the sole enemy mentioned in these verses. He is joined by all his angels. We commonly think of angels as forces offering protection, but we are told that the angels under Satan's command are sources of destruction to all people.

It is important to understand an enemy's strength and abilities. As angels, Satan and his followers have been created with superior strength, power, and intellect when compared to humans. And it stands to reason that Satan, as the leader of the angels who are loyal to him, would stand out among those he commands. But Satan is not superior to God. Knowing that Satan and his angel-followers were created by God, we can conclude that they are not equal to their Creator nor do they possess the unique characteristics that belong solely to God (Gen. 1; Col. 1:16). Satan and his angels are *not* all-knowing, are *not* all-powerful, and individually do *not* have the ability to be in more than one place at a time.

God's ultimate power over them was displayed when they were "thrown down to the earth." While the earth may be much loved by us, these spiritual beings find earth, and its inhabitants, unworthy in comparison to their former home and to themselves. Their "great anger" at being evicted from the heavenly realms fuels their hatred of God and gives these adversaries their purpose.

Their purpose is simple. Satan has "declared war against all who keep God's commandments and confess that they belong to Jesus." And the objective of any war is to defeat and destroy the enemy. If we keep God's commandments and confess that we belong to Jesus, we are at war—whether we choose to be or not. And we fight not only for ourselves but for all those we may influence for Jesus Christ.

Maybe you have never thought of yourself as a warrior of any sort, but we are engaged in daily warfare. Sometimes this warfare may involve direct physical situations influenced by our enemy. It will certainly involve battles of our spirit: our fears, thoughts, emotions, beliefs, and attitudes. It is a war waged by Satan through propaganda, deceit, and confusion. Left to our own devices, we would surely be defeated, but God has given us some powerful weapons.

The apostle Paul clearly outlined these weapons and God's battle plan against Satan and his angels in Ephesians 6. Surprisingly, many Christians never take up these weapons. Don't be one of them! Start by being aware and alert—not indifferent, unconcerned, or skeptical. Do not pick and choose from the weapons we have been given, but "use every piece of God's armor to resist the enemy" (Eph. 6:13). Review each of your weapons to determine if any are in need of attention. Do you believe that our salvation is through Jesus Christ? Do you always tell the truth? Are you obedient to God? How is your faith in God and His promises? Do you study the Bible? Are you ready to share the Good News of Jesus Christ? Do you pray fervently? We need not fear this enemy if we are prepared.

As followers of Jesus Christ, we are either actively engaged in battle against Satan and his forces—or we are A.W.O.L. Are you a warrior?

WEEK 165

A Strange Blessing

Habakkuk 1–3; Zephaniah 1–2; Psalm 145; Revelation 14

Habakkuk was a righteous man who lived in a sin-filled society. As a citizen of Judah, he knew the stories of the times when the people had trusted and obeyed God wholeheartedly. But those times were long gone. Disobedience to and disregard of God was rampant.

God had been patient with these people, providing them with opportunity after opportunity to turn away from their sin, but they had not responded to His loving mercy. Now God was ready to change direction. He declared, "I will destroy those who used to worship me but now no longer do. They no longer ask for the Lord's guidance or seek my blessings" (Zep. 1:6). These people had gone from being in close relationship with God to being in line for God's punishment because they had stopped asking "for the Lord's guidance" and no longer sought His "blessings."

When you no longer care about the Lord's guidance, you no longer care about pleasing Him. It is the beginning of a journey where the next step leads to ignoring God and the following one leads to trusting in something or someone other than Him to provide your blessings. That was exactly the downhill path followed by the people of Judah.

The people did not stop asking for God's blessings because they feared being selfish. They stopped asking because they had become proud (Hab. 2:4). They no longer felt they needed God to provide for them. In fact, they no longer relied on Him at all but put their trust in themselves or in other things (Hab. 2:18-19).

The journey that leads away from God and toward suffering and regret is not one taken only by the people of ancient Judah. It is a pathway that beckons to each of us. Here are two lessons we can learn from the mistakes made by Judah.

First, we should never stop asking for and obeying God's guidance in all things. Today's society, like Judah's, makes obeying God seem like a boring, unnecessary, even a foolish thing to do. But the truth is that when we live by God's guidelines, we find life becomes more satisfying, not less. And yes, there will be times when we either do not understand or do not want to follow God's guidance. If we obey in spite of not wanting to or not understanding why we should, we benefit doubly as our trust and faith begin to develop muscle.

Second, we should never hesitate to ask for God's blessings. It is not a selfish thing to do. God wants us to seek His blessings. His blessings can be quiet, easily taken for granted, almost unnoticeable ones. Or they can be spectacular, knock-your-socks-off blessings. But sometimes, they may be different from what we think of as blessings and difficult, at first glance, to recognize.

We see this reality played out in the life of Habakkuk when he asked God to bless Judah by bringing an end to the out-of-control sin that was destroying the nation. God promised to honor Habakkuk's plea to bless the people of Judah. But what a strange blessing it would be! God was going to end the wickedness of Judah's people by sending a "cruel and violent nation" to "march across the world and conquer it" (Hab. 1:6). The people of Judah would suffer greatly.

Stunned at first by how this blessing would take shape, Habakkuk could only ask, "Is your plan in all of this to wipe us out?" (Hab. 1:12). You can almost feel his hope slipping away. Although he had the promise of God's blessing, it surely did not look like anything he had imagined or wanted.

Like Habakkuk, we probably have our own moments when God's blessings look nothing like the ones we had envisioned. They are the times when our world feels like it is falling apart, our worries are stacking up, panic is setting in, and it is hard to understand why God does not bless us with the specific material goods, physical healing, emotional help, or spiritual fulfillment we feel we must have. The question then becomes: can we trust God enough to believe that the outcome of His blessings will always be beneficial to us in the way most needed?

Habakkuk had this kind of trust, and he eventually understood that God's plan was not to completely destroy Judah but to use this punishment as a blessing to bring back those who would return to Him. The blessing of Judah being conquered by a violent nation was probably still not the one Habakkuk would have chosen, but he trusted in the answers he received because of what he knew about

God. "I have heard all about you, Lord, and I am filled with awe by the amazing things you have done. In this time of our deep need, begin again to help us, as you did in years gone by. Show us your power to save us" (Hab. 3:2).

We, too, *need* God's guidance and blessings. We, too, can *trust* God's guidance and blessings.

Week 166

Busy Doing What?

Zephaniah 3; Haggai 1–2; Zechariah 1–2; Revelation 15–16

Life is busy, isn't it? It seems hard to catch our breath at times as we rush from one obligation to the next. Fatigue, stress, and a feeling that our schedule is out of control are common to many of us. And then we start over the next day.

The Israelites of Haggai's day were not so different. They had been in exile in Babylon, longing to return to their homeland, Judah. After seventy long years, they finally did. There was only one condition to their freedom. They were to rebuild the Temple of the Lord in Jerusalem, the Temple where the Spirit of God had resided among the people before their exile. They were going to be busy people.

And so they made the long and difficult journey to Jerusalem and, as promised, immediately began to rebuild the Temple. Before long, their work stalled—due to intense opposition from the people who had taken up residence in Jerusalem during the Israelites' seventy-year absence. Finally, with only the foundation completed, they stopped work altogether on the Temple, deciding that "the time has not yet come to rebuild the Lord's house—the Temple" (Hag. 1:2).

Being industrious, they turned their attention to other tasks that did not generate as much opposition. Yes, they were busy people. And they were busy with essential things: raising their families, making a living, building their homes—all good things, except for one problem. They became so busy that they left God behind.

After patiently waiting ten years for the people to resume rebuilding the Temple, the Lord had an important point for them to think about: "Consider how things are going for you!" (Hag. 1:5). They needed to consider that even though they worked hard, they had little. Although they had food, drink, and clothing, the supply was never adequate to meet their basic needs. While they earned money, it was never enough to make ends meet. In case they missed the connection, God laid out how these shortages were tied to their neglect of their relationship with Him. In their attempt to gain more, they had pushed God to the sidelines of their lives.

God had a solution for them. "Now go up into the hills, bring down timber, and rebuild my house" (Hag. 1:8). What would they do? They could stubbornly continue with their own busy pursuits, or they could change their priorities. They chose wisely, for "the whole remnant of God's people obeyed the message from the Lord their God. And the people worshiped the Lord in earnest" (Hag. 1:12).

They became people who put God first in their lives. They were still busy, but their priorities were in order. As they headed out to gather the timber needed for rebuilding, pleasing God was their top priority. God knew their sincerity and responded to it: "I am with you, says the Lord!" (Hag. 1:13).

As we rush from one thing to another, do we ever sense the quiet voice of the Holy Spirit saying, "Consider how things are going for you"? Or have we become so busy that we have crowded the Lord God out of our daily lives?

"I am with you, says the Lord!" There are many ways for the Lord to be with us. He may fill our lives and thoughts as we continue our journey of learning to obey, love, and trust Him. He may be nothing more than an afterthought in our busy lives, or He may be someone we deliberately try to shut out of our lives and thoughts as we step away from His guidance. Worst of all, He may be someone we have totally rejected...even as He continues to call to us in love and warning.

God is with us. Are we with Him?

WEEK 167

Facing Death

Zechariah 3–6; Psalms 146–147; Revelation 17

First-time experiences can be unsettling, can't they? But they can also be exhilarating, depending on the situation and your personality. Remember your feelings on the first day of school, the first day on a new job, the first date, or the first time using a new skill? But there are "firsts" that are always difficult, such as the first time we face our own death.

Death was not a stranger to David. Early in his life he faced the possibility of his own death as Saul doggedly sought to kill him (1 Sam. 19). He also experienced the death of his closest friend, Jonathan (2 Sam. 1). And David saw the gruesomeness of death over and over again on the battlefields where he fought.

Perhaps it was his many experiences with death and near-death that made David resolve to "sing praises to my God even with my dying breath" (Ps. 146:2). In the prime of his life, David decided what he wanted to do on the day of his death. David could make this vow because it reflected his trust in God for all aspects of his life—even his death, for you must trust God to genuinely praise Him.

David trusted God because he understood something about God that brings hope and peace and comfort. David understood that the Lord "is the one who keeps every promise forever" (Ps. 146:6). He knew that all the promises made by God were available to him every hour of every day, including the day of his death. It may have been that as David thought about his death, he remembered God's promise to *always* be with those who love Him.

I wonder if David got to fulfill his desire to praise God with his dying breath. We know David lived to be an old man, but we are not told the details of his final hours on this earth (1 Kings 1–2). It may be that his wish to sing praises to God was granted. Or it may be he was physically or mentally incapable of doing so. Either way, we know God understood the desire of David's heart. So whether his praise was silent or audible, it would have preceded him into the loving presence of the Lord.

Most people do not share David's attitude concerning death. They fear death and what it demands from us: the possibility of pain and suffering, loss of control, separation from those we love, and the many unknown aspects of the transition from this life to the next. That is understandable. Even David was not nonchalant about his eventual death.

Facing death is a hard thing, and David knew it. Scripture contains many verses where David pleads with God to rescue him from his brushes with death, but these verses also reflect his confidence that the experience of death for a child of God is softened by the promises of God and by His love. After all, God promises His children that their death is also their birth into the splendor and delight of Heaven.

When you think about it, birth and death have similarities. Birth, while joyous, comes about through a time that is painful. The baby being born, if loved by his or her parents, is about to experience all the joys and beauty of this world, things of which the baby knows nothing. Death, too, may come about through a time that is painful, and we, who are loved by God, know little of the joys and beauty of Heaven. Like a baby being born, we know best what we are about to leave behind. It will take our trust in God to look ahead to our dying breath with the thought of praise for Him on our lips.

If we worship the same God as David, there truly is reason to praise Him with our dying breath…and our every breath.

WEEK 168

Searing Images

Zechariah 7–10; Psalm 148; Revelation 18–19

Over the years four photos have been seared into my memory. They have a common theme but do not share similar endings.

The earliest of these images is that of a young child in Sudan. It is 1993, and the child is starving; she is withered and gaunt, her muscle and fat completely gone. As if she were already a skeleton, each bone is clearly visible, and each arm and leg is no larger than a small stick. Her head is enormous in comparison to her shrunken body, as is her empty, swollen stomach. The child is trying to crawl toward a feeding station but has collapsed face-forward on the ground. But there is another image in the picture. Sitting a few feet away from this child is a well-fed vulture, eyes fixed on her, patiently waiting for her to die. Wretched suffering is captured in this photograph, and there is no one to alleviate it.

The second image is that of an adult. This person is also starving and is not much larger than the Sudanese child. The man is sunk-down, face-forward on the ground with one arm reaching forward in an attempt to grasp a cup. The effort to lift and stretch his frail neck toward the cup is clearly visible. Both longing and hopelessness are captured in his reach for that desperately needed cup. But, as with the first image, there is more to this picture. Two more hands are seen, the hands of someone who is not starving. One hand is helping to hold up and steady the head of the starving person so he can drink from the cup; the other is reaching out to help support the person's arm. The arm being supported is no wider than two fingers on the better-fed hand. Wretched suffering is captured in this photograph, but it is lessened by the caring hands that are cradling the starving person.

The third image is that of a twelve-year-old Sri Lankan. Unspeakable grief is etched on every muscle of her body. Her head is thrown back in anguished weeping, as she sits on the floor with her arms tightly enfolding her legs to her body. This young person's family, home, and village have been destroyed by the 2004 Indian Ocean tsunami, and all that she loved and knew are gone. But, once again, there is more to this picture. Sitting beside her is a shelter volunteer, eyes fixed on this suffering child, arms wrapped around her. Overwhelming sorrow is captured in this photograph, but there is also compassionate understanding.

The fourth image is that of another small child in Sudan whose name is Little John. It is 2008, and Little John thinks he is five years old. He may be unsure of his age, but since he has seen his family members die, he has no doubt that he is an orphan. This wary child stands completely alone beside a narrow dirt lane in front of high brush. The brush is his safety net, where he can slip away from the many dangers of his land. There are hyenas and other wild animals who would hunt Little John, but he is more afraid of the prowling gangs who freely roam the country, kidnapping children and making them slaves or child soldiers. Little John is staring into the distance, waiting for many things…for a safe place to stay because he has no home, for food because he is hungry, for someone to show him tenderness and caring because he is alone. The directors of a nearby Christian orphanage desperately want Little John to come and be part of their family, but there is not enough money to care for the 450 children already there, and their pleas for financial help have gone unanswered…leaving every child vulnerable who is currently in their care. For now, Little John is truly alone in his hostile world. Fear and abandonment are captured in this photograph, and there is no one to alleviate it.

What do all four of these stories have in common? They are stories of great suffering. They are stories that are repeated over and over and over in our world. But they are also stories that give us opportunities to make a difference.

God told the Israelites that the behavior that pleased Him and the evidence of their true obedience to Him were their acts of justice, mercy, kindness, and care for "widows, orphans, foreigners, and poor people" (Zech. 7:10). These things still please God.

As His children, let us resolve to take the actions that are pleasing to him. Pray for those who are suffering. Ask God to break our hearts by the things that break His. Ask God to keep us from becoming fatigued by or hardened to the hunger, pain, and anguish that make up so many people's lives. And ask God to show us ways in which we can do more, not less, for those who have so few of this world's comforts. God will answer these prayers.

And then we should act. And keep on acting. We may be tempted to think that what we are doing makes only a little difference, but that little difference means everything to someone like Little John…and all those like him. As for me, I have kept these four photos so I do not become complacent but, rather, remember what God asks of me.

"This is what the Lord Almighty says: 'Show mercy and kindness to one another'" (Zech. 7:9).

Will we?

Three Reasons to Believe

Zechariah 11–14; Malachi 1; Revelation 20–21

"This message is from the Lord, who stretched out the heavens, laid the foundations of the earth, and formed the spirit within humans" (Zech. 12:1).

Some people question whether there is a God, while others are convinced that no God exists. In this verse God gives three distinct reasons to believe.

Who "stretched out the heavens"? To determine the answer to that question, we have been invited to "look up into the heavens" (Isa. 40:26). So astounding is the vast array of stars, planets, and solar systems that it has intrigued humanity throughout history. Equally astounding is the manner in which these heavenly bodies operate in relationship to each other, helping to regulate our world's light, darkness, climate, tides, and calendars. The heavens are not chaotic but move in a manner that is so orderly that people have always depended upon it. The beauty, the role played in our survival, and the dependability of the heavens have even led some to worship various heavenly bodies as gods. The heavens clearly point to a powerful, intelligent, and involved Creator. God names Himself as that Creator and tells us not only that He made the stars but also that "He brings them out one after another, calling each by its name" (Isa. 40:26). The heavens shout out that there is one true God.

Who "laid the foundations of the earth"? To uncover the answer to that question, we turn our thoughts to the principles that regulate the foundations of the earth. These laws of physical science are the glue that holds our world together, helping to stabilize and sustain life. Even slight variations in the foundations of the earth principles can begin a chain reaction of significant magnitude. Physical laws regarding gravity, energy, motion, light, speed, and chemical reactions are complex, and the highest achievement of humans pertaining to these principles is to be their discoverer. It would take a being infinitely superior to humans to actually create these principles, and God names Himself as that Creator. The foundations of the earth shout out that there is one true God.

Who "formed the spirit within humans"? Scientists and geneticists may unravel DNA. Genes may be cloned. Psychiatrists and psychologists may influence the working of the mind and emotions. But who can shape or heal the illusive "spirit" that sets each of us apart from every other living thing? This spirit, the soul of a human being, can only be satisfied by its Creator. The human spirit either looks in vain to other sources for fulfillment or shouts out with joy that there is one true God.

Our God, the Lord, has a message for each of us. "'I have loved you deeply,' says the Lord" (Mal. 1:2). Never forget that God, the mighty Creator, wants to be in relationship with us. We are wanted and cherished.

But do not forget that relationships run both ways. God has not hidden from us that there are only two possible fates that await us and that our ultimate destiny is determined by our response to His loving offer of salvation. Those who are not in relationship with Jesus Christ will not find their names "recorded in the Book of Life" (Rev. 20:15) and will be separated from God for eternity. The names of those who are in relationship with Him will be found in the Book of Life, and they can rely on the promise that "I will be their God, and they will be my children" (Rev. 21:7). Forgiveness, comfort, healing, power, and eternal life with God can be found in a relationship with Jesus Christ.

God's great love is as much of a fact as the heavens, the foundations of the earth, and the spirit of human beings. This Good News is not to be kept tucked away. The fate of others should matter deeply to us. God is waiting for someone we know to become His child. To whom can we tell God's story of love that leads to forgiveness and freedom?

Week 170

Beginning Again

Malachi 2–4; Psalms 149–150; Revelation 22

You started your Bible reading with the words, "In the beginning God…" (Gen. 1:1). You end your reading with the words, "I am the Alpha and the Omega, the First and the Last, the Beginning and the End" (Rev. 22:13). Everything needed to live successfully can be found between these two verses.

Do you want to know who God is?

Do you want to know how to have a relationship with God?

Do you want to know how to please God?

Do you want to understand your purpose in life?

Do you want to understand what comes after this life?

Do you want to find peace, strength, wisdom, healing, comfort, guidance, and encouragement?

Then read God's words.

You are now at the end of your reading, but you are also at a new beginning. I urge you to begin reading through the Bible once again. There will be stories and passages that are familiar to you, but there will be many verses that will seem as if you are seeing them for the first time. No matter how many times we read God's words to us, the Holy Spirit will make what we are reading applicable to what we are experiencing at that point in our lives.

One of my favorite stories regarding Scripture was told by the well-known 19th century preacher and author, Charles Haddon Spurgeon. He wrote, "True Bible readers and Bible searchers never find it wearisome. They like it least who know it least and they love it most who read it most. When one of our missionaries had to read a certain Book of the Old Testament through a hundred times while he was translating it, he said that he certainly enjoyed the hundredth time of reading it more than he did the first, for he understood it better and it seemed to him to be fuller and fresher, the more familiar he became with it."*

My fervent hope is that you have drawn closer to God by reading His words, that you have a greater understanding of God, and that your desire to live your life by His principles has grown.

"And now, all glory to God, who is able to keep you from stumbling, and who will bring you into his glorious presence innocent of sin and with great joy. All glory to him, who alone is God our Savior, through Jesus Christ our Lord. Yes, glory, majesty, power, and authority belong to him, in the beginning, now, and forevermore. Amen" (Jude 24-25).

* http://spurgeongems.org/vols55-57/chs3246.pdf; Sermon 3246 entitled God's Thoughts and Ours, a sermon published on Thursday April 20, 1911 and delivered by C. H. Spurgeon on March 19, 1868. Adapted from *The C. H. Spurgeon Collection*, Ages Software; accessed August 7, 2015.

Appendix A

Reading Schedule

	Week 1	Week 2	Week 3	Week 4
Day 1	Genesis 1	Genesis 6	Genesis 10	Genesis 15
Day 2	Genesis 2	Genesis 7	Genesis 11	Genesis 16
Day 3	Genesis 3	Genesis 8	Genesis 12	Genesis 17
Day 4	Genesis 4	Genesis 9	Genesis 13	Genesis 18
Day 5	Genesis 5	Psalm 1	Genesis 14	Psalm 3
Day 6	Matthew 1	Psalm 2	Matthew 4	Psalm 4
Day 7	Matthew 2	Matthew 3	Matthew 5	Matthew 6

	Week 5	Week 6	Week 7	Week 8
Day 1	Genesis 19	Genesis 24	Genesis 28	Genesis 31
Day 2	Genesis 20	Genesis 25	Genesis 29	Genesis 32
Day 3	Genesis 21	Genesis 26	Genesis 30	Genesis 33
Day 4	Genesis 22	Genesis 27	Psalm 7	Genesis 34
Day 5	Genesis 23	Psalm 5	Psalm 8	Genesis 35
Day 6	Matthew 7	Psalm 6	Matthew 10	Matthew 12
Day 7	Matthew 8	Matthew 9	Matthew 11	Matthew 13

	Week 9	Week 10	Week 11	Week 12
Day 1	Genesis 36	Genesis 41	Genesis 46	Exodus 1
Day 2	Genesis 37	Genesis 42	Genesis 47	Exodus 2
Day 3	Genesis 38	Genesis 43	Genesis 48	Exodus 3
Day 4	Genesis 39	Genesis 44	Genesis 49	Exodus 4
Day 5	Genesis 40	Genesis 45	Genesis 50	Psalm 11
Day 6	Psalm 9	Psalm 10	Matthew 16	Psalm 12
Day 7	Matthew 14	Matthew 15	Matthew 17	Matthew 18

	Week 13	**Week 14**	**Week 15**	**Week 16**
Day 1	Exodus 5	Exodus 9	Exodus 13	Exodus 17
Day 2	Exodus 6	Exodus 10	Exodus 14	Exodus 18
Day 3	Exodus 7	Exodus 11	Exodus 15	Exodus 19
Day 4	Exodus 8	Exodus 12	Exodus 16	Exodus 20
Day 5	Psalm 13	Psalm 14	Psalm 15	Exodus 21
Day 6	Matthew 19	Matthew 21	Psalm 16	Matthew 24
Day 7	Matthew 20	Matthew 22	Matthew 23	Matthew 25

	Week 17	**Week 18**	**Week 19**	**Week 20**
Day 1	Exodus 22	Exodus 27	Exodus 31	Exodus 36
Day 2	Exodus 23	Exodus 28	Exodus 32	Exodus 37
Day 3	Exodus 24	Exodus 29	Exodus 33	Exodus 38
Day 4	Exodus 25	Exodus 30	Exodus 34	Exodus 39
Day 5	Exodus 26	Psalm 18	Exodus 35	Exodus 40
Day 6	Psalm 17	Matthew 27	Acts 1	Psalm 19
Day 7	Matthew 26	Matthew 28	Acts 2	Acts 3

	Week 21	**Week 22**	**Week 23**	**Week 24**
Day 1	Leviticus 1	Leviticus 6	Leviticus 10	Leviticus 15
Day 2	Leviticus 2	Leviticus 7	Leviticus 11	Leviticus 16
Day 3	Leviticus 3	Leviticus 8	Leviticus 12	Leviticus 17
Day 4	Leviticus 4	Leviticus 9	Leviticus 13	Leviticus 18
Day 5	Leviticus 5	Psalm 20	Leviticus 14	Acts 8
Day 6	Acts 4	Psalm 21	Psalm 22	Acts 9
Day 7	Acts 5	Acts 6	Acts 7	Acts 10

	Week 25	**Week 26**	**Week 27**	**Week 28**
Day 1	Leviticus 19	Leviticus 23	Numbers 1	Numbers 6
Day 2	Leviticus 20	Leviticus 24	Numbers 2	Numbers 7
Day 3	Leviticus 21	Leviticus 25	Numbers 3	Numbers 8
Day 4	Leviticus 22	Leviticus 26	Numbers 4	Numbers 9
Day 5	Psalm 23	Leviticus 27	Numbers 5	Psalm 26
Day 6	Psalm 24	Psalm 25	Acts 13	Psalm 27
Day 7	Acts 11	Acts 12	Acts 14	Acts 15

	Week 29	Week 30	Week 31	Week 32
Day 1	Numbers 10	Numbers 15	Numbers 19	Numbers 24
Day 2	Numbers 11	Numbers 16	Numbers 20	Numbers 25
Day 3	Numbers 12	Numbers 17	Numbers 21	Numbers 26
Day 4	Numbers 13	Numbers 18	Numbers 22	Numbers 27
Day 5	Numbers 14	Psalm 28	Numbers 23	Psalm 30
Day 6	Acts 16	Psalm 29	Acts 19	Acts 21
Day 7	Acts 17	Acts 18	Acts 20	Acts 22

	Week 33	Week 34	Week 35	Week 36
Day 1	Numbers 28	Numbers 33	Deuteronomy 2	Deuteronomy 6
Day 2	Numbers 29	Numbers 34	Deuteronomy 3	Deuteronomy 7
Day 3	Numbers 30	Numbers 35	Deuteronomy 4	Deuteronomy 8
Day 4	Numbers 31	Numbers 36	Deuteronomy 5	Deuteronomy 9
Day 5	Numbers 32	Deuteronomy 1	Psalm 32	Deuteronomy10
Day 6	Psalm 31	Acts 24	Acts 26	Psalm 33
Day 7	Acts 23	Acts 25	Acts 27	Acts 28

	Week 37	Week 38	Week 39	Week 40
Day 1	Deuteronomy 11	Deuteronomy 16	Deuteronomy 21	Deuteronomy 25
Day 2	Deuteronomy 12	Deuteronomy 17	Deuteronomy 22	Deuteronomy 26
Day 3	Deuteronomy 13	Deuteronomy 18	Deuteronomy 23	Deuteronomy 27
Day 4	Deuteronomy 14	Deuteronomy 19	Deuteronomy 24	Deuteronomy 28
Day 5	Deuteronomy 15	Deuteronomy 20	Psalm 35	Deuteronomy 29
Day 6	Romans 1	Psalm 34	Romans 4	Romans 6
Day 7	Romans 2	Romans 3	Romans 5	Romans 7

	Week 41	Week 42	Week 43	Week 44
Day 1	Deuteronomy 30	Joshua 1	Joshua 6	Joshua 10
Day 2	Deuteronomy 31	Joshua 2	Joshua 7	Joshua 11
Day 3	Deuteronomy 32	Joshua 3	Joshua 8	Joshua 12
Day 4	Deuteronomy 33	Joshua 4	Joshua 9	Joshua 13
Day 5	Deuteronomy 34	Joshua 5	Romans 10	Joshua 14
Day 6	Psalm 36	Psalm 37	Romans 11	Joshua 15
Day 7	Romans 8	Romans 9	Romans 12	Psalm 38

	Week 45	Week 46	Week 47	Week 48
Day 1	Joshua 16	Joshua 21	Judges 2	Judges 7
Day 2	Joshua 17	Joshua 22	Judges 3	Judges 8
Day 3	Joshua 18	Joshua 23	Judges 4	Judges 9
Day 4	Joshua 19	Joshua 24	Judges 5	Judges 10
Day 5	Joshua 20	Judges 1	Judges 6	Psalm 40
Day 6	Romans 13	Psalm 39	Romans 16	Psalm 41
Day 7	Romans 14	Romans 15	Mark 1	Mark 2

	Week 49	Week 50	Week 51	Week 52
Day 1	Judges 11	Judges 15	Judges 19	Ruth 3
Day 2	Judges 12	Judges 16	Judges 20	Ruth 4
Day 3	Judges 13	Judges 17	Judges 21	1 Samuel 1
Day 4	Judges 14	Judges 18	Ruth 1	1 Samuel 2
Day 5	Psalm 42	Mark 4	Ruth 2	1 Samuel 3
Day 6	Psalm 43	Mark 5	Psalm 44	Psalm 45
Day 7	Mark 3	Mark 6	Mark 7	Mark 8

	Week 53	Week 54	Week 55	Week 56
Day 1	1 Samuel 4	1 Samuel 9	1 Samuel 13	1 Samuel 18
Day 2	1 Samuel 5	1 Samuel 10	1 Samuel 14	1 Samuel 19
Day 3	1 Samuel 6	1 Samuel 11	1 Samuel 15	1 Samuel 20
Day 4	1 Samuel 7	1 Samuel 12	1 Samuel 16	1 Samuel 21
Day 5	1 Samuel 8	Psalm 46	1 Samuel 17	1 Samuel 22
Day 6	Mark 9	Psalm 47	Mark 12	Psalm 48
Day 7	Mark 10	Mark 11	Mark 13	Mark 14

	Week 57	Week 58	Week 59	Week 60
Day 1	1 Samuel 23	1 Samuel 27	2 Samuel 1	2 Samuel 6
Day 2	1 Samuel 24	1 Samuel 28	2 Samuel 2	2 Samuel 7
Day 3	1 Samuel 25	1 Samuel 29	2 Samuel 3	2 Samuel 8
Day 4	1 Samuel 26	1 Samuel 30	2 Samuel 4	2 Samuel 9
Day 5	Psalm 49	1 Samuel 31	2 Samuel 5	2 Samuel 10
Day 6	Mark 15	1 Corinthians 1	Psalm 50	1 Corinthians 4
Day 7	Mark 16	1 Corinthians 2	1 Corinthians 3	1 Corinthians 5

	Week 61	Week 62	Week 63	Week 64
Day 1	2 Samuel 11	2 Samuel 16	2 Samuel 19	2 Samuel 24
Day 2	2 Samuel 12	2 Samuel 17	2 Samuel 20	1 Kings 1
Day 3	2 Samuel 13	2 Samuel 18	2 Samuel 21	1 Kings 2
Day 4	2 Samuel 14	Psalm 52	2 Samuel 22	1 Kings 3
Day 5	2 Samuel 15	Psalm 53	2 Samuel 23	1 Kings 4
Day 6	Psalm 51	Psalm 54	1 Corinthians 8	Psalm 55
Day 7	1 Corinthians 6	1 Corinthians 7	1 Corinthians 9	1 Corinthians 10

	Week 65	Week 66	Week 67	Week 68
Day 1	1 Kings 5	1 Kings 10	1 Kings 14	1 Kings 18
Day 2	1 Kings 6	1 Kings 11	1 Kings 15	1 Kings 19
Day 3	1 Kings 7	1 Kings 12	1 Kings 16	1 Kings 20
Day 4	1 Kings 8	1 Kings 13	1 Kings 17	1 Kings 21
Day 5	1 Kings 9	Psalm 56	Psalm 58	Psalm 59
Day 6	1 Corinthians 11	Psalm 57	1 Corinthians 14	1 Corinthians 16
Day 7	1 Corinthians 12	1 Corinthians 13	1 Corinthians 15	2 Corinthians 1

	Week 69	Week 70	Week 71	Week 72
Day 1	1 Kings 22	2 Kings 4	2 Kings 9	2 Kings 13
Day 2	2 Kings 1	2 Kings 5	2 Kings 10	2 Kings 14
Day 3	2 Kings 2	2 Kings 6	2 Kings 11	2 Kings 15
Day 4	2 Kings 3	2 Kings 7	2 Kings 12	2 Kings 16
Day 5	Psalm 60	2 Kings 8	Psalm 62	Psalm 64
Day 6	Psalm 61	2 Corinthians 3	Psalm 63	Psalm 65
Day 7	2 Corinthians 2	2 Corinthians 4	2 Corinthians 5	2 Corinthians 6

	Week 73	Week 74	Week 75	Week 76
Day 1	2 Kings 17	2 Kings 22	1 Chronicles 1	1 Chronicles 7
Day 2	2 Kings 18	2 Kings 23	1 Chronicles 2	1 Chronicles 8
Day 3	2 Kings 19	2 Kings 24	1 Chronicles 3	1 Chronicles 9
Day 4	2 Kings 20	2 Kings 25	1 Chronicles 4	1 Chronicles 10
Day 5	2 Kings 21	Psalm 66	1 Chronicles 5	1 Chronicles 11
Day 6	2 Corinthians 7	Psalm 67	1 Chronicles 6	Psalm 68
Day 7	2 Corinthians 8	2 Corinthians 9	2 Corinthians 10	2 Corinthians 11

	Week 77	Week 78	Week 79	Week 80
Day 1	1 Chronicles 12	1 Chronicles 17	1 Chronicles 22	1 Chronicles 28
Day 2	1 Chronicles 13	1 Chronicles 18	1 Chronicles 23	1 Chronicles 29
Day 3	1 Chronicles 14	1 Chronicles 19	1 Chronicles 24	2 Chronicles 1
Day 4	1 Chronicles 15	1 Chronicles 20	1 Chronicles 25	2 Chronicles 2
Day 5	1 Chronicles 16	1 Chronicles 21	1 Chronicles 26	Psalm 70
Day 6	2 Corinthians 12	Psalm 69	1 Chronicles 27	Psalm 71
Day 7	2 Corinthians 13	Galatians 1	Galatians 2	Galatians 3

	Week 81	Week 82	Week 83	Week 84
Day 1	2 Chronicles 3	2 Chronicles 8	2 Chronicles 13	2 Chronicles 18
Day 2	2 Chronicles 4	2 Chronicles 9	2 Chronicles 14	2 Chronicles 19
Day 3	2 Chronicles 5	2 Chronicles 10	2 Chronicles 15	2 Chronicles 20
Day 4	2 Chronicles 6	2 Chronicles 11	2 Chronicles 16	2 Chronicles 21
Day 5	2 Chronicles 7	2 Chronicles 12	2 Chronicles 17	2 Chronicles 22
Day 6	Galatians 4	Psalm 72	Ephesians 1	Psalm 73
Day 7	Galatians 5	Galatians 6	Ephesians 2	Ephesians 3

	Week 85	Week 86	Week 87	Week 88
Day 1	2 Chronicles 23	2 Chronicles 28	2 Chronicles 33	Ezra 1
Day 2	2 Chronicles 24	2 Chronicles 29	2 Chronicles 34	Ezra 2
Day 3	2 Chronicles 25	2 Chronicles 30	2 Chronicles 35	Ezra 3
Day 4	2 Chronicles 26	2 Chronicles 31	2 Chronicles 36	Ezra 4
Day 5	2 Chronicles 27	2 Chronicles 32	Psalm 75	Ezra 5
Day 6	Ephesians 4	Psalm 74	Psalm 76	Luke 2
Day 7	Ephesians 5	Ephesians 6	Luke 1	Luke 3

	Week 89	Week 90	Week 91	Week 92
Day 1	Ezra 6	Nehemiah 1	Nehemiah 5	Nehemiah 10
Day 2	Ezra 7	Nehemiah 2	Nehemiah 6	Nehemiah 11
Day 3	Ezra 8	Nehemiah 3	Nehemiah 7	Nehemiah 12
Day 4	Ezra 9	Nehemiah 4	Nehemiah 8	Nehemiah 13
Day 5	Ezra 10	Psalm 78	Nehemiah 9	Esther 1
Day 6	Psalm 77	Luke 5	Luke 7	Luke 9
Day 7	Luke 4	Luke 6	Luke 8	Luke 10

	Week 93	**Week 94**	**Week 95**	**Week 96**
Day 1	Esther 2	Esther 7	Job 2	Job 7
Day 2	Esther 3	Esther 8	Job 3	Job 8
Day 3	Esther 4	Esther 9	Job 4	Job 9
Day 4	Esther 5	Esther 10	Job 5	Job 10
Day 5	Esther 6	Job 1	Job 6	Psalm 81
Day 6	Psalm 79	Luke 12	Psalm 80	Psalm 82
Day 7	Luke 11	Luke 13	Luke 14	Luke 15

	Week 97	**Week 98**	**Week 99**	**Week 100**
Day 1	Job 11	Job 15	Job 20	Job 24
Day 2	Job 12	Job 16	Job 21	Job 25
Day 3	Job 13	Job 17	Job 22	Job 26
Day 4	Job 14	Job 18	Job 23	Job 27
Day 5	Luke 16	Job 19	Psalm 85	Job 28
Day 6	Luke 17	Psalm 83	Luke 19	Luke 21
Day 7	Luke 18	Psalm 84	Luke 20	Luke 22

	Week 101	**Week 102**	**Week 103**	**Week 104**
Day 1	Job 29	Job 33	Job 38	Proverbs 1
Day 2	Job 30	Job 34	Job 39	Proverbs 2
Day 3	Job 31	Job 35	Job 40	Proverbs 3
Day 4	Job 32	Job 36	Job 41	Proverbs 4
Day 5	Psalm 86	Job 37	Job 42	Psalm 89
Day 6	Psalm 87	Luke 24	Psalm 88	Philippians 3
Day 7	Luke 23	Philippians 1	Philippians 2	Philippians 4

	Week 105	**Week 106**	**Week 107**	**Week 108**
Day 1	Proverbs 5	Proverbs 10	Proverbs 15	Proverbs 19
Day 2	Proverbs 6	Proverbs 11	Proverbs 16	Proverbs 20
Day 3	Proverbs 7	Proverbs 12	Proverbs 17	Proverbs 21
Day 4	Proverbs 8	Proverbs 13	Proverbs 18	Proverbs 22
Day 5	Proverbs 9	Proverbs 14	Psalm 91	Proverbs 23
Day 6	Colossians 1	Psalm 90	Colossians 4	1 Thessalonians 2
Day 7	Colossians 2	Colossians 3	1 Thessalonians 1	1 Thessalonians 3

	Week 109	Week 110	Week 111	Week 112
Day 1	Proverbs 24	Proverbs 28	Ecclesiastes 1	Ecclesiastes 6
Day 2	Proverbs 25	Proverbs 29	Ecclesiastes 2	Ecclesiastes 7
Day 3	Proverbs 26	Proverbs 30	Ecclesiastes 3	Ecclesiastes 8
Day 4	Proverbs 27	Proverbs 31	Ecclesiastes 4	Ecclesiastes 9
Day 5	Psalm 92	Psalm 94	Ecclesiastes 5	Psalm 95
Day 6	Psalm 93	1 Thessalonians 5	2 Thessalonians 2	Psalm 96
Day 7	1 Thessalonians 4	2 Thessalonians 1	2 Thessalonians 3	1 Timothy 1

	Week 113	Week 114	Week 115	Week 116
Day 1	Ecclesiastes 10	Song of Songs 3	Song of Songs 7	Isaiah 2
Day 2	Ecclesiastes 11	Song of Songs 4	Song of Songs 8	Isaiah 3
Day 3	Ecclesiastes 12	Song of Songs 5	Isaiah 1	Isaiah 4
Day 4	Song of Songs 1	Song of Songs 6	Psalm 99	Isaiah 5
Day 5	Song of Songs 2	Psalm 97	Psalm 100	Isaiah 6
Day 6	1 Timothy 2	Psalm 98	Psalm 101	1 Timothy 6
Day 7	1 Timothy 3	1 Timothy 4	1 Timothy 5	2 Timothy 1

	Week 117	Week 118	Week 119	Week 120
Day 1	Isaiah 7	Isaiah 12	Isaiah 17	Isaiah 22
Day 2	Isaiah 8	Isaiah 13	Isaiah 18	Isaiah 23
Day 3	Isaiah 9	Isaiah 14	Isaiah 19	Isaiah 24
Day 4	Isaiah 10	Isaiah 15	Isaiah 20	Isaiah 25
Day 5	Isaiah 11	Isaiah 16	Isaiah 21	Isaiah 26
Day 6	Psalm 102	2 Timothy 3	Psalm 103	Titus 2
Day 7	2 Timothy 2	2 Timothy 4	Titus 1	Titus 3

	Week 121	Week 122	Week 123	Week 124
Day 1	Isaiah 27	Isaiah 31	Isaiah 36	Isaiah 41
Day 2	Isaiah 28	Isaiah 32	Isaiah 37	Isaiah 42
Day 3	Isaiah 29	Isaiah 33	Isaiah 38	Isaiah 43
Day 4	Isaiah 30	Isaiah 34	Isaiah 39	Isaiah 44
Day 5	Psalm 104	Isaiah 35	Isaiah 40	Psalm 106
Day 6	Philemon	Psalm 105	Hebrews 3	Hebrews 5
Day 7	Hebrews 1	Hebrews 2	Hebrews 4	Hebrews 6

	Week 125	**Week 126**	**Week 127**	**Week 128**
Day 1	Isaiah 45	Isaiah 50	Isaiah 55	Isaiah 59
Day 2	Isaiah 46	Isaiah 51	Isaiah 56	Isaiah 60
Day 3	Isaiah 47	Isaiah 52	Isaiah 57	Isaiah 61
Day 4	Isaiah 48	Isaiah 53	Isaiah 58	Isaiah 62
Day 5	Isaiah 49	Isaiah 54	Psalm 108	Psalm 110
Day 6	Psalm 107	Hebrews 8	Psalm 109	Psalm 111
Day 7	Hebrews 7	Hebrews 9	Hebrews 10	Hebrews 11

	Week 129	**Week 130**	**Week 131**	**Week 132**
Day 1	Isaiah 63	Jeremiah 1	Jeremiah 5	Jeremiah 9
Day 2	Isaiah 64	Jeremiah 2	Jeremiah 6	Jeremiah 10
Day 3	Isaiah 65	Jeremiah 3	Jeremiah 7	Jeremiah 11
Day 4	Isaiah 66	Jeremiah 4	Jeremiah 8	Jeremiah 12
Day 5	Hebrews 12	Psalm 112	Psalm 114	Jeremiah 13
Day 6	Hebrews 13	Psalm 113	Psalm 115	John 4
Day 7	John 1	John 2	John 3	John 5

	Week 133	**Week 134**	**Week 135**	**Week 136**
Day 1	Jeremiah 14	Jeremiah 19	Jeremiah 23	Jeremiah 27
Day 2	Jeremiah 15	Jeremiah 20	Jeremiah 24	Jeremiah 28
Day 3	Jeremiah 16	Jeremiah 21	Jeremiah 25	Jeremiah 29
Day 4	Jeremiah 17	Jeremiah 22	Jeremiah 26	Jeremiah 30
Day 5	Jeremiah 18	Psalm 117	Psalm 118	Jeremiah 31
Day 6	Psalm 116	John 7	John 9	Psalm 119
Day 7	John 6	John 8	John 10	John 11

	Week 137	**Week 138**	**Week 139**	**Week 140**
Day 1	Jeremiah 32	Jeremiah 37	Jeremiah 42	Jeremiah 48
Day 2	Jeremiah 33	Jeremiah 38	Jeremiah 43	Jeremiah 49
Day 3	Jeremiah 34	Jeremiah 39	Jeremiah 44	Jeremiah 50
Day 4	Jeremiah 35	Jeremiah 40	Jeremiah 45	Jeremiah 51
Day 5	Jeremiah 36	Jeremiah 41	Jeremiah 46	Jeremiah 52
Day 6	John 12	John 14	Jeremiah 47	John 17
Day 7	John 13	John 15	John 16	John 18

	Week 141	Week 142	Week 143	Week 144
Day 1	Lamentations 1	Ezekiel 1	Ezekiel 6	Ezekiel 12
Day 2	Lamentations 2	Ezekiel 2	Ezekiel 7	Ezekiel 13
Day 3	Lamentations 3	Ezekiel 3	Ezekiel 8	Ezekiel 14
Day 4	Lamentations 4	Ezekiel 4	Ezekiel 9	Ezekiel 15
Day 5	Lamentations 5	Ezekiel 5	Ezekiel 10	James 3
Day 6	John 19	John 21	Ezekiel 11	James 4
Day 7	John 20	James 1	James 2	James 5

	Week 145	Week 146	Week 147	Week 148
Day 1	Ezekiel 16	Ezekiel 22	Ezekiel 25	Ezekiel 30
Day 2	Ezekiel 17	Ezekiel 23	Ezekiel 26	Ezekiel 31
Day 3	Ezekiel 18	Ezekiel 24	Ezekiel 27	Ezekiel 32
Day 4	Ezekiel 19	Psalm 120	Ezekiel 28	Psalm 123
Day 5	Ezekiel 20	Psalm 121	Ezekiel 29	Psalm 124
Day 6	Ezekiel 21	Psalm 122	1 Peter 3	Psalm 125
Day 7	1 Peter 1	1 Peter 2	1 Peter 4	1 Peter 5

	Week 149	Week 150	Week 151	Week 152
Day 1	Ezekiel 33	Ezekiel 38	Ezekiel 41	Ezekiel 46
Day 2	Ezekiel 34	Ezekiel 39	Ezekiel 42	Ezekiel 47
Day 3	Ezekiel 35	Ezekiel 40	Ezekiel 43	Ezekiel 48
Day 4	Ezekiel 36	Psalm 126	Ezekiel 44	Psalm 129
Day 5	Ezekiel 37	Psalm 127	Ezekiel 45	Psalm 130
Day 6	2 Peter 1	Psalm 128	1 John 1	Psalm 131
Day 7	2 Peter 2	2 Peter 3	1 John 2	1 John 3

	Week 153	Week 154	Week 155	Week 156
Day 1	Daniel 1	Daniel 4	Daniel 9	Hosea 1
Day 2	Daniel 2	Daniel 5	Daniel 10	Hosea 2
Day 3	Daniel 3	Daniel 6	Daniel 11	Hosea 3
Day 4	Psalm 132	Daniel 7	Daniel 12	Hosea 4
Day 5	Psalm 133	Daniel 8	Psalm 135	Hosea 5
Day 6	Psalm 134	1 John 5	Psalm 136	Hosea 6
Day 7	1 John 4	2 John 1	3 John 1	Jude

	Week 157	Week 158	Week 159	Week 160
Day 1	Hosea 7	Hosea 11	Joel 1	Amos 3
Day 2	Hosea 8	Hosea 12	Joel 2	Amos 4
Day 3	Hosea 9	Hosea 13	Joel 3	Amos 5
Day 4	Hosea 10	Hosea 14	Amos 1	Amos 6
Day 5	Psalm 137	Revelation 2	Amos 2	Psalm 140
Day 6	Psalm 138	Revelation 3	Psalm 139	Psalm 141
Day 7	Revelation 1	Revelation 4	Revelation 5	Revelation 6

	Week 161	Week 162	Week 163	Week 164
Day 1	Amos 7	Jonah 1	Micah 1	Micah 6
Day 2	Amos 8	Jonah 2	Micah 2	Micah 7
Day 3	Amos 9	Jonah 3	Micah 3	Nahum 1
Day 4	Obadiah	Jonah 4	Micah 4	Nahum 2
Day 5	Revelation 7	Psalm 142	Micah 5	Nahum 3
Day 6	Revelation 8	Psalm 143	Psalm 144	Revelation 12
Day 7	Revelation 9	Revelation 10	Revelation 11	Revelation 13

	Week 165	Week 166	Week 167	Week 168
Day 1	Habakkuk 1	Zephaniah 3	Zechariah 3	Zechariah 7
Day 2	Habakkuk 2	Haggai 1	Zechariah 4	Zechariah 8
Day 3	Habakkuk 3	Haggai 2	Zechariah 5	Zechariah 9
Day 4	Zephaniah 1	Zechariah 1	Zechariah 6	Zechariah 10
Day 5	Zephaniah 2	Zechariah 2	Psalm 146	Psalm 148
Day 6	Psalm 145	Revelation 15	Psalm 147	Revelation 18
Day 7	Revelation 14	Revelation 16	Revelation 17	Revelation 19

	Week 169	Week 170		
Day 1	Zechariah 11	Malachi 2		
Day 2	Zechariah 12	Malachi 3		
Day 3	Zechariah 13	Malachi 4		
Day 4	Zechariah 14	Psalm 149		
Day 5	Malachi 1	Psalm 150		
Day 6	Revelation 20	Revelation 22		
Day 7	Revelation 21			

About the Bible Reading Program

Reading through the Bible was so influential in Arlina Yates life that she wanted to share the experience with others. She and five friends formed an Internet Bible Reading Group with the goal of reading through the entire Bible. The group read one Bible chapter a day with Arlina writing a weekly devotional based on a theme taken from those seven chapters.

A website, www.thewordway.com, was created when the original group expanded throughout the United States. Since 2006, users of the website have found help, hope, and purpose for their lives as they read through the Bible and the related devotionals.

Users of the website have asked to have the devotionals and reading schedule gathered into book format. This is that book.

CPSIA information can be obtained
at www.ICGtesting.com
Printed in the USA
BVOW06s2129060117
472888BV00003B/3/P